CONFESSIONS
of a Motion Addict

STEPHEN PETRONIO

ISBN: 1492736546

ISBN 13: 9781492736547

Library of Congress Control Number: 2013919121
CreateSpace Independent Publishing Platform
North Charleston, South Carolina

This Book is dedicated to my husband Jean-Marc Flack and my daughter Bella E. Klein— two souls sweet, loving, kind.

With Special thanks to: Malaga Baldi, David Rosen, Miranda Swartz, and Wendy Perron (author of Through the Eyes of a Dancer) for their encouragement, editorial eyes and expertise; to Jean-Marc Flack for making everything infinitely better; to Claudia La Rocco, Janet Stapleton, Karen Erickson, Daniele and Ron Flack and Janine Antoni for early reads and support; to photographer and colleague Sarah Silver and the incredibly talented team at her studio for years of collaborative spirit, along with photographers Annie Leibovitz, Christian Witkin, Chris Nash, Hugo Glendenning, Stephen Petegorsky, Derek Storm (back cover) and the estate of Jack Mitchell as well as Ted Henigson (cover photo) for their thoughtful work and generous contribution of the photographs throughout this book; and Chris Iannetti for technical help. I'd also like to thank all the cheerleaders on Facebook, particularly the person who read an early post from these writings, then asked the question "When will these be published?", before there was even an inkling of a memoir. Thanks also to Craig Hensala and Yvan Greenberg and all the rest of the staff at Stephen Petronio Company who offered crucial day-to-day administrative support for my dance work, which allowed this book to have the space to develop.

Annie Leibovitz. Stephen Petronio for DIFFA (1992).

CONTENTS

Cowboys In London

"Stephen!"

Whip cracks across a cottony Novocain void...

"STEPHEN!"

Searing pain shoots from ear to ear then rockets up to the crown of my skull.

One eye snaps open on a tighty-whitey close-up: fabric...a pillow...saliva.

"STEEEEPHEN!"

Down deep inside, the voice clangs again.

"Wake up!"

Right, that's me.

I register the sound of air sucking in, then resurface to the pounding glare of an unbearably bright morning. 1989. Awake again. My jaw is slack and my head throbs with the creeping half-memories of yesterday's debauchery: coke (Charlie), E (ecstasy), endless chatter, shards of music (**Bowie, Johnny**

Rotten, X-ray Spex, Morrissey) and violent dancing, belly laughs morphing into deep tongue kisses, massive amounts of Glenfiddich, then vodka w/ white wine (Car Crash), ever growing mountain of fags (cigarettes), Charlie, alcohol, Charlie, alcohol, alcohol, Charlie, then sleepers; spiraling fuck into blackout.... "Artistic research" I slur to myself.

I shift on the bed and a hive of hornets stings my brain in unison. There's a body next to me. Relief. He's still there, tangled in the sheets. I lean into his monster-pouty lips (delectable) for a sign of breath. It's detectable. Barely. He's out cold. Suspended mode.

The body belongs to **Michael Clark**, notorious British choreographer with whom I'm spectacularly in love, a seismic affair. He's deep in the coma I just emerged from. Through my haze I can decipher only one clear thought: "Coffee."

London in the late '80s means no real coffee in our flat in Shepherd's Bush, or in any cupboard across the Commonwealth. It's all about tea. I take an aching deep breath, then exhale; roll off the mattress and onto the floor, gingerly crawl my way up my legs, hand over fist. I achieve vertical sloooo—o—oooow—ly, see-saw to the loo where I plunk a couple of fizzy Solpadeine in water and suck them down in a gulp. Solpadeine, the over-the-counter hangover cure I covet for its dose of legal codeine. "Civilized. I love London." The throbbing fog hints that it might soften and lift.

Codeine aside, I'm in a honeymoon phase with London. A hopeless Anglophile, really, I love everything about it: the accent, the manners, the wonky English name equivalents of mundane things: *crisps* for potato chips and *loo* for toilet. My friends are my *mates*. I'm not exhausted, I'm *dead knackered*. I live for these linguistic twists.

And there's comfort in the clear division between good and evil in the culture: establishment vs. underground. One stratum is so politely mannered and polished, queuing up (forming a line) eagerly without complaint, while another is roiling punk rock, anarchy destroy! The turf is clear as high school. There's no "mincing about" concerning one's place or class. Except for when one speaks. There's nothing direct about social communication. It's more of a minuet that's downplayed, without emphasis:

"Would you like some porridge?" comes the request to have some breakfast to a famished friend.

"I don't mind," comes the reply that translates to "Yes, I'm starving, heap it on."

It's the art of understatement—formal, polite, of not revealing what's obvious. Discreet.

I'm a choreographer as well, a recent transplant from New York who's received generous amounts of attention and support here. In London, this translates to cultural kudos of mainstream order. I also happen to be engaged to the most notorious dancer/punk icon London's ever seen. (That's him drooling in the other room.) The phrase "Bad Boy" comes up frequently in relation to us—the press seems to need it—and we're drawn as counterparts from different sides of The Pond. The irreverent, quite queer, frank and open, fashion-fixated, velocity-addicted *Angry Young Men.*

In truth I'm a well-raised, well-intentioned guy who hopes for the best, expects it and assumes it for others. But I'm at a point where the politics of my sexuality are paramount, on the tip of my tongue, pressing a cultural moment of change. The ground shifts with Michael. The power of two is exponential and there's considerable buzz around our union. Fabulosity.

It's assumed.

It's easy.

It's the way it was meant to be.

I throw on a fresh long-sleeved cotton tee of from the neatly folded pile near the bed, long sleeves for propriety's sake. The bruised crook of my arm is displayed less and less these days, though it's balmy August. I vaguely notice what I'm putting on, the Ariel brand's fresh laundry scent, the over-the-fingertip bondage sleeves that mark the shirt as one of Vivienne's.

Vivienne Westwood, harbinger of punk, just won the Designer of the Year at The British Fashion Awards, after years of shaping what London's youth wear, what they listen to, how they see the world as rotten to the core. She's royally subversive and so much fun. My mind smudges out a little aside: "This'll do for a quick coffee run." Plus Michael and I love wearing each others' clothes when we're not pasted together at the hip.

Out the door and on to Shepherd's Bush Green, the unusual crowd and blaring music remind me that Nottingham Carnival weekend is in motion. It's a Caribbean cultural festival and a bank holiday, a chance for a long weekend, everything shut down and gone fishin'. Bank holidays are perpetually popping up in Britain. Civilized.

I snake my way through the crowd, make it as far as the local chippy (fish and chip shop) when without warning, the world jolts and screeches to an abrupt halt. There in the doorway he hovers, a magnificently sweet vision. He's the blondest, squarest-jawed, sky-blue-eyed, translucent-skinned angel, an oasis in uniform. Standing before me is a perfectly hot Anglo-blond Bobby. He locks right on me, smiles into me; eyes shift down my body, then nods me over. I'm extremely loyal but Michael is asleep back at the flat and I see no harm in a little harmless flirtation.

We're face to face when he tells me: "I like your shirt."

I look down and clock the Wild-West cartoon cowboy erotica on my chest. I look up and thank him, a bit taken aback. Can Bobbies flirt in uniform? London is fabulous. When his Bobby buddy appears out of nowhere, it occurs to me...this is not going where I think it's going. It all turns wrong as he orders: "Please come with me, mate."

Bobbies don't carry guns but it shocks me how much power they retain and I follow along sheepishly. He asks me my name as they escort me to the police van.

"Jack Peroni," I blurt out in a flash of defensive panic that somehow morphs me instantly into the heir to an Italian beer empire (the brew I was drinking all night).

I'm inside their cub van—the wagons used for transporting the riff-raff—driving around the crowded carnival streets, when I hear my perfect blond Bobby report to his station that he has a suspect with a "pornographic jumper" on and is awaiting instructions. It seems my T-shirt has an unseemly message on it. It's not till then that I have a good look down at my chest and the upside-down image shifts planes and comes into focus. It is one of Vivienne's extremely graphic cartoon cowboy/sex shirts with the slogan "Fuck Your Mother," scrawled on the shoulder. A bit of punkish fun with fashion.

Bobby assures me we're just going to drive around a bit, that his superior will have them drop me off eventually to pursue more fractious criminals. When the radio finally crackles back that they need to "Ave a look at me," my Bobby and his buddy are instructed to haul me in. He apologizes in a sheepish way and I realize that I am fucked. My steamy cop porno is suddenly titled *Done by the Old Bill.*

We arrive at Hammersmith Station, just next to the Hammersmith Apollo where every great band has taken a turn. Irony twists the blade as it hits me that we're just blocks away from Dance Umbrella at Riverside Studios, the venue that was my first stage as a dancer in London, the home to my loyal producers and enthusiastic public. How could I be in such intimate proximity to my dancing glory, now standing hungover and shirtless, looking up at a pasty officer, who is in turn looking down at me in disgust from his lofty perch? How can he not comprehend my entitlement, know I'm decent, intentions pure? Can't he see? What he does see is the message in my outfit.

"That shirt is revolting. What would your mum say if she saw you in it?" he bellows in a cartoon British accent.

"She wouldn't say much. My mother is dead," I offer in a return that's too abrupt ("Who said that?"). I mean to state a fact and separate my mother's memory from his crusty mouth. It doesn't seem to help matters. They remove my shirt and I'm forced to stand for ages, bare torso-ed and nipples at permanent attention, surrounded by a flock of London's best-in-blue. Morning drags into afternoon. I demand my right for a phone call and he laughs: "You're an American national and 'ave no rights 'ere in London."

I'm at their disposal. I tell him I'm a well-known American dancer who performs here often, which just seems to deepen his pleasure at retaining me. I make a desperate attempt at release by mentioning I have severe asthma and need my medicine at home. This jostles him enough—I don't think he wants a death on his hand and he arranges to have a police car to take me around to my flat.

Don't know what I am doing here. (I mean really, right now, and in the big picture. I *am* a good guy, loyal friend of the underdog, kind to children, didn't mean for it to...and yet here I stand, strung out, arrogant, arrested and in a sweat in a precinct in London. Alone.) I'm improvising like hell in hopes that I'll see Michael to at least let him know where I am.

My arresting Bobbies fade out and then, replaced by a new team of mixed origin and sex, off we go for a nationally sponsored drug run. We get to the door of the flat and the officer knocks but no one is home. I see the state of the flat in the look of horror on her face. There are beer cans, pizza boxes, books on top of books, videos, sketches and mountains of trash everywhere. In one light "a good weekend," in another, "mayhem."

I go in to get my inhaler and look around to see if there's any incriminating evidence, should they search the place later. Miraculously I don't see any, though it was everywhere when I left.

We get into the van to return and I'm defeated. We start down the street and through the tiny back window in the rear compartment I spot Micheal. I point him out and implore them to speak to him. I'm still concealed in the back as they ask him if he knows a Jack Peroni. He replies a definite and somewhat paranoid "No."

As we pull away I see it dawn on him. Then Michael's ballet-running after us, flailing at the van, but it's too late for them to notice."

They isolate me in a coffin-sized single cell because I tell them I have a compromised immune system (which I don't) to keep myself apart from whatever else I'm certain I'll want to avoid in the communal lockup. I'm hysterically claustrophobic, post-weekend run-down, depressed at the thought that no one knows my whereabouts. Hours crawl by. Finally Michael shows up to demand my release and gets a snicker at his claims of grandeur and fame. In a fit of giggles, the captain mentions the state of the flat. Michael promises to sort me out and I beg for swiftness.

He vanishes for another day.

I am in prison—

In Hammersmith—

On a bank holiday weekend.

It's looking pretty grim.

The night is long, punctuated by waves of panic and indignation. Early next morning, I'm released unexpectedly into the custody of my Michael and Steve A, an American photographer and friend who's dating George Michael. Steve called a friend at the American Embassy and had me liberated. The discharge form reads "Public behavior to incite civil unrest," with a court date set for the following week.

For a few days my knickers are in a twist: paranoid, guilty, without my passport. It's too overwhelming to enlist legal counsel, and then it all eventually begins to fade away. When my day in court approaches I realize I have but one choice. I get up in the morning, groom thoroughly, then dress myself from head to toe in my best Vivienne Westwood gear: jumbo white-on-pink polka-dot shirt and gray lightweight-wool bondage pants (complete with restraint strap connecting my knees) and de rigueur biker boots. Michael and his mum, Bessie (whom I adore), come for support and we all head off to for my day in court.

When my moment comes I'm cleaved from my family and led to the far end of a cavernous wood-paneled hall and up to what can only be described as a tiny pulpit, a perfect stage for the upcoming drama (or is it more like the plank I must walk and prepare to drop off of?). To my left on the main floor, against the wall and halfway down the room, is a rectangular box with the rest of the day's accused waiting for their cases to be heard. At the opposite end of the courtroom, looming even higher and on grander display, is the magistrate, flanked by his minions on either side but slightly lower. Between us the stage is set with great sea of lawyers and an audience of our friends and family, support teams of the day's defendants.

The magistrate asks for the charges to be read and the minion on his left begins:

"Said defendant was picked up on the on Shepherd's Bush Green wearing a garment intended to incite civil unrest.... The shirt he was wearing was emblazoned with the text..."

He pauses. Murmurs and giggles.

"And there was depicted the drawing of two cowboys engaged in a lewd act: One cowboy had his fist..."

Pause.

The whole courtroom seems to tip forward in their seats.

"I— I— in..." he halts and stammers.

Then, like putrid gas that slips from twixt his pinched and puckered lips he decries: "Cowboy 1 is lording over Cowboy 2, who is reclining with his legs akimbo.

Cowboy 1 has his fist inserted to the forearm into the...anus of Cowboy 2."

Up rises a great din of laughter and cheering from the crowded room that completely disrupts the proceedings in the most delightful way. I am now certain I forever love London.

When the court settles down, the magistrate asks me for a statement and I offer this: "Your Honor, it was an innocent mistake. I was quite hung over when I got up and threw the shirt on without a thought, to pop out for coffee. No malice at all was intended. And besides, Vivienne Westwood, London's own beloved designer and cultural hero, has recently won fashion's highest honor. As an American, I'm proud to wear her clothes. *Pause here.* And in my own small way, *genuflect here,* I'm doing my part to fuel the economy of the British Crown." Pause 2, 3, 4.

The court breaks out in hysterics once again.

A barely discernible smile tempts his stern lips as he rules the charges "Overstated. Case dismissed."

I shoot my hand up and urgently but politely ask, "Your Honor, Your Highness, sir...my shirt? It was quite expensive and one of my favorites. May I have it back?"

He looks back at me with a stony stare and proclaims in measured rhythm:

"The COURT will KEEP the SHIRT. *You* get the story."

Photo: Hugo Glendenning. *Half Wrong Plus Laytext* (1992).
Dancer, Stephen Petronio.

Start

The story...
How does it start?
It starts like this: one word at a time. A story builds.
So too in dance, one step at a time set in motion, ideas become flesh. Ether and breath, untouchable, form just out of reach. Written on air, a dance appears.
Ready?
And begin.

I remember the moment of knowing that I am here and the world is out there. I'm swinging on my backyard swing set, hurling high up in the air, little pelvis penduluming up and down through space, a tiny body measured against the charcoal-gray corduroy texture of the shingled wall that is my house. This is me, and all that is everything else. I am a single, separate person in space, my body apart and in motion. FLYING PUMPING SOARING HIGHER to dizzy heights of...

I'm the son of a truck driver from New Jersey—the second son of a second-generation, Italian-American blue-collar hero. I have a traditional loving family but something is decidedly off. I can't sit still. I'm uncomfortable in my skin from as early as I can remember: What's in front of me is simply not for me. I feel awkward—out of rhythm with the world-as-I-know-it in Nutley, where I spend my childhood. The dilemma's not what I will *not* become, the kind of son who stays close to home and finds a solid job from the selection of options available in my hometown. I simply understand that I can't do that. But more disturbing is that I have no direction, no anchor. I'm lost in a vague and anxious state of feeling without option, without place and without company.

My sense of gender is adrift in relation to what I see around me. I'm restless as hell. I feel my body but have zero interest in sports, the physical mandate for boys in my caste. Baseball, football, soccer, hockey, basketball? "*NOOOO!*"

I love men—just not in "that" way. My body keeps calling from an uncharted place. I need to move, travel, to feel the speed of forward motion, my body cutting through space to feel at all. I'm the restless second son of a truck driver and I want to move on.

Caught in a Kodak klieg-light glare: me spinning in the pink dress shot through with gold thread that's got pink-plastic buttons up the front, flaring out like a parachute to land me in crashes on the green-gray carpet of our living room floor. I kiss my brother between bouts of tornadoing around the room, dizzy with laughter, squinting against those camera lights, always smiling or crying into to that blinding glare.

I come from a large extended Italian-American family. Everyone's on high volume, the calmest conversations seeming like riotous arguments to my friends. "It's just how we speak." And there's lots of it. Every single thought is to be discussed at length in a familial ritual of communication and purging. Secrets? Never. Quiet? Rarely. Emotions? High. That's just the way it is in my family...abundant, warm and connected.

We're Italian-American *New Jersey*. My mother, Lorraine, has three sisters: Genevieve, Christine and Phyllis, all with husbands and kids. They and my grandparents, Marie and Phil, meet at our house every Friday for dinner, my mother like some magnetic loving force drawing everyone into her warmth. Dinner's always meatless, Catholic Friday, something that stretches a long way at a large gathering: pizza made fresh from dough Lorraine picks up at the bakery that morning to rise in the oven, stretch out before dinner and bake while everyone arrives—great rectangular sheets of crust, sauce and mozzarella. Or peas, onions and scrambled eggs, zucchini, summer squash, tomatoes, onions and potato. Or white rice with tomato sauce and cheese. All the dishes are like that—starchy and abundant, comforting to no end. I love these Fridays, the whole family checking in weekly at a social moment that's chaotically large.

There's a whiff of glamour. Camera pans right onto phantomlike relatives adrift in a stylish celluloid limbo. Here is my perfect Italian family and its sprawling extended web. We are caught at birthdays, communions and weddings...where every woman's makeup is perfect and hair coiffed to the nth. They float on monochrome peau de soie *stilettos that match their narrow-waist dresses while the men wear muted awkward grins and stand in proper trousers and dress shirts.*

Friday's dinner invariably segues into "Friday Night at the Fights," Marie and Phil sparring over ...something: the structure of their long life together, their kids, their losses, wading through the Depression and barely scraping by, or perhaps my grandfather's continuous drinking, or some nameless indiscretion I'm too young to perceive. Marie is a virtuoso, a matriarch, a dramatic force in these fights, voice as loud as a foghorn as she gets every last thing off her chest. Phil stays quiet.

The epic battle scene is at the dinette table. It puffs and blows like a steam engine roaring uphill, building to a pinnacle. Marie now possessed by innate animal rage and howling with the operatic range of a prima donna soprano, tears open her dress in a jolting unrestrained flash. Faux pearl buttons fly everywhere.

Phil, unmoved, sarcastically grumbles under his breath, "You should live a hundred years." She almost does.

Somehow I can still sense what it was all like before: oneness, a lack of separation, a merging with the all. Baby powder and ointment, milk, sweet smells, innocence and hard tears melt together. And always there was the perfect true-red of my mother's late 1950s Monroe lips, always young and fresh, always hovering, detached from the rest of her face, omnipresent, beautiful, somewhere just above. My mother is Maya in lipstick, Revlon's Cherries in the Snow.

With my brother Thomas (1958).

I will listen to what you have to say. I will listen longer than I need to as a show of support, exactly like my mother. Lorraine finished your sentences, echoing them while you spoke, her way of showing that she was with you. She expected that back, an allegiance. She mostly got it.

Fragile. She often seemed on the verge of a breakdown when I was little. Lived a sheltered childhood and married my father at twenty-one. Pictures of her from the period before her wedding portray a constructed sophistication well beyond her years. The permed hair, dark lips and penciled brows above a twin set and cultured pearls paint a picture of maturity that is oddly out of sync with her experience.

Her young world was restrained: couldn't roller-skate, didn't play sports and as an adult she couldn't drive a car until she was in her thirties. In her forties she determines to learn to ride a bike. It was a giant three-wheeler, neatly skirting the issue of balance.

But she does know how to disappear. When the grind of two small boys becomes too much, she pours herself into the corner of their bedroom, facing inward, between the bureau and the wall. Or grabs her large white leather purse with the gold clasp and bolts out the door to take refuge at a neighbor's, or burrows into the midst of a group of teenage girls hanging out on the street around the block.

Crazy clean, scouring our home continuously, she wraps everything in plastic like it was an exhibition to be preserved for viewing. The couches and chairs (Mediterranean style) remain spotlessly new as a result, even after years of display. Her wall-to-wall carpets lined with plastic runners placed along the beaten paths are my first performance runways: *Stephen at the Palace*, a fledgling performer, testing out new moves.

She mostly leaves me on my own with my other homework, but when it comes to art projects, she jumps in with gusto. She especially loves pastels (how they blend so satisfyingly) and paints, makes a mean sugar-cube igloo and complex Popsicle stick structures. She sinks herself into my art projects, because she wasn't going to do her own. How could she do her own? Who would assign them?

She joins the paint by numbers craze in the years when she shows more troubling signs of wear: the spontaneous fits of tears; not arriving to fetch me from school until hours after I was out; the gut-wrenching noose that I was too petrified to mention to my father or brother when it appears in the basement, hanging between her sewing machine and the furnace. The burden of that discovery was crushing and I still can't fathom if it was real or a fabrication of my fragile young mind.

The family doctor recommends a hobby to soothe her frazzled nerves and to provide her homemaker life some kind of creative relief. He prescribes art with her steroids and vitamin B-12 shots. Those paint-by-number masterworks, sad clowns and wild horses, catch so clearly the psyche of a woman isolated, overwhelmed and searching. She never hangs them. They stay hidden in the basement.

Lorraine Geronimo (1946).

It's late winter, afternoon, dinnertime, and the light is fading fast. I'm with my mother at the front glass storm door in our living room and it is freezing. I can feel the cold against the front of my body and my heat pushing back at the door. We're calling for my brother, who is playing down the street. It's filled with snow from a recent storm and the white is still squint-blue-bright in the fading light. My body is up against the glass, my breath fogging it, and suddenly I remember I am three years old. I hold three fingers of my right hand up against the glass (index, middle and ring), press them in and drag them down the pane in a single deliberate path. Three strokes appear in the damp mist stain of my breath. I am three. I am three.

Uncle Joe arrives at Ellis Island on Christmas Eve, 1937. He's seventeen and spends two nights there in jail because no one comes to claim and sponsor him, usher him past the statue and into his promised future. He weeps when he can't buy the "two Hershey Bars for a dime" offered by the vendor that night when he makes his Christmas rounds. He arrived in America with only five cents in his pocket and just can't understand.

He's a tailor slash barber, the real deal. A greenhorn my father calls him. He has a thick accent, a volatile temper and a thin pencil mustache. Uncle Joe—a sweeter man would be hard to find—was born on St Joseph's Day, the eighteenth of March, one day before my father, two days before me, a perfect trifecta of spring birthdays. Uncle Joe cuts everyone's hair after dinner on those epic Friday nights—man, woman and child (only the dogs escape). While the Flintstones' "Yabba-dabba-doo time" blares in the background, Fred bang-bang-bang-banging on his front door, calling "Wilmmmma!" to let him in to the house he just got locked out of by Dino, everyone gets cleaned up, a little off the sides. I beg him to buzz me down to the scalp every time, and he always does, despite my mother's protests. My father laughs...my hairline is so low it looks like I have horns on my now-exposed forehead. Eddie Munster, baby Dracula.

The bells of the Good Humor man sound in the distance and the stampede outdoors to a hot Jersey night is set into action. All the neighbors with their respective social groupings are out too and it's a regular summer block party on Briar Lane. Ice cream is bought, games are played, the breeze is shot, and when the mosquitoes are bad in high summer the "Sprayer" comes. He's in a regulation Army jeep loaded up with DDT that sprays billowing clouds off the back—up and down the street and through our neighborhood, a fog so thick you could hide in it. We always do, pretending we're soldiers on a mission, spewing verbal bullets out of our automatic finger weapons into an exotic, fogged-out land—Germany or Russia most likely. We chase the sprayer for blocks screaming "Sprayer! Sprayer!" at the top of our now-damaged lungs that inhale so much DDT in direct proximity. (This still happens in many states, the potential damage so ethereal compared to the fear of West Nile virus. Asthma anyone?)

In that day we have men, a battery of men who deliver. And they deliver to the home: Bread Man, Milk Man, Egg Man, Dugan's Man (hang the yellow card with the giant black "D" on your front door for donuts and cakes), Charlie's Chips (potato chips, pretzels and such) and my favorite of all, the Cheese Man. He delivers what his name demands, imported cheeses, right to the door, the same time every week. He arrives with a vivid and fragrant selection to choose from, all for the discerning homemaker. He is, of course, from the "other side" (as in the other side of the ocean) and includes in his wares, of all things, clothes for the lady of the house. Polyester and brightly colored things, sleeveless shell blouses, paisley pantsuits, these are the height of fashion in working-class Jersey. And he has those most curious of items, the ever-desirable "housedress" or "duster," somewhat like an artist's smock for the homemaker. Where have these gone? All in all, a deliciously suburban idea: cheesy fashion with your ripe cheese. Life is filled with convenient home shopping, well-stocked, well-dressed wonderful! It's most definitely a social call and my mother loves to sit and have demitasse or regular coffee, "a touch of anisette?" with the Cheese Man, one of her own kind, and a man who doles out attention so lavishly in the long desert of a lonely housewife's day.

The first dance is me in rubber pants, no shirt, running wildly around the living room— still unable to speak fully. I'm dancing some rhythmic shape/flow thing for the Friday night company, bouncing furiously at the knees. The motor in my body is turning over and over but can't seem to start yet into full action—unbridled energy will have to do. I stop in place before each relative, giggling/jiggling and holding out my canister bank, hawking for dimes and quarters, understanding at that tender age that I had a captive audience and they had me.

Sweet Marie, she is my benevolent protector, and I her youngest and favored grandchild during this period. She's loving and embracing, with pizza-dough triceps that she lets me jiggle to my heart's content. Her countenance is so soft and lightly wrinkled, creases so friendly and inviting, pendulous breasts that seem godly and human all at once. Her hues of silver, gray and blue, and her scent of Estée Lauder *Eau de toilette* are enough to drop my pulse into a Buddhist trance.

Heaven is the occasional weekend at my grandmother's, an away from home, special treat, no sibling or parent, just me and the grandparents on a welcome and exotic vacation from the daily pummeling of my brother, and a break for them from my incessant yelping in response.

I stay in the upstairs bedroom of my aunt Phyllis, the youngest of four daughters, my mother's little sister, now married and gone. There is an enormous stuffed black bear, heroically bagged at some carnival by her sad-sack fiancé when they were courting. Now it's covered in plastic and hovering over the bed like a furry centurion guarding my respite. In the wrong light this cuddly love bear is one chromosome away from a character in several of my worst nightmares.

Grandma. I nearly die when a neighbor tells me she has a name and it's Marie. "No, that's Grandma!" Why would she deceive me like that?

Grandma—sacred source of all lovely things to eat, a breakfast of toast with sweet whipped butter from a large round Breakstone tub (apple butter optional) and that exotic elixir, Del Monte prune juice. Afterward, how easily she coaxes me into the kitchen sink for a mid-morning bath. Tiny and naked, with the tap large and close to me, I am giddy from the water running onto my skin. How rich to be bathed in the kitchen with her calloused hands and sweet demeanor!

Marie Geronimo, in our basement, Nutley, New Jersey (1969).

It's a vivid morning. I'm in the throes of the coveted bathing-in-the-sink ritual only Grandma can provide, a long and magic moment that is our and ours alone. The spell is abruptly shattered by a knock...who? The omnipresent Cheese Man! Selfsame intruder piercing our private bond and catching me in all my naked bliss, coming to rip her attention from my pureness, to display a variation on his goods at Grandma's. The Cheese Man gets around. How does he know where they all live? The ladies seem to offer no complaint.

Phil appears on summer afternoons after lunch and we head out to the vegetable garden. ("Don't sit on the cool ground—you'll get piles—you'll get worms," my grandmother bellows from the kitchen.) We weed in his corn, or prune his prize, the singular fig tree that he loves so well and wraps with brown paper and cord during winter. Dedicated to his drink with a quiet passion, by mid-afternoon Phil and I inevitably head down to the local corner bar named Binkie's, his reward and solution to my daycare. He sits me on a stool and orders me up a ginger ale and bag of pretzels. "I'm hanging with the BIG guys," I chirp. "Hanging with the BIG guys."

"Sta facendo il pappagallo," he says to me (you're making like a little parrot), 'cause I'm driven to repeat everything at least twice.

It's Phil who inadvertently gives me my first glimpse of a vocation in the arts. "Get up on the bar and dance for the guys," he says. "You put on a grass skirt as a costume. They'll laugh at you but never mind. While they are laughing, you just go on dancing and pick up the money they throw at you..." He has no idea how profoundly he is shaping the underpinnings of my future performing persona and my aesthetic inclinations.

Philip Geronimo (1948).

Marie is a prudent provider, pasta for twenty at a moment's notice and a tight budget? No problem, Marie can lay it out in a jiffy with grace and a smile, meatballs that set her apart from the best (she does not fry them first but lets them slow-cook in the gravy all day), bones and *brasciolla*—thin steak rolled with raisins, pine nuts and cheese, oh joy! And she bakes like a pro, just part of the turf of Grandma-ness: cheesecake, ice-box cake, cannoli and cookies too numerous to name. And forget about Christmas with her pièce de résistance—*struffoli*, that tiny golden nugget of sweet egg-yolkie bliss, deep-fried then covered in honey and sprinkles. What could be better? She is legend for having baked all the cookies for all her daughters' weddings, three hundred guests per and easily an assorted mass consisting of 20 different kinds of cookies per tray decorated with tinsel, and pastel-colored candied almonds to boot.

I love the way that she instantly recites any recipe that produced the delicacy she sets before you as if it were nothing at all, no matter how special or how complex. She recites them methodically and quietly by heart, as she would a mantra or prayer, generously revealing all her secrets because she has a million more, she is infinite.

Struffoli is her Christmas specialty. Equipment and ingredients procured and in place, she starts quietly, with a kind of knowing about what she's doing, that she is good at it and the pleasure she knows it will bring. She wears a housedress under her apron along with a little smile. She moves about the basement kitchen with effortless authority and I can tell that she loves me watching her most magic act. She measures out her flour, weighing it on the green baking scale, ingredients on the top plate that moves the black hands on white dial round to their appropriate resting place. She builds a mound of flour on the dusted pastry board and drops many egg yolks (no whites, as so many other recipes call for, that was her twist, her secret to the soft texture that separated her product from the herd) beaten with Crisco, salt, baking powder. With her soft bare hands she mixes, squishing and kneading a magically solidifying ball of deep yellow dough ("gently, not too rough!") that I know is sweeter and more melt-in-the-mouth than the salty Play-Doh I can never resist sampling when alone. Later she divides it and rolls it out into long round snakes, then cuts these ("blade away from you!") into small half-inch nuggets.

When she amasses army of the tender little dough balls, she drops them into the 375-degree hot oil of a deep fryer and waits the short wait until they transform into the dark golden prize that bobs on a roiling, stormy sea. Then onto paper to drain before being mixed into a bowl of heated honey to coat them completely, and arranged on large platters into mountains of pleasure, sprinkled with multi-colored round sprinkles. I eat struffoli to my heart's content, addicted to the indescribably firm, not crunchy, pellets of pastry and honey sweetness that come to represent all the joy of Christmas and the love of my grandmother rolled into one colossal source of pleasure. I spoon them in by the plateful with milky coffee until I can eat no more, making them my Christmas morning breakfast, savoring their flavor alone at the kitchen table in a quiet reverie after the hysteria of the presents on Christmas morning. It is then that I can call my best friend, Kenny, to compare booty and ask him "Whadja get?

Marie's Christmas Struffoli as made by her daughter, my Aunt Chris Durante (foreground, with Jean-Marc Flack (background). 2012

I am perched at the edge of a diving board over the chlorinated water of a pool in a motel courtyard somewhere in Rocky Mount, North Carolina, on a yearly migration from New Jersey to Florida. I am giddy with the promise of flight, and only vaguely cognizant of the assurance of a safe landing into the arms of my father, treading water below. I am young and still unable to swim, but equally unable to resist the drunken rush of hurtling through space and into his safe strong arms. (He lost his wedding band while catching me that day.) This is the game we play more than any other. Me perched somewhere, the top of a staircase, the edge of the couch, the diving board of a pool, makeshift schools for flight that cultivate a deep appetite for a life of plunging into empty space, the irresistible, the unknown.

My father is Tarzan to me-six smiling feet of handsome V-shaped manhood. He's out of the house before we get up, home just in time for dinner, then asleep in front of the TV until bed. There's a movie star aura about my father, his easy smile flashes like a lighthouse beacon in the gloom, brightens everything in its path. He works hard, laughs and flirts a lot, and although seldom there, he's always present. He rules the house, has a joke a minute but can turn on a dime in a flash of hot sternness if called into disciplinary action. He's fearsome, irresistible and everybody loves my father Tom.

The youngest of five and the only boy, dad was raised to be served by the women who adore him. He wears this privilege with easy charm. He never cooks a thing, has no knowledge of my mother's domain and rules the neighborhood with confidence, challenging evil neighbors, abusive husbands and wanton housewives. All the kids are magnetically drawn to him and he would toss a ball around with anyone who walked to our end of the street.

My father looms large but has more of an imposing cameo role in my life. He's alien to me, the sports he likes, the hours he keeps, his swagger in the world. He's a man's man, one who relishes hanging with the menfolk while watching fantasy versions of themselves slaughter each other over some ball or other. (I'm my mother's son and I'd rather cling to her and the aunts in the kitchen).

Tom drives a sage-green step van delivering clothes for a small dry cleaner in town called **A.Tozzi &Sons**. Everybody knows him and many are fond of him. His relaxed charm allows him to enjoy a kind of local celebrity status. He's very popular with the ladies, a most anticipated and welcome guest in many homes on a regular bases. Translation: His offspring have to be extremely well behaved, can get away with zero and are screwed if they veer off track.

He's hardworking lower middle class, proud of the independence he has in a job that keeps him roving around town all day out in the fresh air, walking and socializing and connecting himself with a wide variety of townspeople. He's a young husband and father, a capable provider for his family, and seems to revel in it all immensely.

Tom, Thomas, Tomooch, Sonny, Son, Guidano, Tommie Tozzi, uncle Tommy: my young mind is exhilarated by the prospect that my father has so many names and roles, something for everybody. Sonny is my favorite, not imagining it's a diminutive title, his tag as the youngest child and only son. In my mind it's spelled S-u-n-n-y, because that's how I see him—warm and luminous.

His relationship with my mother is romantic. They flirt and laugh as if they were kids and like so many in the 1950's, they can social dance like pros. My jaw drops when they break out into alien personas whose bodies speak this foreign language, assume a deeply charged poise, his box office physique molding perfectly to my mother's zaftig grace. They hunker down to set off to slice a very mean rug, jitterbugging or fox-trotting through some wedding or anniversary celebration. All the while they're swirling and laughing, swirling and laughing. When did they rehearse?

He's an avid Democrat in these days. When JFK appears on the evening news on our black-and-white RCA TV, my father puffs up with pride, not particularly responding to his politics, but to the man filled with youth and vitality. He's Catholic, like us, and never wears a hat, like him. "I just don't trust the ones that wear hats." I think it significant that hatlessness could mean so much. The power and freedom that clothing in general come to represent stays with me to this day.

Sometimes Dad invites me to work with him on a Saturday or during summer break, riding up front with him as we drive through town dropping off and picking up clothing. It's fun to hang with him, though he doesn't take me as he disappears into each house with an armful of clean, pressed clothing and returns with a bundle tied up by the legs of trousers or the sleeves of a shirt. While he's gone, I climb into the back of the van and hide in the freshly pressed and cleaned clothes, inhaling dry-cleaning fluid smell and hoping to spring out when he returns, or remain concealed, forcing him to wonder where I disappeared to. I always come out of hiding prematurely, doing a jiggle pee-dance in search of relief. He sometimes gets tips that he lets me keep as pay for my company. These are oddly relaxed days, free of any domestic tension or hassles about our roles as father and son in the family unit, or over sports or school. It's just him and me alone, me being relatively quiet (for me) and getting an up-close picture of my father in the action of his life.

At Christmas, his customers tip him with gifts for his trusted service all year, either an envelope stuffed fat with cash or a bottle of Four Roses or Seagram's 7, until the floor of our hall "liquor closet" is overflowing. It's a treat to sit at the dinette table and open envelopes with hope and anticipation of the rewards my father earned from so many people.

Thomas Petronio (1946).

Christmas Eve belongs to Lorraine. She bills this night as the main attraction, the ultimate display of family togetherness and celebration (the birth of Christ for Chrissake), and she pulls out all the stops. Of course it would be hers. Our house is *the* social gathering place with a relaxed air of fun, and she is the sister with the heart and skill and the easygoing husband to pull it all off. It calls for a multicourse dinner for around thirty, all at one large table in our newly finished basement, in our newly built little home, in a newly built neighborhood in New Jersey. She toils valiantly to create a sense of tradition in the newness. Christmas Eve beckons to all of my parents' siblings, their spouses and children, plus anyone attached to them floating solo. This holy night is not meant to be spent alone.

Her preparation starts in November and builds steadily. The planning and shopping are methodic, guided by some unwritten script that only she knows. Christmas Eve dinner is meatless and white in accordance with Italian-American/Christian doctrine, so the mainstay array of meats or tomato sauce is absent. This is a catalyst for excursions to the fish market and I go along with trepidation. My personal experience with fish is limited to tuna sandwiches on white bread on Friday's or the occasional Mrs. Paul's Frozen Fish Sticks. The fish market is another world completely and reminds me of the doctor's office, its whiteness and crowded, somber air. There are unidentifiable, glassy-eyed whole fish lying in state on beds of ice alongside pale tentacle-y things at rest, and an oddly deflated smell that chokes the room. I find it hard to believe this smell comes from something you're supposed to find appetizing. This is my most direct exposure to primary resources on the food chain. My reference to food is processed and disguised, divorcing what I eat from any credible whole source. It is a cruel world where dead things are delicacies.

The table is set for the evening with flawless care, not using the good silver because we are too many, but festive beyond belief. There is always some new centerpiece theme for the table that gets positioned every few feet: a *Reader's Digest* accordion Christmas tree or the puffy angel made from recycled dry-cleaning bags or a candle with holly and gold pine cones. Each guest has a homemade placeholder that my mother outdoes herself to concoct each year: the clothespin reindeer, the macaroni angel or the snowball Santa. She produces these things invisibly and with meticulous care as if her life depends on it. In retrospect it just may have.

Cocktails at 5 p.m. and God help the selfish souls who are late, who cannot get to her show on time. The hors d'oeuvres include provolone, cold salami and prosciutto, wine-laced cheddar cheese concoctions and that cream cheese ball armored in chopped nuts. They're a tease in comparison to the thing we all long for: *zeppole, la zepl, pizza fritti*, wads of pizza dough deep-fried in boiling oil then drained and dusted with powdered sugar, crispy golden on the outside and fluffy air clouds on the inside. This oil-boiling made-in the-moment production is impressive considering that everybody loves them and everybody always wants more.

Now seated, we move to the Dadaist "shrimp trees," great cones of Styrofoam in 3-D tree shape, covered with lettuce then pinned with cold pre-boiled shrimp, festive and convenient for keeping the natives pacified while she cooks spaghetti alia olia (very thin spaghetti with garlic, oil and herbs—crushed red pepper optional) for the first hot course. The precision and élan that it takes to pull this off for thirty raucous Italians, by now lubricated by champagne punch, and to do it in a timely fashion, is amazing. Lorraine accomplishes it with a believable smile, as if she had not been screaming and cursing and promising for weeks that "this year it was canceled," that she would just not do it, and beyond that, this was the very last year if she did it at all! The hysteria carries on right up until the first knock on the door at 5 p.m., when she transforms instantly into the unrecognizably sweet, smiling host she is born to be.

Then comes the parade of fish: *baccaloa*, (dried cod reconstituted into a vinegary salad), squid and *squingelee* (octopus and stuffed squid), then a beautiful sole with lemon sauce and mushroom caps studded with breadcrumbs, egg and cheese. Other vegetables? I don't recall any, apart from raw carrot sticks and raw wedges of *finocchio* (fennel) that are deliciously crunchy, licorice-y and succulent at once.

Just after dinner Santa is penciled in to arrive. The cold facts hit me at about age seven, when I somehow see beneath the cotton beard that my Uncle Vinnie doesn't apply carefully enough and glimpse his street shoes peeking out beneath the PVC leg warmers. I'm crushed with the weight of looming grownup-ness. When I hit puberty I begin to direct the "Santa Moment." Orchestrating the magic of artifice, replacing faith with spectacle, I plot with whoever is playing Santa and sneak him away to transform him for the present crop of innocents. At show time I race back down with a GIANT-size coloring book of *'Twas the Night Before Christmas* to read the story aloud to the entire family, who often recite along with me. The agreed-upon cue "And then in a twinkling, I heard on the roof the prancing and pawing of each little hoof..." never fails to bring Santa clumping and ho-ho-ho-ing down the steps to greet the cheering throng of innocents, the suspicious or the adults. With the aid of some drunken elf from the crowd, Santa cajoles and distributes the mountain of presents that rises up so high around the tree it touches the ceiling. And in a wave of flashbulbs, winks and cheers, he is gone in an instant.

Petronio/Geronimo Clan, Christmas Eve (1970's). Left to right: Me, Seth Petronio, Joseph Credico. Tommy Petronio, Tom Petronio, Chris Durante, Marie Geronimo. Patti Durante Petruzellis, Tara Petruzellis, Jimmy Durante, Phyllis Dragone, ?, Craig Dragone, Lorraine Petronio, ?, Gen Credico. Sal Petruzellis, Marc Dragone.

We roll on to dessert: the prized struffoli, the dessert calzone (deep-fried sweet ravioli stuffed with chestnut and chocolate paste), green Jell-O/cream cheese mold with pineapple and chopped nuts and finally, the roasted chestnuts that are the prelude to the trip to midnight Mass. For those that stay behind, Grandma might do *Maloic*, the magic healing prayer that removes the evil eye and headaches, and whose secret formula can only be revealed at midnight on Christmas Eve.

It's somewhere before 12 and I am upstairs, away from the crowd and lying under the Christmas tree. The magical twinkling mini-lights emit the only light in the room. My head is on the white cotton and silver glitter tree-skirt, positioned next to the manger, eyes heavy as I let go, drift off and float up amongst the tinsel and ornamented branches, the balls and elves and icicles that transport me out of this world and into a place of unbelievable joy. I fight to stay awake for the midnight hour when the plaster baby Jesus will miraculously appear from behind the crèche to occupy the empty crib. I hover at the edge of sleep, floating in and out of focus, and my eye fixes on the red-blue iridescent translucence of my favorite Christmas ball, the one with letters arched in silver glitter script: *N O E L.*

The dream comes frequently and with sickening regularity. I am on Milton Avenue, the farthest boundary and outer limit of my neighborhood. Beyond this is a foggy void. The high-walled villa at the bottom of the hill is forbidding, the brown stone and mortar wall laced with glittering mica so alluring in its hint of treasure beyond.

I approach the gate expecting it to open, and a large, dark and dangerous presence creeps into the edge of the frame, towering above and casting a long, fearsome shadow. There is a tug on the air all around me like a tidal pull and a gut-wrenching chase up the hill begins. I run as hard as I can, pumping my legs in high-kneed strides but I am weighted, my feet in my beloved maraschino-red rubber snow boots, fastened with an elastic loop and a button at the calf. My favorite boots have turned against me and my legs are stuck in an invisible muck that renders my stride a slow-motion scream. The shadow looms closer larger till I snap awake in a real-time pool of sweat.

"Steeeeephen..."

My mother's sweet voice calls me back to consciousness. Her tone and the light strokes to my cheek while rousing me in the morning are an existential irritation. My mood softens instantly, though, when the smell of breakfast hits me. It's always a five-stack of pancakes or French toast swimming in a pool of Aunt Jemima and Mazola. Every morning. I'm swimming too: An ocean of memories, dreams and restless desires sloshes around in the container that is me. I can't form these vaguely erotic, ambitious impossibilities: flight, achievement, control, conquest. I'm a bundle of possibilities rushing forward to leave behind a bundle of experiences that might not be enough. I'm hungry, empty, without respite. I want. Stimulation. I'm awake. "Next!"

I'm three years old when I escape my backyard and my mother isn't looking. Along with my best friend Kenny (three) and his brother Gary (four), we trot down to the Garden State Parkway to play just on the edge of our neighborhood. The game is "run back and forth across the lanes through the roaring traffic, laughing and holding hands," taking time out to throw the little white pebbles from the side of the road at passing cars, clueless at how close we are to death. Fade to black. Next frame opens on a close-up of a trooper's holstered gun well above my eye level as it swings at his hip. His hip and butt seem enormous, deep, dark blue. I can't see up to his face but he holds my hand as we walk back up the street, to my house, to deliver us to another fate. It's his miraculous intervention that rescues us, and my mortified mother meets us at the end of our driveway. What transpires is vague but it ends with me tied to our beloved stepstool (the thing that makes me higher, taller) in our darkened basement, where former blissful scenes crumble into a terrorizing nightmare of the unknown, so that I might have some time to ruminate on the scope of my transgression. See her legs ascending the stairs, the last thing I see; is she really leaving me behind in the dreaded darkness, as she never has before? Listen to the gagging tears, the ear-splitting sound of me wailing as it all fades out to black...

My father is alerted through his omnipotent social grapevine and within the hour he's home in the middle of the day to wreak havoc. I don't recall his reaction, but the stepstool is forever.

My brother is Most Valuable Everything. He's funny and popular, the easy all- around athlete. Thomas is his father's son, the high water mark against which I'm measured. I'm a mama's boy/bookworm and he's a jock who hates school. I'm pretty much allergic to land sports of all kinds, unsure if I suck because I just plain suck, or my motor skills are light-years behind his. When I'm occasionally included in some practice session like catch or punting, I'm the lead balloon, spastic, less-than-worthless-than-shit. Or maybe my queer gene is pointing me along an as yet undiscovered path, a future fabulous.

He's only three and a half years older than me and I can't understand his disdain at my following and parroting his every move, for wanting to be involved in all his activities, for being with him wherever he goes, for being with him nonstop like we're meant to be. How can he not want these very things that make my heart beat faster?

He takes great pleasure in tormenting me whenever possible, punching me senseless (or so it seems) if the mood strikes, farting on my head or dropping a booger in my mouth when my eyes are closed and my tongue out waiting for the surprise he promises if I follow his orders. It's a real giggle when he talks me into eating a Milk-Bone dog treat ("they're really delicious, I swear"). But I love and idolize him blindly. I get into the back seat of our '62 aqua-blue Pontiac Catalina, his eager passenger even though he's only ten or eleven years old and we're taking the car for a spin against all good judgment when my parents are out for the evening. I know how wrong/dangerous/punishable/*insane* this crime is— nevertheless, I follow him into fire because he invites me. He's my hero. His audaciously fearless brio is a shock to my innocent mind. I couldn't fathom doing something that so obviously challenges my parents. But there I am in the back seat.

With Thomas Petronio Sr. and Jr. (1958).

Joseph is the youngest of five rowdy boys, his mother, Anita, my father's youngest and most fragile beauty of a sister they all call "Babe." They live an hour away and my mother and I often visit them when Joseph and I are toddlers, the other siblings safely sequestered in school. I love Joseph's soft vulnerability; it's familiar though I'm a couple of years older. He still can't speak, so it's like having a little toy brother who doesn't answer back. Suddenly I have an upper hand. I'm used to the privileges and drawbacks of being the youngest: spoiled, forgiven, doted over or ignored, misunderstood, forgotten, tortured by my brother. I'm ambivalent and a little bruised by someone in the family taking my place.

Their house is modern, pastel colors with magic lazy Susan shelving in the cabinets. We drink juice from brightly colored aluminum cups and play in Joseph's room while my mother and Aunt Nita talk in the dinette over coffee. Once during our games, I bend his thumbs back a little to make him cry, half out of love, half from a burgeoning sadistic need to mirror my brother's dominance over me. "I have no idea why he's crying, he just started!" comes my flimsy defense.

We both like dolls. When I finally convince my mother to buy me a Barbie dressed in a red-sparkle mermaid gown with tulle trim, I'm complete at last! After a few weeks though, she coyly suggests that Joseph would really like it *very* much as a Christmas gift. The holiday is rapidly approaching and how could I refuse? I love giving Christmas gifts, constructing the elaborate lists and he is my little cousin and I am innocence. We carefully wrap it in tinfoil and a red bow and off Barbie goes into the wide-eyed grasp of Joseph. My Barbie is gone, and my mother's problem temporarily solved. But Joseph's parents? Not sure what they say about my sacrificial gift. Joseph and I both blossom as the family homos, proud and unapologetic.

We have little contact after Aunt Nita "passed away," an expression I cannot fathom beyond a vague fading, a picture disappearing slowly. But her absence is sudden. (We learn later that she hung herself after a long battle with postpartum depression, electric shock therapy and everything just short of lobotomy.) Louis, her eldest, is around ten, when he comes home after school to find his mother, our Aunt Nita, hanging from the curtain rod in the family bathroom. He cuts her down, holds her in his arms, sobbing, and administers mouth-to-mouth resuscitation learned in Boy

Scouts...but she's gone. Anita's suicide has a devastating impact on everyone in her circle, but my mother, who spends so many afternoons alone with her, is shattered by her action. She's left with an unshakable fear and sadness.

The boys are mythological to me after that, spoken of in worried fragments: "It's a shame about the boys," "Who's cooking for the boys?" "Joseph has no idea what happened," "Louis is shattered—he found her and can't get right." The pictures are vivid and fraught, but all secondhand accounts—we lose access to our cousins, now infamous and motherless as "the Boys." Their father (short, muscular Uncle Lou) gets the blame for her death: "too many perverted demands," "would not leave her alone," "he was always at her, made her do disgusting things." He remarries quickly and the boys are even less accessible to us, carried away by tragedy and circumstance. It all becomes unbearably difficult and emotional for the rest of the family.

Joseph and I reconnect in our twenties out in the Hamptons. He's molded himself into a buff bodybuilder, surprisingly like his father. We flirt with a novel and forbidden attraction that we consummate before long. The first time we do it, it's a bit like kids playing doctor, but it shifts to something blindingly magnetic. Are we really face-to-face, our forbidden bodies melting into each other? We're easy together in bed; there's something deliciously familiar about the texture of his skin, the intimacy of his breath. I understand his body automatically, but it's also oddly off in its awkward reflection of my DNA. After a week or so it becomes what it was: something we were compelled to do. And when we do, the necessity evaporates.

We see each other infrequently after that. A handful of years go by without contact. The next word of Joseph I hear is that he was diagnosed with AIDS (well before the new drugs to fight the virus are developed). *Shock* when I see him again—I can't look directly at him for fear of him reading the reaction so obvious in my eyes. His muscular Adonis physique withering to its preadolescent stage; it's like watching him move backward in time to his more "innocent self." He spent his last Thanksgiving with us at Aunt Norma's, one of my father's sisters. He was vulnerable and angry, declaring we'd all get what he has, testing and goading our tolerance of him. There was trepidation but mostly blind stubborn love in return.

Toward the end there's a rumor that he's denounced his sexuality and come home to the Lord. I'm suspicious but have no idea what happens when death looks you in the eye. At the funeral, the fear of AIDS is palpable in the room. He's buried too quickly and in a closed coffin because in those early days of AIDS, the Embalmers Union, one of the most powerful in New Jersey, does not allow embalming of people with aids for fear of the unknown parameters of the virus. My family, the brothers and sisters and cousins who rally as his circle, mourn him as their own lost child. The memory of his long-gone sweet mother Anita is sharp in the uncomfortable room. Everyone's in uncharted territory. Is it my family's characteristic warmth or stunning naïveté that mourns him with such open tenderness, without harsh judgment? I'm there with my boyfriend Justin Terzi and somewhere in me lurks the unthinkable fear that we too may be vulnerable. But that's buried down impossibly deep, and I come away from this day with the supreme sense of luck for having come from such a family.

Joseph, my soft, sweet lamb of a cousin, sometimes pops up in random psychic readings that I have, traveling with Aunt Anita and my mom. He's identified by his physique and goofy grin and checks in to make his presence felt, always smiling and assuring us that he's fine.

Colored eggs and hollow bunnies, black and white—the hunt, the find, the prizes (and tears)—Run, Bunny, Run! Then into sharp new suits and hats for an endless parade of antipasti, manicotti, turkey roast, rice and ricotta pie. Hard to beat, Resurrection is the ultimate product. It's spring now; up, up and away...

No, my father and I do not have sports in common, apart from swimming. In the water and away from the confines of gravity, I turn from pansy to shark and can rarely be beaten. But the sports link ends there. What we really have in common is a love of my mother and a passion for food. We bond over the Italian-American cuisine that is our manna, me insisting that I have portions equal in size to his. If dinner is the only time I see him, I will play on his turf. It doesn't really matter, we happily eat whatever it is, from the mandatory pasta variation served three times per week minimum, to the veal, chicken or eggplant parmigiana. If it has red sauce (gravy in our Italian-American-ese) it's fine with us. Other nights Lorraine moves gingerly to more American fare like meatloaf and mashed potatoes, cube steak and canned vegetables, or to her more exotic expeditions like Chung King chicken chow mein with noodles. We love it all, we eat it all, and we always come back for more.

After dinner, TV. My father falls into a coma, and at some point later in the night he's caught standing before the kitchen candy cabinet inhaling peanut M&Ms, Mary Janes, Tootsie Rolls or Reese's Peanut Butter Cups. He's the Somnambulist of Sweet. Ice cream didn't stand a chance of surviving very long in his mitts. In this, I am my father's son. Many a half-gallon is spooned away on the front porch in summer or at the dinette table year-round, while Daddy and I bond over sugar.

I'm the odd man out, the youngest in the family with tastes that raise eyebrows, even those that are plucked and penciled. My heart races at the prospect of watching *The Judy Garland Show* on Sunday nights, which is up against my grandmother's choice of *The Lawrence Welk Show*. I cannot abide watching those boorish and anesthetizing orchestrations that lull you to sleep while Judy is self-immolating in front of a live audience on CBS. Judy doing *chassés* and time steps, wrapping herself in a knot of microphone wire angst and landing in that pelvis-forward, torso-back, defiantly wide, woman power stance. When I do win the lottery and get my way, the rest of the family evacuate the room, shaking their heads in wonder about how I could be drawn like a moth to a flame to such destructive pain? This is **Judy** and with **Frank, Barbra** and a host of other talents too big to comprehend, too moving to bear. This is Dorothy, all grown up and finally over the rainbow in some deranged lullaby land that I long to be a part of. I have to be there on Sunday nights to witness it. It's mandatory.

The last incarnation of the *Judy Garland Show* plays against the wildly popular *Bonanza*, Western dreck, an alien language that I cannot comprehend, except for the vaguely attractive son Adam, always in black, dark and sideburned, sophisticated and hapless at the same time; always drinking and gambling. There's also **Nick Adams** as Johnny Yuma, the Rebel, the one with the Civil War map that catches fire and burns from underneath in the beginning credits. I love that graphic depiction of the South's death by fire. Johnny is a slight, blond ex-Confederate soldier who wanders the old West after the end of the Civil War. He is a tough loner in a wild and lawless time, a precursor to the Beat generation's alienated wanderlust, and a man that I would not say no to, though I am too young to really know the question. I love being introduced to **Johnny Cash**, who sings the theme song for the show. Or **David McCallum** as Illya Kuryakin: He is "The Blond from Uncle," the pouty sidekick on *The Man From U.N.C.L.E.* who breathes new life into black turtlenecks for me.

My obsession with vampire movies runs deep, with me watching every one I could find on late-night network TV, staying up long past my family, scared silly, then to bed with a crucifix around my neck just in case. And on weekdays there is *Dark Shadows*. How my young heart stirs at the thought of studly Quentin Collins and Angelique's blonde curls! I'm unsure of whom I desire more, but how I long to be bitten and welcomed into eternal wanderlust and nocturnal flight.

My other need is **Elvis**. I'm ridiculed about my obsession and unabashed crush on The King. My brother torments me for my devotion until I leave for college, and then swipes my vinyl collection, realizing that my finger is on some cultural pulse and that my unnatural love for Elvis could prove valuable someday. Elvis as hoodlum, roustabout, stagehand, dishwasher, down-and-out Everyman, slugging his way to the top: His handlers so smartly build his rise from nothing to powerful into every film, recreating that narrative in real life, whatever that is for Elvis. It's so obvious to me, even as a child. Effective nonetheless.

I'm dumbstruck by *Viva Las Vegas* with **Ann-Margret**, (that sexy precursor to *American Idol*): Who do I want to be more? Either role is fine with me, and a winning one in the end. I make my father, quite a clotheshorse himself even though he drives a truck, shop with me for days to try to find the custard-yellow jacket that Elvis wears to court Ann-Margret. We come to the sad realization at some point that I would not find it in Bamberger's, Sears, Alexander's or even Harry's Men's Shop. I need a costume shop....

Singing is the thing that wins my early devotion, and though my untrained voice is monotone flat, the superstars I admire sing so effortlessly, they assure me I could too. The fearless megalomania of my natural bent propels me into a vivid illusion of vocal talent, where only passion, heart and desire reside. It's in these early singing extravaganzas, elaborate routines carved out on plastic runways that protect our wall-to-wall carpet, and in front of the living room mirror, that my performing chops are honed. My instincts are natural, spot-on. I'm just working the wrong art form.

It's Sunday night and we are returning home from Aunt Chris's house, one of those late-night rides in the back of the car in my pajamas. I love visits there. She and my Uncle Pat are hysterically funny, his humor X-rated and rapid-fire, loves something he calls *snatch* that makes my parents and Aunt Chris howl whenever he mentions it (and that's often), and there is always good cake at their house. Aunt Chris, the blue-eyed, high-cheekboned image of my grandmother, is a master baker.

We arrive home and I am climbing the hallway stairs when my mother announces with premeditated glee, "Oh, tomorrow Stephen starts school!" It is dark and time for bed, no time to prepare or plot some way out of what I instinctively fear. In a panic, my world begins to sway, my carefree hang with Mom and have milk with a touch of coffee, visit with the neighbors, hang out under the table examining their legs and listening to their lady gossip. My "watch a.m. cartoons and play around the house all day" world is fading like a murky sunset. I'm coming through the side door halfway up the steps, little hands touching faux-wood-paneled wallpaper, mortified at this announcement, betrayed by the suddenness and finality of the close of this chapter of my life. I'm beside myself, furious at my mother's obvious plot to push me out of "our very own private world," just her and me, and out into the world that I thought she would guard me from willingly and forever.

Mrs. Denoia is my glamorous kindergarten teacher and sweet mater suppono at Holy Family School. She's a tall brunette with great legs and the required early-'60s four-inch heels; her sidekick Mrs. Morgan is blonde but more matronly and stern. It's always the brunettes that I fall for, Mrs. Denoia and the show-stopping Mrs. Mazziotta, in third grade, with her hourglass figure and killer calves that are hard to beat, cloaked in clouds of heady perfume. Oh, what is that scent that makes all homework seem an effortless mission of love at the end of which are the extended arms and up-flip of Mrs. Geraldine Mazziotta?

I'm a Catholic school child and I'm built to perform. Please, excel, despondent over defeat, respond to fear and guilt.

I am built to appease, please, achieve-

I want to be a priest, to be chosen, to see miracles that no one else can,

to see the statue move when no one else is looking, to wear white robes, be a missionary in Africa or South America.

I pray silently when people swear and this mantra sets up an incessant meter behind all activity.

I walk on my toes, wear my mother's open-toe clear plastic Cinderella pumps or her five- inch true-red stilettos, follow her constantly. I am

43

the second son, not the favorite, and I need attention. Achievement is reflexive.

God performance gender, God performance gender, God performance gender!

I'm a die-hard young bookworm. (All brain and no body—unphysical.) Miss Ann Troy is the seventy-year-old librarian at Holy Family School, the parochial institution that I attend for K through eighth grade. I'm a mote in the second grade, and she's towering, grandmotherly, well-read and proper, less Italian than my own gran. Her white/gray hair is set in a bird's-nest do, flat at the center and curled all around the periphery. She wears shan-tung silk, sleeveless women's suits with long skirts below the knee, armholes rimmed with sweat, and she speaks with a slow, high inflection that sounds smart, melodic. She has an unthreatening way, takes you into her confidence, speaking to our little minds with respect rather than authority. She often meets our class in the library to read to us, to introduce us to the "prac-tice" of reading, as well as to discuss specific books of interest she's found.

At the conclusion of one of these early trips she singles me out, taking me aside to reveal "Stephen, I think you will make a very good reader," and how much she thinks I would like to read my very own book. She takes me over to the shelf and makes a selection. I, *Adam*, my first novel, just for me and it launches a long and passionate adventure through a world of books. The smell, the touch, the escape into lives and worlds far from home and everything I am not. How can I resist Miss Troy and the treasures she uncovers? I'm free while reading late into the night, the rest of the family perched at the TV. Miss Troy and I remain friends all through my school years, our bonding over literature, poetry and ideas.

Kids in the neighborhood are like plantings propagated every few years, creating groupings of souls, networks loosely bound by age, traveling in packs. For a time I'm the leader of the Briar Lane Gang. In the scheme of things, it's a mid-level assortment of boys who live in a three-block radius of our new tract houses, born in 1956. I'm probably the smallest of our crew (two Kennys, Gary, John, Colin and Brian), but I have a mean mouth and a tough stance. It's a new and exhilarating rush of power to be out of the house where I am the youngest and weakest, and on the street where I am king. It's understood that I could take anybody down regardless of my smaller size, though nobody puts me to the test. It all ends abruptly one winter after a major blizzard that leaves giant pyramids of snow along our block at the ends of our driveways. I build a full-on igloo in one and Kenny K comes by to suss mine out and throws an attitude that rubs me the wrong way. It escalates to fists and he beats the crap out of me, bending me over backward onto the snow dome of the igloo with my head buried in its roof. My extreme claustrophobia and asthmatic fear of suffocation annihilate me. I'm toppled just like that, coup d'état in an instant. We become mortal enemies for a few days while the sting of his victory hangs in the air, but he doesn't have the temperament to flaunt his power and it's all forgotten after a while and we just resume playing.

My best friend, the other Kenny, has a father who's a part-time ice-cream man and he parks the instantly recognizable white truck in his driveway on our block. It is unthinkable that we should have such a mobile palace of pleasure in our very midst, a kind of backstage access to such a significant monument in our lives. Mr. M., however, is not a very forthcoming man and my image of him is smoky and vague. He's one of those ghost fathers on the block. Faded. Never really present, never playing on the street with neighborhood kids. He keeps us at a distance and I can't ever remember tasting the merchandise he must have sequestered in his truck. It's an odd form of torture to have the actual truck in our sights all day without ever winning its prize. We could, however, play on the white truck all we wanted, whaling on the steering wheel as if in a thrilling, high-speed chase ("Don't ring the bell, my mother will kill us!"). Along the way, one of us discovers that if you slide the guard aside on the locked cap to the gas tank, it exposes a keyhole that leaks the heady aroma of gas. We take turns huffing at that keyhole, our noses pressed up against the cold, fragrant metal as if it were the most normal thing in the world. Why doesn't everyone do it? It smells so good. If we can't have ice cream, then we will have gas.

One afternoon when I am seven or eight, we're hanging around with sweet fuck-all to do and a kid from around the block says, "I've got this great new game." I take the bait: "What? What?"

"It's called blow," he says.

And we do. A lot. Whenever we could, wherever we could. Shortly after, he figures out it must be wrong so he won't play anymore. But I will, with whoever I think might be up for a new game. In basements, at after-hours construction sites, out in the tall grass of field down by the parkway. It is surprising what a popular game it turns out to be, how good I am at it, and how many people are up for playing.

Boundaries are set by adults and wrought from social mores. But when kids cross a line, who's looking? After sampling the intimacy of sensual, physical closeness, moving back from it feels like punishment and denial to me. "If you like me, you love me = I want physical access to your most private self."

Norma is my father's sister. She's one of four, along with Agnes, Pearl and Anita. But Norma is a natural competitor for my mother—very close to my father and my parents spend the early years of their marriage living at Aunt Norma and Uncle Mike's house. She becomes a go-to baby-sitter for me during my mother's disappearing acts and has an attic full of costumes for me to model on our lone afternoons together. She's an apt seamstress and makes all my early Halloween attire: the Ballerina with

46

full-on powder-blue tutu with tights, or the Flapper, a red-fringed Roaring Twenties dress that aces me first prize in kindergarten's costume contest.

Norma has two daughters, Michele and Joanne. Women rule their house as much as men rule mine. There's a giggly sorority amongst them and it's alluring. We're all clothes obsessed, but they mirror the fashion moment with an immediacy that only women can. My envy is clear. In the early sixties they are junior Jackie O: pastel party dresses with tight sleeveless bodices and flaring full skirts that fall above the knee. Pointed stilettos and postures that are easy and in repose while standing, chests hollowed, shoulders rounded, weight thrust forward and into one hip and arms crossed across the waist, their spiked heels tipped back, digging into the green mottled linoleum of our kitchen floor. They are women and seem foreign in our house, my mother slightly off balance with them yet slightly relieved. They always tell her she had great legs. And she does.

Later on, when the British Invasion takes hold, they transform into the Mod-est dolls for miles around, foreign and fashion forward in our suburban warp. Their dark hair is ironed out and mid-chest, bangs to the top of their thick-lined eyes and their skirts are micro-tight rectangles of thick corduroy, belted with white leather belts only slightly less wide than the skirts themselves. The boots they wear are flat or small heeled, to the calf, and white or black. Everything else is purple. Tights, skirts, ribbed poorboys and jumpers. Purple, purple, PURPLE. As they get cooler, they get closer to my mother, confide in her and welcome her into their world. She likes purple too. Purple reigns.

In 1965 I'm nine years old. It's a Christmas Eve and when the evening's feast winds down and there's that warm feeling that all is right in the world. This freezing world is punctuated with color, the irresistible glow of holiday lights when they come on at dusk and pierce the black suburban night.

After dessert, I meet up with a small collection of kids at the construction site of the house that's going up on the edge of our neighborhood. We break in behind the plywood barricades to enter the house-in-progress. Not really treacherous but we have to ascend on catwalks to the top floor where the walls are still part stud skeletons. It feels raw, a dangerous charge in the air. I assume Santa's not watching when we burrow in and begin to pair off in far corners to mess around, breath visible as we grope and grind each other through our festive clothes in the cold dark. It's sexual without really having sex— more animal or primal, a collective testing out of the perimeters of sexual behavior. We're not really even aware of orgasm yet, not even masturbating on our own yet. These moments are about intimacy, pressing up against the idea of a future possibility of sexual power. "This is what a dick feels like when erect," as if exploring my partner is more believable than exploring my own body, whose power isn't yet apparent to me. We're acting out of instinct, an erotic, fraternal bonding behavior, a rite of passage to our future sexualized selves.

My taste for love in the dark outdoors, in the marginal territories, gets entrenched in my psyche. And all mixed in with the holiday cheer that's carrying on back at home. How did we figure out these sexy scenarios at such a tender age?

One of my sidekick sodo-mates is a foster kid from around the corner named Ferdinand. A blond, wiry science nerd with black-framed early-'60s glasses, he's only a little older but seems to know a lot more and has hobbies that are highly detailed. He's always building complicated things, models and electronic devices beyond my capability, things that require jerry-rigged batteries. He raises gerbils in his basement and has the filthiest mouth in the neighborhood. Hyper and brittle and kind of a loner, used to entertaining himself, he's just my type. Ferdie is more obsessive than me in every way and wants to mess around constantly. He moved around a lot in foster care, is jaded by that. It's kids against adults, no matter who they are.

So we're in the middle of it one day and he suggests that we try kissing too. A surprising new boundary appears out of the great-unknown rulebook that reveals itself spontaneously. I have no idea how these prepubescent lines are drawn, but it's best not to wonder at this point. "ABSOLUTELY NOT!"

I will pop his pencil dick in my gob at a moment's notice. But kiss? Swap spit? Revolting!

The enigma of identity is severe for a young boy drifting in the middle-class suburbs. As the younger son, I'm with my mother a great deal and identify with her in many ways. I go with her on her social calls on her coffee-break housewife network and am coddled, pinched and often told how cute I am. Then I pretty much am invisible for the rest of the time and free to do what I want. Check out the house unsupervised, rummage through drawers that hold personal things, artifacts of personal identity. Silk and cotton briefs, jewelry, coins and such. Who am I? I am my mother's son and prefer being with her to venturing outside and fending for myself on some sports field or other. I lock myself in the bathrooms wherever we visit, check out the medicine chest, stare hard into the mirror, mix a stew in the sink with powder, shaving cream and whatever else I can find. I rummage through the hamper to get close to the most personal artifacts of our host's existence. What is it like for them? Who am I? I look down at my smooth, shirtless body and am comforted by its texture, hairless like my mother's and its feminine aura. But is this normal? The guys in my class are talking about hair "down there" and my father and brother seem to have veritable triangles of tangled hair that rest mockingly at eye level when we shower together. What's wrong with me that feels so right? Conflicted, I start to shave above my penis at the first hint of downy peach fuzz, hoping at once to erase and accelerate any signs of manliness to come. My mother tells me that when she shaves her legs it thickens the hair so I gamble...

Jump ahead to early puberty and I am in another bathroom in a more advanced stage of this locked-in privacy. The bathroom, the only place in suburbia where complete self-examinatory solitude can be achieved. The place to get real, examine and ponder every inch of being and transformation. I strip off my pants and check out the now full patch of pubic growth, and there it is, a hint of a trail forcing its way up from my genitals to my navel. When did this happen? How? I just checked yesterday and the road was clear and pure. The shock is profound. Mortification sets in at my body's betrayal. I am a man and will be hairy. It hits me hard that there's no turning back.

Summers include the obligatory long drive from Jersey to Florida, packed into the weeklong vacation my father gets at the end of August. His family lives in, so we caravan with the Senecas (Aunt Norma, Uncle Mike and Michele and Joanne), arriving in Tampa for a bout of communal life with my paternal grandparents, Millie and Muzzio. We leave in the early Saturday morning hours and are there by Sunday night. The trip is fast and continuous, dotted with breaks for roadside food and a short motel nap somewhere at the midpoint. Perfect for my wanderlust.

It's these trips that hone my taste for pecan pie and spark my wonder at why I can't enter the bathrooms marked "Colored" when it seems so much more exhilarating than the ones marked "Men" or "Women." Or why I can't have the primate child I long for as we pass the chimpanzee and gator farms that crop up in makeshift sideshow markets housed in trailers along the way. Or why I can't take home in a jar some of the eerie Spanish moss that hangs like ancient whiskers in the branches of the trees along our route. We're foreigners in this world and pass through with excitement and brisk disdain that whet my appetite for more.

And it's on one of these endless sweltering, air-conditioning-less summer trips, hurtling along Highway 301S, past Pedro's Place at South of the Border, where every hour is breakfast hour and no one ever sleeps, no matter what time we arrive to stock up on fireworks that are illegal up north, through muggy everglades and swamps, petrified forests and dark people hunched over cotton fields, it's on one of these family trips that I sleep in the sweating back seat. And I dream, long and fitfully...

Running through warping landscapes with a foreign soundtrack from the radio that plays in the real world, interjecting something unusually classical for my family's taste. And I dream of...ballet? A ballet, I think, it is, it must be. It comes in focus, up close and in progress, though I've never seen one, or had an interest in doing so. But there it is. I am as surprised as anyone, it's as vivid and detailed as can be...stiff bouncing white tutus and striped tights, movements in rhythms that are exotic and sure: light-footed petit-allegro and switchblade cool *jetés*; duets surrounded by rings of dancers who circle in the opposing direction from the ring outside it. When I awaken in wonder, we're still barreling forward through some fetid swamp deep in Georgia, I'm sweating, perplexed and oddly embarrassed. A ballet.

Muzzio is a young chemist in Italy, just outside Naples in Sant'Agata di Puglia. One afternoon he boards ship in Naples with his fiancée's dowry and skips out to America. With a degree that's worthless when he arrives in the new world of New York, he embarks on a long journey of adventures in product invention, marries my grandmother Millie and raises five kids. He eventually founds Petronio's Shoe Products in Newark, New Jersey, and invents a successful line of shoe polish and shoe care products. Shady partners, in a tale that includes a suspicious explosion that sidelines him for quite a while, allegedly swindle the business away from him. When he recovers, he heads to Florida to procure additional financial backing, is hit by a taxi and is left lying in some hospital for more than six months, "every bone in his body broken." Amnesia to boot. Without word for so long, the family mourns him as dead and his partners gain control of the business. He returns to everyone's shock but his partners won't relinquish the business, Muzzio can't seem to fight and he never regains control.

I end up in grade school with the granddaughter of his former partners, to whom I'm not allowed to speak. Their family still runs the legacy that belongs to my paternal grandfather, Muzzio.

He's an ancient, weathered brown man with a giant nose, short, with spindly arms and legs and a large protruding stomach, the result of an enormous hernia that he refuses to have tended. He shuffles slowly in his ever-present flip-flops, pelvis tucked and shoulders round, gentle and silent like so many men in my family. He has a cigar store Indian vibe to my young mind, which is enforced by the fact that my father seems to smoke only Tiparillo cigars on these trips.

Muzzio's disposition is ultra-calm—he's ruffled by nothing (unlike his wife Millie, who's a tightly wound type-A matriarch). English broken and smile sweet, he loves to take me onto the back porch or their modest, aqua cinderblock ranch house in Tampa, asking me to stir the giant kettle o' concoction that's cooking slowly, transforming into the bathroom and bowl cleaners he peddles on a route of local buyers. Sunshine Products is his last grassroots business and it keeps Muzzio and Millie going in the later and poorest period of their life. The last time I see Muzzio, we're at the end of one of our visits, suitcases piled on the front step of Aunt Aggie's fancy new white-columned colonial, the arm-swinging awkwardness of departure is in the air. Minutes before we get into the car, he leads me to the end of the driveway where it meets the street. Muzzio takes my tiny hand into his leathery mitt, and gently presses a silver dollar from 1882 into my awe-struck palm. We freeze in time together, wordlessly bonded. I can still feel the silver against my skin. Fifty-odd years later it remains tucked safely in a drawer with my handkerchiefs and socks.

Muzzio Petronio, above; Agnes Pepe, below (1961).

Aunt Aggie is a platinum blonde with a killer body and a quick smile. My father's oldest sister, she's the benevolent caretaker of their family and minds the grandparents in their late years. The family teases her about the mild guilt she retains from her childhood reign as proxy mommy and of her domination of the brood with acts like positioning my father's stroller in the sun while she plays, forcing him into a sweaty sleep. She has the easy nature of Muzzio, and the combination of her looks and temperament make her a general knockout on every level. She's built for fun and games— the kind of aunt who could dance herself out of her black Chantilly lace dress, leaving it in tatters on her body, the result of a wildly abandoned jitterbug with my dad at a family shindig.

She lost her husband, Uncle Al, when they were in their thirties and she raised their daughter, Patricia, a Southern beauty, on her own. Aggie molds herself into an independent professional, turning survival into success as a beautician when she starts a salon called The Tiki Hut. Her assistant Carmen and several other "girls" work the chairs. I marvel at the matter-of-factness of these working women in control of their lives, led by my heroic aunt. This independence makes her ever-changing tints of blonde (pink, platinum, honey, white) seem more glamorous and exotic for the control she herself wields over them. She imagines a salon of beauty, and wills it so.

But the Petronio branch of my family remains a distant interlude in my life, visited once a year, a haven of riotous stories and laughter. My father left home in his teens to join the Army, to marry, to start a family. He struck out for points unknown and behind is where his family remains.

Disappearing must be a genetic prompt in my family because my brother, Thomas, definitely has it too. The moment arrives out of the blue—he detaches himself from us, from me, with resolute speed. When he hits his preteens he's gone. I don't know where, but he's gone after school, shows up for dinner, then he's gone again, infiltrating new neighborhoods with new friends and experiences beyond my reach. There's a host of mysterious pubescent guys in his world and girls begin calling the house non-stop. His voice lowers to discuss their secrets, and I realize that I'm abandoned by my idol, uninvited to new world he inhabits. The sting is harsh. How can he leave me behind?

Thomas butterflies into the smoothest of operators away from of the scrutiny of the family unit. He's a rampant Casanova with girls tucked everywhere. His raison d'étre is hormonally driven and his powers are apparently impressive. One of his current targets, Marguerite, turns out to have a friend with a little sister my age, so my brother resurfaces abruptly and announces his need to have me with him more: "Come and hang with us, it'll be cool."

It's now summer '67 and I'm just eleven years old. I have nothing better to do and how can I resist the playboy glamor of my Mystery Date Bro? He wants me back under his wing so I jump at the chance, my chaffed feelings a childish memory.

The friend I'm matched with is Rosemary Joaquin, a wiry guida beauty with teased hair who's way too wise for my naïve self. She's foreign and magnetic. I want to do stuff with her, anything to solve her mystery. No longer urged to play sweaty boy games here, strings of long summer days are spent languishing in lower class **Jane Austen** configurations, *Sense and Sensibility* for the suburbs, practice romantic reveries to prepare us for the real thing someday.

This, however, is the summer of 1967 in New Jersey, the summer we're interrupted by the shocking not-distant-enough rumble of the Newark race riots in the next town, a few miles from our home.

Violence intensifies and spreads over the course of these seven days that are formidable in the shifting tide of civil liberties of the early '60s. In this unprecedented social territory, an elemental tension is laced through the heat of August. My mother is fraught with fear and racism. One nervous afternoon she can contain herself no longer and makes an unforgivable appearance in our Boys to Men world in the next neighborhood, where we're idling with our womenfolk. Petrified that civil unrest will spill out and up the road to the white suburbs of Nutley, she whisks us home. It never does so we're released from lockdown in a few days, but slightly emasculated, our swagger toned down.

Toward the end of the summer we fall into twilight games that drift between childhood and adolescence—Hide and Seek, Spin the Bottle and Seven Minutes in Heaven (where winners pair off to do whatever they please for the prescribed time). I get my first make-out session with one of the older girls in the group behind the Joaquin's furnace, where winning pairs retire for some private time. Until that moment I talk a mean game beyond my experience, but when I press my lips to my partner's soft mouth, I'm not really sure what the follow-through should be. Definitely no tongue (that would be a sin, even though just a *venial* one). I simply wait in suspended animation without the imagination to go farther. But it was sweet and innocent—my first real hetero kiss.

Later in my early teens I'm in pink-brushed cotton hip-huggers with that wet stain on front from dry humping Lori. She's my girlfriend in eighth or ninth grade and we spend a lot of time rubbing around on each other and practicing horizontal dexterity. It's an interesting period of what feels almost like love, while beginning to figure out how our sexual parts might someday work. It's a starter relationship that's serious but on training wheels in preparation for ones anticipated. She's a lucky find, and although we move on to more advanced research with other people, I'm grateful for such a kind blonde beginning.

In high school I move easily from group to group. Football jocks, wrestlers, hippies, nerds and geeks. I have little trouble assimilating into these worlds and find interest and camaraderie in each, but I'm a visitor in these groups and never feel quite like "I am home, this is me."

The horn honks and I dash out the front door in a flash to squeeze into the back seat of Joey's red Alfa Romeo, crammed in together with my jock friends (Steve C and hippie heartthrob Vic, all athletes except me). As we screech off, I have my first taste of pot in a social setting with them, wrapped in pink candy-flavored rolling paper. Looking down at the ash, I taste bubblegum sweetness as I suck in a hit in disbelief: "I'm spliffin' with football hunks." I was on the road with these guys and they seemed as genuinely open and as drawn to me as I was to them, stoned on the freedom of our hot wheels and teen hormones. Anything seemed possible on those nights, even if they ended in their usual way, a trip to Mickey D's (over three million served).

But my first joint was alone—one I pinched from my brother when I found his stash above the molding in our closet. It's seventh or eighth grade and I'm bent on smoking it to practice for when I'm in a social moment. Still all Catholic about it, I decide to light up on my way to confession so I can cleanse it all away before I have time to maybe drop dead and burn in hell for eternity for the multitude of infringements lighting up might reap.

I'm halfway up East Passaic Avenue on the way to St. Valentine's Church— the unpopulated stretch seems a safe bet—so I light up and toke away. On my second, guilty pull (is it working yet?), I spot a friend's mother, the stern Mrs. Merook, heading straight toward me. Divine intervention? Is it possible that she can't see what I'm toking on? I dump it as she nears, and we exchange stiff, suspicious niceties before I jackrabbit to confession. She never lets on if she knew what I was up to. More importantly, the deed is done—I have tasted weed!

I drop (ingest) blotter acid (LSD soaked into a half-inch square of blotting paper) by my junior year of high school. In 1973 I'm seventeen, an excellent student, intelligent with a curious mind, but innately aware that there must be something other than what I can see from my low perch in suburbia. I feel it my duty to search and research. LSD didn't seem bad to me at all and I don't recall considering its legality. It was just part of a culture of expansion. I'm driven to experiment—it's as simple as that. There aren't many warnings or media blitzes on the downside of recreational drugs in those days—it's still a brave new frontier in my estimation and I'm heading west, no fear or regret.

My first trip is textbook. A few buds and I decide to take the leap and drop it at my house, then jump in my copper-beige Rambler American for our great adventure. We have no idea what to expect. Nothing for a long time, and the anticipation begins to wear off. We're tooling along trying not to seem disappointed. "Is that something? No...do you feel anything? I don't know. Maybe. No, not really..." when BLAMMMMM it hits like an earthquake, an adrenal wave rushing from the pit of my stomach up through my chest and out the top of my head.

I immediately pull over and park the car in an abandoned lot and we step out. Everything is vibrating. No, literally— those handheld, image-trailing, independent film school tracking shots, but in over the rainbow Technicolor that I can't believe. My friend whispers, "Do you feel them?"

"Feel what?"

"Cobwebs," she replies, with glee.

And there they are, skimming at the surface of my exposed skin, face, arms and hands, a gossamer curtain wrapping gently around me as I move gingerly forward through space. I raise my arms in a slow-motion benediction to bring my upturned palms together in front of my chest. In that instant appears a bedazzled emerald spider that fills my open palms with glimmering magic. I freeze in gap-mouthed reverie, then realize it's a gargantuan SPIDER! As I pull my hands apart as it radiates into cosmic dust and we're off and running, frolicking and laughing through the parks and dales of our town like it's some distant planet. Everything is new, improved, sharp-focused and screaming to be discovered. Eventually we end up locking down at a friend's house whose parents are gone for the night, where we roar on for twelve more hours, then skid into early-morning dawn with notebooks full of arcane poetry and undecipherable observations. Though the comedown is worse than a screeching nosedive landing in zero visibility, our grins are shit-eaten for days.

I go through school with her from kindergarten and by high school I'm her slave. She was the Alice Underground of my youth, a queen of hearts and a genuine country hippie girl living in our suburban town twenty minutes from NYC. She is a cloth-weaving, bead-stringing, clay-throwing, God's-eye-making, finger-pickin', **Leonard Cohen–Bob Dylan–Phil Ochs–Joan**

Baez–listening, contra-dancing, **Kerouac**-reading, psychedelic-substance-dropping woman. She's got a sparkle in her eye that steals my breath and I want to be in on all her intrigue. She's kind of short with thick black hair, often braided or pigtailed, shapely and slender, with narrow hips and never-brassiered torpedo breasts that count her a woman beyond our tender years. I am dedicated to her. Ridiculously. Enamored on a deep level and would follow her off a bridge.

She draws me into all things folksy, grassroots, down-home, Native American, Aztec and Eskimo. We demonstrate Lummi sticks, carve kachina dolls, and read **Carlos Castaneda**. We go camping, attend readings in Passaic to hear the fathers of the Beat Generation: Beat poets **Allen Ginsberg**, **Peter Orlovsky** and **Gregory Corso**. She's wide-open wise, changes like a prism when I look at her, so I can rarely get a read on her. It draws me to her all the more.

Spliff and hash, opium and THC, acid, mushrooms and peyote, white crosses and black beauties. She's my playmate, my pen pal, my judge. She laughs uncontrollably when I show up at her house crazed on speed in a teal-blue wife-beater, hipster bells, aviator sunglasses and a shoelace headband, to announce that I'm off to the park to practice hatha yoga that I learned from a book. She understands the depth of my ridiculousness and has no mercy on my soul as I submit to her, tolerating the men she takes as lovers in high school: V, the older Kowalski-like hood who eventually runs off to join the Army; M the Southern hippie, then on to A, whom eventually completes our triangle. The three of us are inseparable, together 24/7 after school and in many of the same classes together.

I lose my boy-girl virginity at sixteen in a walk-in a closet at her house, but not to her. Her friend S takes me on. She's a year older and I'm shit nervous (I haven't even masturbated yet, it's wet dreams till seventeen), nor am I really aching for her, but I'm willing to accommodate as always when it comes to my body. Slick, quick and over, I'm nonplussed my first time in. I can't admit it when we're in the throes, but it's not really her I'm thinking about. Our relationship lasts a little longer than that first encounter.

Our triangle is insulated from the outside world, and I don't want it any other way. Even though the there's a massive amount of confusing feeling on my part, I'm in love with a couple and feel quite free. Along with a fourth friend, the redheaded B, we purchase land in upstate New York in hopes of some vague alternative future.

Then oddly, on one of the rare evenings we're apart, the evening designated to have my yearbook photo taken, they're busted for possession in a public park that runs through the town center. I'm dumbfounded by the coincidence and my luck, but a gap of suspicion opens between us. Things dissolve further toward the end of high school when B and I don't ever really couple as planned. The final blow comes when I break our pact to boycott the senior prom and ask a longtime crush, sweet Debbie Mitrovich, to be my date. Eventually, our land gets sold, the dream of a commune remains just that. Our friendship evaporates into mist.

A large, squarish woman swathed in beige and gray lumbers down the corridors of Nutley High School. Her sensible, orthopedic shoes belie a petty righteousness, a sadness of spirit and a muggy air of disappointment clings to her like faded perfume. Mrs. Clement is meant to facilitate my future path as my guidance counselor in high school. She has no idea what she's in for when she takes me on. She knows my grade point average and my test scores, maybe reads an essay or two of mine (I doubt it), but she's in the dark about the reality that I have, in fact, mysteriously fallen from the cosmos.

I'm born in a leap year on the first day of spring at zero degrees Aries, a fire monkey with Scorpio rising to boot. A germinating seed pushing up furiously through the pavement, I will not be restrained, I cannot sit still and it cannot happen rapidly enough for me. If I want something, I choose the fastest and most direct path to it, even if there is a brick wall between it and me, and I will go crashing through that barrier in pursuit of my goal. I'm certain I am somehow misplaced in my family/life and most definitely do not fit in easily at the moment.

I start researching colleges two years before I need to, and explore hundreds of even the remotest of avenues possible to jump ship and make my way to some brighter foreign future that I know must be mine. It is all too obvious to me that some mistake was made when I was dropped into Nutley. Am I really meant to grow into one of the guys, taking a place shoulder-to-shoulder at a local factory, or even finding considerable fortune at the local Hoffmann La Roche Pharmaceuticals, IBM or IT&T, home to so many of my family and peers?

Bruce Springsteen is growing up not far from me—down the shore, in Long Branch, New Jersey, and even he's "Born to Run" but it's years before that song hits the charts. **Martha Stewart** is across town in Nutley, and although my father delivers dry-cleaning to her house, I don't know her. But she certainly isn't *Martha Stewart* yet and has not shined a guiding light on the mythical tunnel out of town. I'm clueless about my future and my untested skill set but innately certain my future is not where I am. I have a perfectly loving family and enjoy my upbringing more than most, I suppose. Still, there is a yawning gap of deep emptiness. I know I need to move out into the world and sniff around.

I'm good-ish at a lot of things, well read and ambitious, but where so many of my friends dig into a seemingly clear life direction rather early on, I feel void. Passionate guitarists, potters, artists, writers and athletes surround me. Nothing sparks me beside the freedom of books. I'm desperately passionate about finding something to be desperately passionate about.

I am a blue-gray parakeet flapping through the room, a high-ceilinged simulacrum of my family doctor's waiting room (Dr. William DiGiacamo, Dr. Bill). The wait there could stretch into four-hour marathons of fearful anticipation and boredom. Torture. I am chased throughout the room by an INVISIBLE THING and I am flapping frantically to rise and I do, slowly at first, then deftly into the air, I skim the ceiling of the room, hovering like a helicopter, the backs of my wings beating gently against the ceiling above me. Out of reach but unable to escape.

By sophomore year at Nutley High School I begin obsessively scouring college guides and journals for the sweet spot that will launch me into some magic stratosphere where I belong. I try on so many possible lives and majors at so many universities, Ivies and privates. Mrs. Clement vehemently discourages such endeavors as useless. I'm an "average" student with "average" SAT scores and "You'll be happiest at a local college or community-level endeavor."

"NOOOOOOOOOOOO!!!" echoes like thunder off the sides of my skull. I'm meant to be far away in some unknown top-level school with engagingly idiosyncratic characters and can never be average. Never be average, even if I want to and I often long to be. Am I a dysfunctional misfit or a rare bird undiscovered? The jury is still out. But I'm already well acquainted with the searing pleasure/pain of outsider status, jumping nimbly from social circle to social circle, experiencing the limitlessness of LSD, art and the seed for extensive sexual experimentation. I will not stay home.

I stumble across Hampshire College in *The Underground Guide to Colleges*. New, small, "experimenting," it is the brainchild of the older, more traditional institutions that partner it (Amherst, Smith, UMass and Mount Holyoke) without the competitive and solitary focus on number scores. I write my way through the portal to my dreams. Full scholarship.

I work summers during my high school years, usually some town service–type job my father can wangle through his well-connected web of movers and shakers in Nutley's civic life. My favorite is working as a grass cutter on the New Jersey Turnpike, cutting the grass along the parkway with enormous tractors that drag primitive blade systems to do the job. These tractors are large and intimidating with many gears, clutches and blade levers, and have to be ridden on the highway and precariously tipped onto the banks of grass that need to be cut regularly. Its cutting blades are bands, steel and dangerous, and not a few tractors are prone to taking a roll. The amphetamine-giddy truckers back then pick off road workers for sport, so you have to watch your back at all times. I love the random assortment of guys who work the road crew, none of whom I know, but who bond in the reality that we have indeed scored such a coveted job. Interesting to be in a fraternal structure of strangers my age, kind of a soft prison sentence. I feel certain I don't belong in this line of work; however, I mentally try this life path on as I do with almost every possibility. Rising to the position of tollbooth attendant suddenly seems a prize, a noble gig with good benefits, "set for life." I get a lot of pleasure from being somewhere I don't really belong, and it is fun to try to master the tractors, a vehicle decidedly against my natural inclinations.

One afternoon while tooling down the turnpike near the Vince Lombardi rest area I find a full baggie of weed along the shoulder of the road, obviously dumped in a panic as the law approached the guilty vehicle. I snatch it up for home, and when I roll my first taste later that night I am urgently transported, more stoned than I've ever been. It's obviously treated with something very special. I call it Devil's Weed and smoke it sparingly all summer when I want to get paralyzed. It is the ultimate perk of my civil service.

This summer before I'm off to college feels epic. *Waiting in the wrong place.* Everything moving too slowly, or lightning-fast, and Devil's Weed contributes heavily to the warp. One Jersey Shore weekend that August, I share a joint with my cousin by marriage, a sarcastically beautiful "bad girl" prototype. Cindy is rail-thin, irresistibly lank, longhaired irreverence. I'm lost to her. We shag deliriously through those transitional nights before going our separate ways into the future, a sexual balm and rite of passage, enjoying the high together and the forbidden danger of being somewhat related. We fancy ourselves far too sophisticated to be bound by family law. Is it me, or is every family like mine? Did I lust after an inordinate number of near and distant relations while growing up? Is this normal? Seems like a natural extension of my large, loving clan. Or am I the Devil's spawn?

My cousin Michele is several years older than me but we form a close bond growing up. She is an eccentric beauty, in a *Women in Love* kind of way: wildly full mane of dark curling hair that she piles on top of her head, sensual, exaggerated aquiline profile and severe eyebrows. She speaks with animation, smokes stylishly, reads voraciously and is somewhat of a libertine. She's curious and not afraid to forge a new model for herself and her willingness to do so seems natural and unforced. Although she's ultra-warm and sunny by nature, restlessness is palpable beneath the surface. She straddles the border of the generational shift between the '50s and '60s but she conducts her rebellions in the context of needing to stay connected to her family base. She will carve out a different reality for herself, attend university, bridle against a preordained role, but she doesn't seem determined to trash where she came from on her way out the door.

Michele takes the unspoken role of mentor with me, decides it's her duty to wake me from my suburban slumber. She senses I'm marginal, as she must feel of herself, and gives me certain prompts, "opportunities," shall we say, to expand out of the world I'm born into: the books she suggests, the friends she introduces me to, the clothes she wears and the dance steps she copies. By high school she hijacks me for outings to Greenwich Village for the sake of debauchery and art. She turns me on to **Herman Hesse, Ayn Rand**, black Russians, *Cabaret* (the movie), and occasionally takes me to an improvisational dance class taught by a woman called **Edith Stephan**.

Edith is bohemia personified. She wears the multicolored tights, crocheted jumpers and thick eyeliner to prove it. She has a tiny studio in the Westbeth Arts Center on Bethune Street, a massive block of low-rent artist studios and housing where numerous artists are based, including **Merce Cunningham**. She teaches dance/improvisation to New York experimental luminaries like **Yvonne Rainer**, wacky sessions under her guidance, where people assume the role of wild horses on the beach, or run around bopping each other with soft toy hammers that squeak when they find their mark. I think it is wild but never can be convinced to join in. Instead I remain sitting on the periphery in denim cutoffs and Western-checked shirt, back against the wall, the serious young anthropologist of real life.

It's Michele that takes me to see *Sleeping Beauty* at Lincoln Center for my high school graduation in the summer of 1974, right before I leave for college. **Rudolf Nureyev** dances the Prince that night and although I know the gist (in this epitome of grand story ballets, a work that strives to tell a tale through narrative and character, the cursed Princess lies in slumber waiting for her savior to awaken her with a kiss), it's a foreign and muted language to me. I'm lost in the rush of activity, the mimetic display, and I don't understand a thing from my perch in the second mezzanine. It may as well be pure abstraction as far as I know, except I haven't delved into the concept of abstraction just yet. I am an outsider looking in at the heart of classical dance as portrayed by the legendary prince and masculine icon. Nureyev is over the top, an animal athlete, mannered unlike anything I've ever witnessed. His leaps are a riot of height, and when he rises impossibly high onto his toes he is a refined giant. But it's his "style" that endures. I am certain of only one thing, as I watch him in his gleaming white tights: Rudolf Nureyev is gorgeous.

Family Reunion (1975): Mike Senneca, Joanne Griswold, SP, Michele Seneca, Lorraine Petronio, Norma Senneca, Grmaine Griswold, Eileen Petronio Thommy Petronio, Millie Petronio, Thomas Petronio, Patricia Pepe, Agnes Pepe, Peter Griswold.

The day finally arrives, and Tom and Lorraine drive me up to Hampshire to launch me into a new life. Though none of us say it, we all intuit that I won't go back home, that I can't. This rupture in my until-then-predicted trajectory to manhood in Nutley is a cataclysmic one. We check into the hotel with the orange-tiled roof (Lorraine says, "You know what to expect at Howard Johnson's") and have a quiet dinner of deep-fried something. We're sharing a room that night and there's expectation and tension in the perfumed air. They're conflicted about all this, happy at my ambition and achievement, but not happy about Hampshire and my independence. "Why do you always have to instigate trouble?" They prefer the local state college with me living at home, but there was no arguing with me, or my full scholarship. We fall asleep eventually but in the middle of the restless, pitch black night, the muffled sound of my father's tears and my mother's whispered consolations is a muted nightmare I can't let in.

Dance chooses me because it's certain that I will be a slavish lover, a loyal, sensitive and malleable partner who won't let it down. It's certain of my dependence on it, my attraction to its elusive nature, my political arousal by its shortfall in generating a product, my compulsion to shift locations, mimic what's around me, draw strength from not being able to solidify or settle on just one thing. I am slippery like dance—hard to pin down. Dance sees me coming a mile away.

Life In Motion

I become a dancer while chasing love. Julie is a mirage in a sandpit of desire, my ring of lust radiating out in all directions, the expanding perimeter of a teenage detonation. She is compact, a Chincoteague pony galloping across the channel and into the spray, all rainbows and glow, with me in uncontrolled pursuit.

At Hampshire, I'm thinking pre-med (what else does the first son to go to college do?), but Julie casts a spell on me. The elusive dancer-girl pulls me helplessly in, milks me like a goat night after night, leaves me in a puddle at her feet. We party and dance and screw into the late hours for days at a time. She tells me I should take a dance class, that I am easy, that I can move, that I have good feet. So I do.

My first class in dance is Improvisation I. One of four "beginner" men in a sea of talented women who have been dancing for years, I'm an infant. That first crazy class takes us through uncharted places, both internal and in real space, in studios, galleries and out into cornfields on campus and eventually onto stage. **Francia McClellan** teaches the class, a post-Limón dancer with a deep interest in body/mind awareness. Plus she's no stranger to **Timothy Leary** and the psychodrama of creative altered states. She turns me on to early modern dance pioneers like **José Limón** and **Rudolf Laban**, the German movement analyst, as well as structures for finding an "inner motor" for moving. I'm a young eighteen and this blows my mind. Francia completely disorients me, unleashes torrents of new experience and exposes me to the rudimentary tools I need for digging deeper into my psycho/physical territory that's completely foreign.

One of her specialties is the guided trance journey. We lie on the floor, eyes closed, breathing for a very long period of time. We're urged to "soften our focus" and let go. She describes a door, the door to an elevator. The destination is unnamed, but we're urged to walk up to it and get on when ready, and travel up slowly, floor by floor, until we reach the top. The doors open and out I rush, eyes open, into space, into movement.

And there it is: *the moment.* Waves of goose bumps roll from head to toe, as my surface becomes a finely tuned organ in this newly charged world. Skin contracts with tingling heat. I look down my body and I realize...it's there. I have a body and it is mine. I have a body and do not understand its power or potential or the invisible stories pressing at my skin. I desperately want to move.

Up till now my "self" exists from the chest up, the image I can see in the mirror when I wash my face or shave. This part is full of *me*. Below is an unexplored abyss: torso and pelvis, genitals and back, ass and legs with crazy articulate feet. I desperately need to move.

ON YOUR MARK:

I am at the starting block crouched down in a position of ready

Left leg reaching back, foot up onto the ball,

right leg folded under me in deep flexion,

Deep crease at the hip joint,

Heart pumping

chest pressed against my right thigh

Breath ballooning deeply down to the floor of my pelvis, hands on either side of my foot, my head down, neck long.

—READY—

Heart thump-thumping through my chest and into my thigh, down my shin, through the sole of my foot and into the ground below me, grounded, drumbeat calling.

—SET—

Legs lengthen a little, jacking my ass slightly forward and up, head up and light, eyes fixed on the horizon, some distant point. Pulse quickens, muscles prepare to fire...

—GUNSHOT—

A blast of smoke and

I Spring Forward,

Evaporating into the future.

Was it coincidence that brought **Steve Paxton** to Hampshire College as guest artist that first semester that I found my body? Steve Paxton was a leading member of Judson Dance Theater, a renegade band of experimental thinkers formed in the '60s. These innovators were reshaping how America would perceive dance for generations to come. They smashed the hierarchical world where all things related to center stage in the flat screen of the proscenium, and replaced it with a shifting spherical world in which all information was equal. In short they mounted a revolution in modern dance that eventually would come to be known as postmodern.

Hampshire has a grad student teaching part time, **Eleanor Huston**, a riveting force of her own. Before Hampshire, she was an undergraduate at Oberlin College when Steve was in residence, breaking ground with some of his early experiments in natural and athletic movement. These experiments would later become known as the origins of "Contact Improvisation."

Contact is a highly physical duet form, an "art sport" based solely on the physical fact of two bodies blending weight and moving through a point of contact, a new shared center of gravity. While dancing Contact Improvisation, you soften the focus of your eyes so everything that falls into your field of vision is equal—democratic vision like information taken in on a journey—observed lightly, not sought out.

You lean into a roving point of contact that's shared with your partner, so you're gently pressed in, intimate and warm, but not erotic or judgmental or "creative" per se, but just meditating on pouring your weight like fluid into this shifting point and anchored on the authenticity of the task. You're following that weight wherever it leads YOU. The improvisation is your ability to follow it, through upside-down, acrobatic and disorienting predicaments, free from any particular name or agenda. You're rumbling upside down and inside out and it's all a surprise. There's a sense of journey together through this new center of gravity, an adventure in physics and letting go.

Photo: Stephen Petegorsky. Contact Improvisation. SP w/Randy Warshaw at Hampshire College, Amherst, MA. (1977).

Eleanor brought Steve and his posse to Hampshire frequently throughout my years there and gave me open access to this new world as it unfolded, both academically and socially. And in the periods between Steve's visits, Eleanor and I practiced Contact Improvisation every spare moment we had. We spent a great deal of time falling and rolling around together, honing our skills and developing our personal style. We also became very acquainted with each other's bodies. Contact Improvisation is intimate work but our connection was about work. And adventure. And she was too beautiful and intelligent and so much more fully formed for me to even fathom. Regardless, as I was falling through space, I was falling in love with my new dancing partner. She was fresh and confident and rooted in her body, comfortable, with a moral ground that was high and clearly carved out. A sense of direction that was innate and irresistible. This falling was thrilling and the possibilities daunting. Until Eleanor, I drifted casually through a series of misfires. This felt significantly different.

Steve's ongoing visits to Hampshire provided him with an intermittent base to continue his groundbreaking work. It was also transformational for the students, throwing Hampshire into the center of the exciting new shift that rumbled through the foundations of the postmodern dance world. Along with Steve came his partner **Lisa Nelson**, the bad cop to Steve's good one. Ever the provocateur, it was Lisa who turned to me at the beginning of my dancing life and threw down the gauntlet in terms of the path of my training: "You're just starting, and you're in a unique position as an adult beginning your studies. You can either work like mad to catch up on classical techniques that your peers are already fluent in, techniques you may never be great at because of your late start, then throw it away to begin to innovate within that technique. Or you can strike out on your own, into unknown territory, and find your own forms to develop, find a language of your own."

I choose the latter and I haven't regretted it for one second. I dug into researching a personal language, another level of me that I'd only just begun to catch glimpses of, a kinesthetic me that began to emerge in my improvisational life.

ROLLING UNDER STARS/1975

*I am crouched in the new-car-smell leather pouch of a giant slingshot. Think **Kirk Douglas** in Spartacus or **Brad Pitt's** Achilles outside the gates of Troy. I mean humongous slingshot, and I'm the ammunition. Folded into a vibrating ball of excitement, contracting against the moment of release, it springs without warning, great surge of unleashed force vaulting me over all walls and up through space on a high diagonal thorough the air into the clouds and beyond. Not prone (head-first Superman), rather torso first, chest tearing through space, the pleasure of speed pricking through my skin, and I keep going farther up and farther past anything expected, reveling in the joy of flight through crazy elevations to a weightless apex...*

I glance down in awe as it dawns on me that I've given no thought to the return trip.

It's an exciting/overwhelming first year at Hampshire. Independence! I'm reading like a maniac, dancing nonstop and partying in every other available space. The spring semester, I'm cast as an inmate in the play *The Persecution and Assassination of Jean-Paul Marat as Performed by the Inmates*

*of the Asylum of Charenton Under the Direction of the Marquis de Sade. Marat/
Sade*, a consuming production, is a political musical set in a loony bin that
has new resonance, given my experience of dorm life on campus. Inhabiting
an insane inmate in a faux prison all spring takes an emotional and physical toll on me. The result is an irrepressible need to break out, break away
and stretch my legs.

This same spring, I research organic farm programs at other colleges,
as a group of us want to start one at Hampshire. Exhaustion and green
interests are all the rationale necessary to cook up a cross-country trek
for July. My goal is UC Santa Cruz, which boasts an impressive operating
organic farm on campus.

July arrives with no one to say good-bye to. I set off that first morning from campus with a map, a small tent and sleeping bag, peanut butter
and jelly and $100. I thumb it up US 91 and make it easily to downtown
Montreal by sunset. I check into a youth hostel (my first ever) and hunt for
food, alone in a new city and feeling excited and melancholy. I am a man
traveling, free of responsibility.

No schedule.

Vague itinerary.

Alone.

I sit at the counter of a café and realize the menu is in French. "Merde."
Clueless, I order a "Pizza Nature." I am vegetarian so I think, "Very cool:
natural, whole wheat." Out comes a flaccid/anemic plain disc (nature =
plain) and note that fake-speaking French might be amusing but I really
shouldn't try to fake-understand it.

The next morning I'm back on the road. I choose Canada Highway 1,
which stretches across the width of all ten provinces of the country. Picture
a skinny, longhaired kid jittering by the side of a zooming, multi-lane highway of a city that he's spent only one night in. Large signs loom ahead indi-
cating opposite (I think) directions: EST > to the right and OUEST < to the
left. "*Ouest* must be west, almost sure," I nervously reason, so I roll the dice
and get into the first truck heading Ouest. I'm on the road!

Crossing Canada on Highway 1 (emblazoned on the maple leaf) in
1975 is a trip of awesome beauty. Outside of Montreal the road thins out

and my surroundings become bucolic. The big picture of the adventure hits me, a giddy moment of splendor, a benchmark in my life: a man traveling through a foreign world. I hitch all day and sleep in youth hostels or camp by the side of the road at night. I eat oranges and almonds, PB&J open-faced on whole wheat and fall in with random groups of nomadic kids for nightlong entanglements, jamborees even. The impermanence is a celebration, cut loose from expectation in a way that I've never known, comforting in its nonattachment. There are blaring sunstroke-sunny days, heaving-mad storms and a sparse, slow stream of vehicles migrating west, business travelers and lovers, families on holiday and me together with them but apart, humanity cut free and caravanning to the continent's edge.

The faces of this journey are mostly vague now, but one has lingered. In Manitoba, just outside of Winnipeg, a red Datsun 240Z swerves to a stop. I can hardly believe my luck. The door swings opens and inside is Mark, a handsome collegiate who invites me to travel out to the coast with him. Now in a buddy film, we warm up to each other, tentatively dealing out small parts of our stories as we jet west through a blur of Canadian beauty. The particulars are insignificant— for the most part it's the bliss of silent bonding I recall in the close quarters of his hot, hot wheels. The reverie is broken at some point by a flash storm so frightening that we have to park under a bridge, huddled together to wait it out while lightning of biblical proportions ricochets all around. It's cinematic and surreal. Under this bridge I notice that my toe, which has been kind of tender in my Vibrams, is now warm and achy, swelling quickly.

We continue on and so does my toe, inflating with throbs beyond reason. Mark offers to drive me to an ER to treat it, and we locate one in a hospital in Medicine Hat, Alberta. He's kind and we are bonded now; he tells me sincerely not to worry, no big deal, it's probably nothing and he will wait for me to continue on. When I limp back out of Emergency a little while later with my toe freshly lanced, antibiotics in hand, he's vanished. I understand this about the male species but I'm still oddly and secretly let down. Then I realize there is no one to keep my disappointment hidden from. Mark is gone and so is pretense. OUCH! It's painfully familiar. Disappearing men. Men I can't get a hold on. Grinning at this, I stiff-leg it to the edge of the city, free again and back on the road.

On through Alberta I climb, into British Columbia, the Canadian Rockies, to Banff, Lake Louise and up into Jasper. I arrive at a pulsing hippie campground at the peak of summer insanity. It is the night before the infamous August meteor showers and the middle of an underground festival called Egglust. Egglust is a state of mind that only trekkers can tap into, the howling celebratory psyche of wanderlust, of the road, food, drink and the freedom of the wild nirvana high up in the thin air of the mountains at the peak of summer. At the camp's center is a huge cauldron, giant and communal, bubbling away with the most delicious Mystery Stew for all travelers' sustenance. I'm dirty and tired and up to here with fruits and nuts. I can't say that I've ever tasted anything quite so... savory... and wonderful before. I pitch my tiny tent and meet a curvy California girl, blonde and game. We hit it off and hang out, hook up, and make love through the frosty night by the light of the hyper sky, showers of meteors charging and Etch-a-Sketching so close, we can touch the stars with the tips of our outstretched open arms.

The next morning I head out to Vancouver Island and find the lone road that crosses the island from Nanaimo to Tofino. I leave my ride halfway across the island.

"The middle of nowhere," he warns me. "Are you sure?"

I am.

I disappear into uncharted wilderness for the first time in my life. Woods can make me nervous, reflect my weakness and hopelessness in the face of the natural world, impotence I can conceal in civilization. Not this time. It's supremely quiet in the woods, a quiet that I've never heard before. I'm alone, off the map. It's a tangle of trees and vines. Brambles pull at me, and the smell is sunshine and organic matter, greens and peat. When the thicket opens up I come to a river whose depth I can't judge but it's not too wide. I decide to cross, hoist my backpack, that holds all that is currently me, over my head and forge out into the surprisingly strong current that rises quickly to my chin.

Momentum drives me forward, while I'm wondering if I'm in too deep. I decide in a flash to continue. The music gets louder and violent as I fight and push forward across while being dragged well downstream. I reach the other bank in now quiet relief. The solid ground under my feet restrains a chuckle at my naïveté. How quickly nature veers out of control to *emergency* and returns again to gentle breeze–quiet calm. Unpredictable, unforgiving yet serene. I head farther into the woods for the night. It's pitch-dark, nightmare-black chilly when it occurs to me I'm clueless—a nineteen-year-old student completely, joyfully unprepared. (Fortunately I'm not destined to be the antecedent of Christopher McCandless, the hapless guy from Jon Krakauer's *Into the Wild* who ventures into unmapped Alaska and accidently poisons himself on what he thinks are wild edibles.)

From Vancouver Island I decide to take the ferry out of Victoria down into the U.S. It's over five hours on deck through the dove-gray, wind-whipped northwestern wet. I speak to noone, keep a silent reverie by the rail peering into mist. We stop at Anacortes, and go on through the melancholy Puget Sound to Seattle. I decide to circumvent this city and head down US 5 into Oregon. I live on wild blackberries that grow fat by the side of the road, smashing them into a sweet-tart paste that I spread on Peanut Butter and whole wheat. A former Hampshire roommate/bromance Tom Williams is from this part of the world and speaks constantly of this Willamette Valley as the Fertile Crescent of the Western world. I savor the richness I've heard so much about and think of my friend Tom.

Night is falling and the faucet is fully open, drenching my sorry self at the side of the road. Night is falling quietly and perfectly this night, the wait in the rain now part of the beauty, the rhythm of living outside, untethered and with no real place to be. The rat-a-tat-ping-ping-ping of the drops downbeating against the hood of my poncho, loud and constant, keeps me buoyant on the long, wet wait where I'm stopped. Everything around me seems to jet by.

Eventually a VW bug stops and I jump in to meet Jeff. He's a sparrow-framed twenty-year-old blond. He's cozy dry and asks me if I'd like to ride out the storm at his home not far down the road. His kindness is quiet and sweet at his apartment as he offers me a towel and fresh clothes, hanging my wet ones to dry. We share some cheese, bread and a bottle of wine, talk about my travels, and when it comes time for bed he invites me into his. I'm pleased at the prospect of a warm body, though I haven't slept with but a few men before this, mostly early experiments. I nod happily but before we undress he hesitates, his pause apologetic and insecure.

"I've got something to discuss."

There's a wary drumroll in my head as I urge him forward...

"What's up?"

"My penis..."

Now my curiosity is piqued.

"My penis is...extremely large."

Silence smiles across the room. Jeff is small, about five foot seven and very trim, and I can't imagine his problem is as large as he indicates. Ever supportive, I tell him to relax and let's just hit the bed. Lights go out, clothes come off, and we fall together...

Holy shit, his penis is enormous!

Well beyond the large side of my projected estimate. He's as large as my forearm and easily as thick. I instantly take it on as my job to make him as relaxed and comfortable as he's made me. I was raised to be supportive, but I'm not very experienced with men as it is and I have no idea where that thing is going. Certainly not near any orifice I'm in charge of. We kiss tentatively, tenderly...and I wrap him in my arms and press into him and get to know where he's coming from. He's sweet as pie but he's a two-fisted love and as I take him in my hands I am finding it hard to believe his predicament and mine.

Once we get to know each other's terrain, we settle into a manual rhythm and that does the trick. I fall asleep wrapped up around him knowing that somewhere out there is a mate for him, someone eager to have his wealth. In the morning there's fraternal closeness with no worry of attachment. Glad for the night, I'm happy to be on the road after break-fast. I've never seen Jeff again but he is still there in my endless scroll of images. His special stature hasn't been rivaled in the thirty-five years of travels since that dark, wet night outside of Portland.

I head down to Eugene and stop at Mama's Truck Stop, the legendary hippie diner that's a must for the discerning freak. Behind Mama's is a car-nival breaking down and I have breakfast at the counter with several rig-gers, exchanging transient stories from the road. They tell me the carnival is hiring. "Hmmm, a carney," I drift into reverie about the possibility...

Like all good Aries, I must try to try on every possible lifestyle as my next incarnation. I wonder what it would be like to join up with them. Rugged, long greasy- haired, forearm-tattooed men in their twenties; wiry, Camel Straights kind of men. It's tempting all through my Swiss and broc-coli omelet with home fries, but I remember eventually that I have zero mechanical skills. I would have to learn to handle a wrench somewhere in secret before facing the rig of a carnival ride. We say good-bye at the cash register and I'm back on the road.

I enter Northern California on US 101, perhaps one of the prettiest highways in the country. It sits beside the blister-blue Pacific and winds and sails at the edge of the world like an eagle in the air, soaring above the crashing waves. With a nylon-sheer drop to the sand below, Highway 1 rides the vastness of nature in its beauty and danger.

Somewhere outside of Mendocino is prehistoric redwood country and I'm Lilliputian beside the immensely giant beauty that surrounds me. An old Chevy picks me up and inside is a dark, young earth mother and her toddler; she offers me their home for the night. I'm the recipient of so much goodwill on this trip yet it doesn't seem out of the ordinary. People just want to adopt me for an hour or a day or as long as I might like, to make sure I'm safe and fed and.... It might be something to do with my aimless, rambling venture and their need to talk to roving strangers. Maria and Jeb are no exception. We drive off trail and deep into the woods. When we stop at a tree, I spot, high up in the branches, one of the legendary Mendocino tree houses I've heard about. It's their home. Up we go and it is an amazing two-room Tarzan fantasy. (You know that Johnny Weissmuller film where he marries Jane and together they have that crazy home in the boughs, Cheetah the chimp and all? Jane gets domestic and makes giant ostrich egg omelets. We are there.) Maria fixes tacos and we talk into the night. She is up before Jeb and me so it's oatmeal with raisins and sunflower seeds for us when we open our eyes. She is kind and open and invites me to stay as long as I like, but I thank her and beg a ride out to the highway where she sets me free, honking as she pulls away.

A nuclear family picks me up on their way south through Sebastopol. The conversation is quick and deep as we move from details to motivations then on to bigger dreams. We hit it off so easily they offer to adopt me for a few days. Their daughter is in high school and their son just starting. It is interesting to me how easily they all open up, befriend me without getting too attached, and find it quite normal that I am camped on the couch of their upper-middle-class house in Petaluma for two days. While Dad seems to like having an older male to talk with, and Mom is sweet enough, the son loses interest pretty rapidly. By the third day our time is done when "why is that dude who my father seems to speak to a lot still on our couch?" begins to leak from his pores.

They drive me into San Francisco and drop me off with warm good-byes, and I sense the irrational pull of mutual attachment release on my way out of the car. I'm in a large city for the first time since Montreal and the survival skill set is different. They drop me in the Castro and I stop for coffee at **Orphan Andy's** at 17th and Castro. A clean-cut, preppy guy working an Adonis-in-the-making body strikes up a conversation, then sweetly offers me a bed for the evening. He gives me an address and asks me to show up for dinner. I can't believe my ongoing lucky streak. Feeling relaxed about a place to base myself, I set out to explore the city through a long, hot day. When I arrive at the address he gave me, it's a quaint old Victorian. I knock on the door and wait in anticipation on the porch of a perfect stranger. The benevolent prince answers after a bit and leads me into his home. Within minutes, his mannerly mask falls away and declares that if I want to stay I will have to screw him. Now he's good-looking enough and well appointed, but his manner is so completely repulsive that I bounce out the door and in a second I am back on the street. It's getting dark and I'm caught homeless in a city I'm not sure how to navigate. The idea of being the urban camper is not in my plans, but I nap at the bus station. At dawn I hit the road and head for Santa Cruz.

I spill straight off the highway and into downtown, sunburned, straggly hair well past my shoulders and my emerald-green backpack. I am Traveler Personified, Wanderlust on Wheels. Or, a Sitting Duck. At a central intersection I meet a group of people who are passing out info about their organic/vegetarian garden and free dinner later that night so I take an invitation and determine to check it out. Meanwhile, I get oriented and head up to UC Santa Cruz to see its organic farm program at long last.

The campus is a Shangri-La of higher education, a mossy-green pillow perched high in the clouds at the Pacific edge of the world. The ocean is the horizon line from this perch, and that infinite blue space seems to call you into it, hinting that if you dive out, you just might fly into the vastness of nature in its beauty and danger, waiting calmly to consume you. I am certain I can see the slight curve of the earth, and it's so beautiful at this campus I can't fathom cracking a book to study anything.

I find my way to administration and a student guide to show me the Santa Cruz Organic Garden Project, the organic garden that is the raison d'être for the entire adventure. I'm pumped by the prospect of finally seeing the legendary place in the Wild West where students are living a reality that we are only dreaming back east. When we get to the rise above the plot, I look down with a drumroll and it is...

Disappointingly meager.

Bone-dry brown.

Unkempt.

Before me is a ghost plot of a garden gone to weed. The students/part-time farmers deserted the bio-dynamically raised beds. They are now off surfing somewhere or photographing Nicaragua. There's no one tending or even associated with the project, so I wander gloomily around the beds like a visit to an abandoned graveyard. I thank my apologetic guide and make my way disappointedly back to town in time for my free organic veggie dinner with the group I met earlier. At least the whole day won't be a waste.

When I arrive at the address there is guitar playing and singing and a large pot of some kind of veggie stew rich with summer squash and zucchini. It's delicious and the singing is kind of kumbaya corny with a little Bob Dylan thrown in. It's well intentioned enough though, so I glide along making friends in the room and enjoying the general vibe. One of the people hosting the dinner asks me if I would like to come back with them to their fully functioning organic farm in Mendocino County the next morning to check out their community. How lucky can I be? UC Santa Cruz was a bust in this respect just a few hours ago, and in the next moment I have the opportunity to check out a working farm. I jump at the chance.

I can't remember where I sleep that night, but I show up at the house bright and early to meet with the farmers as well as several others whom I recognize as new guests from last night's dinner. One guy in particular, Daniel, is lean, handsome with dark skin and eyes, hair that curls in a goofy way. I like him instantly and form a quiet bond with him. We all pile into a white windowless van, sprawl out on mats in the back and set off north for an alternative world.

There's more singing and conversation and general rabble-rousing. About an hour into the journey we make a pit stop and a phone call, after which it's announced that there has been news of a measles outbreak at the farm and we can either go back to Santa Cruz or go on to the Berkeley house, an annex of the farm, to hang out for a day or two to wait out the quarantine. We all opt for north and arrive in Berkeley at a massive and impressive Victorian house with myriad rooms and lots of new faces. We are invited for a three-day seminar but if we accept we must play by the rules of the seminar:

*NO CONTACT WITH ANYONE OUTSIDE THE SEMINAR.

*NO UNACCOMPANIED DEPARTURE FROM SEMINAR GROUNDS.

*NO PHONES FOR ANY REASON.

*REMAIN WITH AN ASSIGNED COMMUNITY BUDDY AT ALL TIMES.

*DROP YOUR JUDGMENTAL MIND AT THE DOOR AND BE OPEN TO A NEW EXPERIENCE.

*NO ALCOHOL, TOBACCO OR DRUGS.

I am excited by it all, the challenge of a new experience in a new place with tons of young crazy strangers. I see Daniel across the room and want to speak with him but it's against the rules. Our backpacks mysteriously disappear but it seems in keeping with the focus of the "experience" and I don't think much of it. We are all assigned chores for the next day and a schedule of lectures, seminars and meals. I'm on some kind of cleanup detail and when I cross paths with Daniel in the hall he whispers that he is on kitchen duty and let's try to meet up sometime tomorrow. At bedtime we are separated by gender and shuffled off into the larger halls to bed down en masse for the night. I go to sleep in anticipation of what might be in store the next day.

We wake up early and we're out of bed fast, corralled into the dining hall for oatmeal, raisins, OJ and toast. The first seminar starts immediately after and they keep coming all morning. *Spiritual Values, World Order, Communal Cooperation*, lunch. Peanut butter and jelly, or tuna on whole wheat. Everything is kind of salty. It's oatmeal raisin cookies for dessert and back into seminars: *World Government, World Religion*, then discussions of our fears and dreams, what moves us, our personal weaknesses.

In the afternoon we go off to exercise in Golden Gate Park. We play a dodgeball-like game where we hurl the ball at each other at close range and get slammed! They call it "love bombing" and during the entire game there was chanting: "Win with love! Win with love! Choo-Choo-Pow! Choo-Choo-Pow! Win with love!" By nature I hate team sports that involve a ball. It's a violent and weird game and I'm completely put off by the supercharged and overly aggressive vibe. My weekend is beginning to ooze suspicion.

On the way back to the Berkeley house, we stop off to sell roses in the streets for world peace and order. It all happens so fast and without discussion. I find myself acting without really challenging the activity and I end up in the streets with this lot, hawking single roses to strangers while my competitive nature drives me to sell. I carry on for an hour and just when I am getting twitchy and uncomfortable about it, we pack off back to the house for dinner.

Back at the Berkeley house I see Daniel alone in an upstairs hall and we exchange updates and observations. Notably, while on baking duty, he is putting a strange white powder in the cookie mix that produces the house favorite oatmeal raisin cookies after lunch and dinner. His guess is that it's saltpeter, and it makes sense since there is no sexual energy in the place at all and we are a lot of people in close quarters for extended periods of time. Yuk.

Dinner is veggie stew then singing and chanting off to bed. Sunday morning is a repeat of Saturday but the day progresses more intensely in the world religion direction, and community members are beginning to target me as an extreme skeptic, delving into my intellectual resistance to spiritual practice. After lunch a Bible comes out in a session and alarms blare in my post-Catholic head: How could I not have seen it coming? Some kind of religious cult!

As the day goes on there is discussion of a joining ceremony and when it arrives it hits like a storm. People are breaking down and crying about their ability to trust and let go. People from the community are at me from all sides, flattering my openness, intellect, looks and critical facilities, while suggesting that these very skills are what are stopping me from experiencing real happiness and depth in my life. I am caught, because we all know by now that I have not been able to become deeply, thoroughly involved, to join something and have it seep into my identity. I'm at ease everywhere, but at home nowhere. I'm a façade with no real central anchor in my life from which to make a contribution to the world. Are they right or are they evil vultures after my soul?

My group leader, Epi, tells me, "Your suspicious mind has never really let you be a part of anything, has it? You never feel you belong, do you?" I can't argue with her, and I tell her so, and I begin to wonder if this could be me? Do I have to go back to my East Coast intellectually aspired pre-med track at Hampshire College, where critical thinking is golden and

CONFESSIONS OF A MOTION ADDICT

questioning authority is at my core? Or can I just stay here and serve something bigger than me?

There are people sitting directly behind me. I can see them in my peripheral vision; they are chanting and shaking some invisible pom-poms of energy at me to try to break me down. Epi keeps working on my fear of alienation, and now other potential inductees are being thrust into the center of a ceremonial circle surrounded by chanting, singing community members. They're being asked, "Are you ready to commit to joining the community? Are you ready to change your life?" It's like some weird war circle meant to sweep you up on the spot and suck you in, and many people are buckling and crying and shouting, "YES! I want to join."

Suddenly I'm in the middle of the circle and the clapping and chanting rise in a crescendo. Sweating tense smiles and imploring eyes are on me, urging me to declare my surrender. I am asked aloud and in the space for a response there is emptiness. I am torn, speechless and can't let myself go. I won't let myself lie. I say nothing and leave the circle, to be replaced by the next potential inductee.

Epi intercepts me like a hungry hawk and says, "You need more time."

"Maybe I do," I respond.

She comes closer to me and whispers: "Promise me that you'll give it more time. Come back to a weeklong seminar at the Santa Rosa house. We think you're extraordinary and can make a huge contribution to our community. You're so intelligent."

I'm not flattered but quickly guess the best way out of this mess is to agree and escape en route when I get my backpack back. I tell her that yes, I'll go with her, and move in to hug her tightly. I can feel the ever-so-slight but perceptible chill, the hardness and retraction in her body. I'm thinking Witch of the East as her legs shrivel under Dorothy's newly dropped house. At this moment I am certain she is powerful trouble. Her body can't lie to me.

I'm shuffled into a group of people assigned to go to Santa Rosa. Daniel is with us, along with another guy I met at the house, Steve, as well as some underlings, a few new members and two other uninitiated prospects. Epi stays behind to finish up business but plans to join us in the morning. "I know you will love this extended seminar. It's an amazing experience. And I'll be back with you tomorrow," she says.

Does she feel my relief? Her pull over me will be absent and make it easier. We pack up into a new van and arrive in Santa Rosa later that night. The prospects are assigned to one room this time with two bunk beds and it's finally lights-out. We begin to whisper as soon as we think it safe. We have no real idea of our location, although I saw a Santa Rosa Village sign flash by from my place on the floor in the back of the van. Steve and I are freaking and suspicious, Daniel and the other guy are curious. Our packs are stowed away in an undisclosed location but Steve pulls out a flashlight from his overnight bag and we search the room and the adjacent dining room.

The house is minimally furnished and oddly undecorated. In the drawer of a sideboard we hit the jackpot: a framed picture of a suited Asian man, official-looking and of obvious import shaking hands with a Midwestern couple. There is a large Korean flag behind him. Not certain but he looks like the **Rev. Sun Myung Moon.** *Moonies!* Adrenaline is flying and both Steve and I are adamant about getting out. The infamous cult is a favorite in the news, and its sophisticated tactics for collecting wayward members are legendary, but we can't believe we are in the middle it all. Their camouflage is insidious. Steve and I plot our exit while the other two remain undecided. The atmosphere is strained but the tension is kind of welcome. We have a concrete foe at last, so we devise a plan for breakfast and fall asleep with resolve and with hope. In the morning we're up early and breakfast is the usual communal experience sitting around the dining room table with three cult members, three female prospects and our male group. There is the familiar mush, OJ and coffee before us. As breakfast begins it's innocent enough, I need my coffee first anyway. There's a discussion of the day's agenda then Steve and I start in: "I'm completely uncomfortable being here," I blurt out.

"Why, what's wrong?" longhaired Jonathan with the British accent replies, aflutter with innocence.

"I feel trapped," says Steve.

"I thought you wanted to continue your studies," says Jonathan.

"Me too," I say. "At this point we're here against our will, you're hiding the fact that you're a religious cult that's controlling our moves. We found a picture of Reverend Moon in a drawer last night and you are fucking

Moonies. This is bullshit and we demand to leave immediately." I am yelling now. "We want out now. And if any of you don't want to be here, come with us right now," I charge, looking right into the eyes of the openmouthed prospects around the room.

Like magic, our backpacks appear out of nowhere and Steve and I are being ushered out the door like we have the plague. *No discussion.* While we're storming down the driveway (Daniel's nowhere in sight), I turn to see another prospect, a doe-eyed buxom blond in her teens, at the door in tears: "I don't understand. I really liked those guys." She cries. "Please come back, you guys!" I feel for her, I really do, but the gate is cracked open and we're through it and down the street in a beat.

Steve and I bolt to our freedom and head out to the highway together in disbelief. We thumb it as far as the outskirts of Las Vegas, where our escape gets stalled waiting on a ramp and we continue replaying our week while getting badly sunburned. Eventually we decide the adventure is over and split up to get a ride faster. I never see Steve again.

It's getting close to the end of August and I need to think about a quick wrap-up to make it back to Hampshire in time for fall semester. I also really want to see my mother.

I skirt around Sin City and head onto Highway 50 across Utah because I hear it's a must-see, then hitch straight across the state, through a beautiful desert with its oven hot breath and lonesome terrain, scorched in the August daylight. Frost and galaxies rule the night, but it's the red buttes and bluffs that linger all these years later. As for civilization, there are tiny towns spaced every two hundred miles or so, or rather stops with a gas station, general store and a bar or two. Not much else. On one pit stop I walk up to the sweet young teen who collects payment for gas. She's wrapped behind a bulletproof Plexi encasement.

"How far to the next town?" I ask.

"I'm not sure," she says. "I've never been out that way."

"Never been to the next town?"

"Never needed to," she answers.

She must be sixteen at least.

I barrel on getting long lucky rides and make it across the Colorado Rockies, climbing from summer heat to a raging blizzard summit. Wet snow and giant hail force cars with their summer tires to snail and slip their way to the inferno below. Then on through Ohio where the rain is so heavy I'm forced off the road outside of Kent State, to a truck stop where I wait out the storm.

While I'm having pancakes at the counter, I ask two truckers if I can hitch a ride and they glance at each other, then grunt their consent. I head to their rig and when the guy riding shotgun opens the door, he silently indicates that I'm sitting in the middle between him and the driver. We head into the dark, wet night; the driver is a curious and wiry old guy. He asks about my travels and finds my openness and naïveté hard to swallow.

"Don't you ever worry about your safety?" he asks.

I tell him idealistically: "If you are open and a good person, you draw the same kind of energy to you."

While he's chuckling, he reaches under his seat and pulls out an eight-inch fishing knife that looks much sharper than me and holds it so the oncoming headlights glint off it like a cold hard diamond. I freeze, trapped between my escorts, then inhale, waiting. He laughs again and puts it back. I exhale.

"Everyone's not what they appear to be," he warns.

I seem to be learning that in the last few weeks. We drive on in silence to Pennsylvania, where they drop me by the side of the road.

I catch a ride from a red Chevy convertible (Mike) and am happy that the morning is breaking and it's a dry one. He's driving to New Jersey, not far from Nutley, and as we warm up to each other he offers to take me the rest of the way home, right to my door. When we get off the highway I ask Mike if he would mind a little lie that would set my mother at ease, and he agrees to play my traveling bud throughout my month-long adventure, concealing the fact that I have been wandering alone by foot and thumb. As we drive up to Briar Lane, my home and my front yard, my safe cradle of young life, the breadth and outlandish reach of my trip hits me hard. I am a man in the world and there on my front lawn is my mother, Lorraine, in madras Bermuda shorts, black tank top and fashion sunglasses, weeding the perennial borders around the front of our small charcoal-gray home. Our house is distinguished by a white ceramic cat caught mid-leap, frozen for all time on our shingled roof.

Mike plays his part like a proper gentleman of the fraternal code and greets my mother warmly. She greets him in return as sweet as she always is to strangers and friends alike, thanking him for acting as chauffeur for me and bringing me all the way back to Nutley, all the way back home. There is a vague exchange about our great adventure and he vanishes up Briar Lane, back into the world from which he veered for his brief cameo in my story.

I walk with my mother up the driveway to our house, and with each step closer, I can feel a transformation rumbling deep inside, molecules recalibrating and rearranging, shifting back again from all that I've been this month: from all the rides, stories, wind-slashed storms and glacial ponds, from the star-clustered saliva-slick passion, camaraderie, suspicion, fear and disappointment, and from the swift, constant path forward, the change from face to place and back, the return to my role as a mother's son in a small suburban-safe home in the embracing town called Nutley.

Later that afternoon, I prepare to take a long-awaited shower in our own pink-tiled bathroom with abstracted phantoms floating on black wallpaper. As I empty out the pockets of my patched, dirt-worn jeans I find a $20 bill left from that original $100 I set out with to travel North America.

About ten years later I am passing Macy's at Christmastime. On the Broadway side of the store just above 34th Street is a display on the street advertising a Community for World Peace that's welcoming new members. I walk up to have a look, as I'm sure it's a Moonie story, and there seated at the display is longhaired, British Jonathan. I approach him and start in about Santa Rosa and the Berkeley house, but he cuts me off and turns away. "I've never seen you before and 'ave never been on the West Coast. You're mistaken."

Back at Hampshire something's changed. I've made hard decisions before, choices of import and consequence, but I'm emboldened by the knowledge of "possibility" that I found on my trip. I shift my study of medicine to nutrition, then to the politics of food systems and how they impact quality of life and health. All the while I'm dancing comittedly and it becomes clear that I am far more creative on my feet in a studio then I'll ever be on my ass in a lab.

I take survey courses of the major modern dance leaders (**Martha Graham, José Limón, Merce Cunningham**), enough to get the gist, but not to become fluent or find reason to do so. But I do find infinite passion in moving bodies through unknown journeys through space, in the sparking of an improvised, spontaneous connection to the world. When I quickly seque into building dances more repeatable, more choreographed, I've never felt closer to my bones. I've hit a center for my life and the passion is addictive.

City Mouse

I zigzag incessantly from the north side of St. Mark's Place to the south, then back again (often on the same block) to have it all. The thought of missing something, someone—the better thing, the right one—is unbearable. Unbearable. It's 1976 and I'm in New York City on a semester off from Hampshire. The city ramps up one of my obsessive dilemmas. What side of the street to walk on? And insomnia; I can't bear the thought of going to sleep at night as a child for fear of missing...whatever. I'm easily awake long past the rest of my family at night while growing up. All are older than me, but with less endurance. How could they shut it down so early? The dark night is full of possibility. And on the nights that I might strain to stay awake, I lie on the couch in the den while my family watches TV, my face to the wall buried in the fantasy of some book that's propped up in my hands. If I dozed while reading no one could tell and I wouldn't be sent off to bed. To bed, to dark alone, unknown, not what's happing now in the room. Something...whatever...anything! From early on I crave things, experience to add up, to fill me up, to make a "me" I can live with. My solace is moving. Anywhere really. Action. Forward motion: "My legs can keep no pace with my desire" but try to. I'm an empty container, a heat-seeking missile hurling toward...toward warmth, light, intimacy. Toward "more." And New York makes me hungry.

I sublet a six-floor walk-up on Lafayette and Grand. The long flights necessitate bringing up groceries one meal at a time. It's three small railroad rooms at the end of a long dark entryway with a claw-foot half-tub in the kitchen next to the sink. The toilet with pull-chain is in a small closet off the kitchen.

I start the day of intensive study with some variation of official Technique Class, (or two) then on to Stretch and Placement at the **Colette Barry and Susan Klein School,** where I get everything grounded and aligned, then to **Louis Falco Studio**, where the technique was fast and dirty and placement was out the window. I thought it was a good antidote to all the "enlightened" bodywork I was doing. Next up was some kind of improvisation class, i.e., **Danny Lepkoff's** Contact Improvisation, then back home to collapse.

I operate on a tight budget (about $50 per week), so it is soup and bread for dinner at home. The proximity of the tub to the stove in the kitchen allows me to stir my Progresso lentil while soaking off the day, then dry off to eat it with a whole-wheat Italian roll. I'm in heaven during these days and I love that the great, seething San Gennaro Feast is in full swing right below my windows in that neighborhood when I move in.

There are throngs of Italian-American tourists in the streets of Little Italy then, eating sausage and pepper heroes and gelato, and playing carnival games for stuffed animals or short-lived goldfish. I lose myself in the din, pressed up close and lumbering along, not knowing anyone but feeling oriented by the look and sound of families from the suburbs with cultural references that I know on a genetic level, that make me feel at home in a strange city.

Eleanor is taking classes here on weekends and we're in a Contact Improvisation class together on Saturdays. I invite her to stay with me when she's in the city. Away from Hampshire we are out of our given roles and simply friends obsessed with dance. After a visit or two we begin to grow closer and I can't believe she's in my apartment, how right it feels to me. I'm in free fall for her. It's out of my control.

We have dinner one night and afterward we're chatting, she on the cushions I keep on the floor as a sofa and me sitting as near as I dare get. Her voice is a delicious rhythm and I begin to skip the words and ride on the lolling sound, drink it in, lean closer and closer to eventually slip into her arms. Softly. We start to make love but in that instant the phone rings and breaks the unreal spell. I pop up in response—is this interruption some cruel chance to reconsider? When I return from the call I can't skip a beat and dive to her, get to feel the extreme silky path of entry immediately once again. It's begun and our relationship continues on all through my semester off.

She was all that I was not: Logical, grounded in her actions, she seemed to excel instantly at every task she approached. You could feel logic in her—it was physical. Firm in her convictions, unshakable really, she always seemed oriented and aware of her relation to everything, vague about nothing. She could articulate her subtlest feelings and was sexy as a tiger to boot. Her laugh was big, her laugh was open, her laugh was infectious. How I craved her laugh. Around Eleanor I felt I could be better than I was at everything and her ease about it all made me eager to try.

I can't believe my good fortune. I've begun a life in New York, am beyond passionate about my work and have found a giant love that's changed the way the world looks to me. It feels perfect in New York and I want to make the move permanent. The idea of going back to Hampshire to finish my BA suddenly seems senseless. It's Eleanor who convinces me that New York will wait, that I have my whole life to struggle, to pay for rehearsal space, figure out how to make rent, how to fight for a slice of the professional pie as an independent dancer and artist trying to make it in the toughest city.

My apartment on Lafayette and Grand is $112 including utilities. I have no idea how cheap this is and how lucky I was to find it advertised on a flyer on a pole on Prince Street. My landlord is a waif of a junkie dating a buff tae kwon do stud whose looks say that killing me would be a pleasure. I choose not to indulge him and vacate the apartment quickly and head back to Hampshire when my unhinged landlord comes by all strung out one night and tells me she needs a place to crash.

My body holds the collection of things that are me, things close to my skin. I am open and my body's a map of where I've been. My comfortableness is there in the slope of my shoulders, the sling of my pelvis. I am sexual from an early age and that shows in my gait. Shy with words then, afraid to speak, but cocky of body. I am easy. Welcoming. Open. I want to greet you then eat you. You better like me, my style, the way I see it, the way I move. I'm aghast then gutted then disgusted if you don't. I'm just a guy from New Jersey.

Like so many major events in my life it happens in a flash. Instantly, complete and without warning, an image blasts into my mind fully formed and it's a shadowy dancing figure fixed in place but spinning and moving in a gyroscopic kinesphere that's at once organic and virtuosic. It's a joining of the spherical model of movement I'm embracing in Contact Improvisation with the extended-out-in-space language that postmodernism rejects because of the context that it comes out of. Yet there it is, my future self, unveiled and dancing in my mind during a caffeinated car trip between Boston and New York, Eleanor driving and I in quiet dance trance brought on by forward propulsion.

I move permanently to New York City in the fall of 1978 and am teaching Contact Improvisation at **Frances Alenikoff's** studio on Broadway between Prince and Spring Streets. Almost as soon as I start, my class somehow becomes the go-to Monday-night class. So many great downtown dancers/artmakers pass through that class: **Ishmael Houston Jones, Yvonne Meier, Jackie Shue, Melanie Hedlund, Vincent Fox** (aka **Lavini Co-op,** always in patterned sheers instead of sweats, a founding member of the critically acclaimed troupe **THE BLOOLIPS**). They are the hot, the awkward, the up and coming, the down and out, the hobbyist and the beginner. In that class I hone my skills as a teacher while passing on the goods I learned firsthand from Steve Paxton, Lisa Nelson and other influential teachers like **Nancy Stark Smith** and Danny Lepkoff.

I start as a pot washer then advance to wait tables at **FOOD**, SoHo's first restaurant and artist haven started by musician **Carol Gooden** and **Gordon-Matta Clark**, the "building slicing" artist (he cuts holes through the floors/

layers of a building to expose new volumes of space). The restaurant was a lone central meeting place in a still undeveloped neighborhood with lots of vacant lofts. It's here that I catch my first glimpse of **Trisha Brown, Lucinda Childs, David Gordon** (dance stars of Judson), members of the theater group **Mabou Mines** and musicians of the **Philip Glass** ensemble, as well as other pioneers living in the neighborhood. At FOOD, employees can eat one meal a day there for free, even when not working. It's a glamorous place staffed with artists, hipsters, British expats and the elite of New Yorks's demimonde like actress-writer **Cookie Mueller**. A job there is akin to an artist's stipend and is the way many are able to survive through their early days.

It's here that I meet the angel-faced **Ron White**, my coworker and the lover of Neo-Geo artist **Ross Bleckner**. We fall in like and he becomes my first friend outside of the dance world in New York. He introduces me to Ross and Rennie (Ross's adorable dog at the time), and affords open entry into the **Mudd Club**. The club is stationed in the building Ross owns and where Ross and Ron live on the top floor. In 1979 it is the epicenter of New York nightlife cool and home for punk music culture. Everybody passes through the Mudd Club but I'm paralyzed shy at this stage and can just soak it all in like a mute sponge. The music, the clothes, the drugs, the superstars and freaks in the belly of downtown. It's an alien and irresistible world.

Later I bake bread and make soups at **Michael's** on Bleecker Street in the Village, then move on to become a waiter, a part-time house-painter and Sheetrock hanger, a figure model and finally a dancer and teacher. Things are looking up. The modeling gigs, arranged by an agent, send me throughout the city to pose nude for various artists and classes. I'm a natural mover with a decent body but sitting still proves to be a monumental challenge. I run across the usual pervs and weirdoes, but my favorite class is an adult education assignment in Harlem. I'm excited to go to a neighborhood that is legend and so far outside my downtown parameter. I get off the subway and am suddenly w-h-i-t-e and feeling very small. It's another city, another country, and I can't believe how incomplete my experience of New York instantly seems. I arrive in class and I *am* small and white. The students are all women, early thirties, quite large and weighty and all shades of dark. I'm asked by the instructor to strip and sit on the unswept linoleum floor. I petition for a sheet of drawing paper from the teacher and sit my skinny white ass down to pose, feeling like a pupa in a rain forest, small and vulnerable. At the break I stroll around in my underwear to check out the progress and uniformly see the skinniest tiny boy with a preternaturally large penis splayed across their sketches. I am an odd mixture of humiliated and enthralled. Alien for sure.

Arrow-straight, chestnut-brown, split in the middle and down to her waist, her hair is like a lightweight cape that accentuates all of her moves. When she wears it in a braid (and that's often), it's a metronome setting the beat for her moves and what's around her. And all of those around her notice the grounded, sure way her compact body moves, cutting into a room with forthright sureness, delivering the most wide open and sky-blue, soft- hued eyes. Eleanor. Midwestern Methodist sweet, she's from a large, handsome family; a kind and upright micro-culture. We remain together during my last year at Hampshire and continue on when I move to New York.

Photo: Stephen Petegorsky. With Eleanor Huston at
Contact Improvisation Workshop. Putney, Vt. (1977).

It's clear that Eleanor has a magnetic power. It's reflected in people's eyes when they speak to her or of her. She's a strong improviser and is performing with Steve Paxton and his inner circle. I'm her boy and I like that she's respected. I don't mind being in her shadow. My time will come.

We try living in Northampton while she finishes her graduate program at Smith and continues teaching at Hampshire. I'm working in a bakery and it grows awkward, vague and I only last a month or two there. Eleanor protests but I can't wait any longer for the move to New York. I'm anxious to start the climb into a new life in dance.

On weekends, she travels between Amherst, Massachusetts, and my apartment. She constantly drives the three hours in a silvery blue Honda Civic like it's the easiest thing in the world. She is economy in motion. And our relationship makes the periods of separation, the hard work, soul-searching and growing pains of establishing a career in New York filled with wonder. I am dumbfounded. She is my mate and I could not be happier.

She likes her soup hot and her prints clear, bold, '70s Marimekko. Wholesome is the word. Open, a fan of perfection, Say it: "Aesthetic perfection." She hones her aesthetic to a pencil-sharp point. Effortlessness. Integrity. Her weight is fully grounded and generously poured in space so that you know where she's coming from and definitely want to go with her when she does. And she does.

The last time I hold her in my eyes we are at the Spring Street uptown E train platform where she drops me. I'm off to class and she's driving back to Hampshire to teach all week. I push through the turnstile to get on the train and as the doors close and the train pulls out I turn back to her where she's planted behind the turnstile, beaming her wide open smile. The train moves forward and I can feel the pull away from her, I can hear the click of a mental shutter freezing the moment; then she's gone.

The ringing phone cuts sharply through my grog the next morning, February 14. It's 7 a.m. and I'm still numb from a long night at work, bussing tables at Vanessa's on Bleecker. I'm loft sitting for my dancer friend

Paul Langland and his lover Colin, so I'm disoriented. I drag my way to the phone in the kitchen and it's our friend Ellen Elias. She's close to both Eleanor and me and is calling from California to see how I am. I can't quite grasp why she needs to know so badly and so early. She realizes I haven't been told and through her tears performs the unthinkable deed of telling me that Eleanor, my lover, her friend, is dead. Killed in a car accident in Connecticut/US 84 on her way from New York to Amherst.

My legs give out and I hit the floor, my left cheek pressed down against the Masonite. It's smooth and cool. Can I get any closer to the ground? I try, I need to, I must. This is the floor of the loft of my dear friends, the floor of the loft that Eleanor had been so happy in with me all weekend, just hours ago. Where we bathed and danced and made love and spoke of the future together. My brain swells to numb. How can she be gone? She can't be gone. She's so clear and real and full of power and her love is so very sweet. I disappear into to the floor now and the air slips out of my chest, the room becomes cloudy gray, then everything fades to black.

I stumble badly in the year that follows, lost and in mourning. I drift from job to job, dance for a while with **Nancy Meehan Company** (an **Eric Hawkins**–related choreographer, who had a lifelong interest in release movement). But I'm too crushed, barely hanging on and I need to leave. Contact Improvisation goddess Nancy Stark Smith takes me to **Naropa Institute** under the guise of serving as her teaching assistant, but it's her kindness that's leading her to keep me afloat.

Naropa is a haven of art and Buddhist study, so I find myself in daily sitting meditation, watching my breath with **Allen Ginsberg, Ann Waldman, Barbara Dilley** and **Valda Setterfield**, whose poetry and dance classes there have a deep impact on me. The community is led by **Chogayam Trungpa Rinpoche**, the eleventh descendent in the line of Trungpa tülkus, important teachers of the Kagyü lineage of Tibetan Buddhism. (Renowned for its strong emphasis on meditation practice, the Kagyü lineage is one of the four main schools of Tibetan Buddhism.)

Naropa is a wild community of insanely talented and intense personalities who come to teach, perform, study, drink copious amounts of Bombay gin and rake each other over existential coals, all under the guise of the march towards enlightenment. It's just what I need at this time, and the first point in my life where I can sit still and breathe on a daily basis.

As a teacher I'm welcomed into the inner circle of Buddhist elites, so I sit and party with Rinpoche frequently. I'm a bit taken aback the first time I see him pull up to an event in a gold Mercedes Sedan. Where is he coming from, why so flash? At first the wealth is an incongruent jolt, but I acclimate quickly. VIP is VIP. Is there a schism between wealth and enlightenment? Is this a lucrative business? It can't trouble me now. I'm unhinged at Naropa, but comfortably so. I'm in the dark, traveling without a map, so all bets are off. Naropa was a powerful balm.

I return to New York City in 1978 and meet Trisha Brown while working as stage manager for a benefit performance for Movement Research. I've not seen her work at that point. When she arrives, I greet her at the door of the theater. She smiles as I take her white metal makeup case and lead her to her dressing room. I can't remember the conversation, nothing much is said—but on that brief walk she completely wins me over.

That night she danced *Watermotor* and a short excerpt of the work-in-progress that would become *Glacial Decoy*. I was floored by what I saw, and not only for its exhilarating beauty—her language was startlingly new, a twisted blend of wild-ass, intuitive sensuality and cool rigor—but somehow I recognized it on a genetic level. I was instantly hooked and somehow knew I was home.

Lisa Kraus is a powerhouse dancer and Buddhist whom I know from Contact Improvisation circles. She also dances in Trisha Brown Dance Company. One day in May of '79 she calls me to mention that Trisha is going to invite men into the company as permanent dancers for the first time. She thinks I might make a good candidate. I say, "Cool" but think, "Hot": what an incredible, amazing, crazy opportunity. Is this possible for me? I call to sign up immediately. Days before the audition I shear off my Prince Valiant '70s hair, buzz it down to the skin in preparation, to clean the slate, to restore my most essential self. I wake up the morning of, to face the pressure of auditioning: I glance at the clock and roll over and go back to sleep. The next day I get a scolding call from Lisa asking what happened. "I balked." And she says, "Let me see what I can do."

By the end of the week I have a private audition scheduled along with one other man. I literally slept my way into a private audition and can't believe the opportunity. I determine to use this one to full advantage.

The day comes and my good friend Ellen, former teacher of a summer class I took in Massachusetts, has a loft on Broadway and Grand called ParkFast Sudio. Ellen and Eleanor were the best of friends and she's taken me under her wing after Eleanor's death. Ellen offers me the loft to warm up in prep for the audition. It's two blocks down from Trisha's studio, and as luck would have it, she and her roommates will be out. She gives me her keys and I go in to warm up.

Being alone in the cool dim and quiet focus of this perfect studio could not be sweeter. The ceilings are high and I sense myself in relation to the walls. Me, alone in space, that singular separate feeing of inhabiting a room. I begin the usual prep to dance, warm the spine breathing deep, then on into a basic series of *pliés* (knee bends), *tendu* (brush with the foot on the floor) and *degagé* (allow the foot to brush and disengage from the floor), joint articulations and extensions, and something shifts and I drop into a powerful state bordering on threatening. The floor is moving and the space around me crackling. It's immense, unlike anything I've felt before but there's no fear. I'm on fire and my body's vibrating, stretching onto a level light-years beyond my current skill: a new zone. Instantaneously I know it's her. I intuit that in those private focused moments, Eleanor, my beautiful, tragically short-lived love, has somehow tripped a switch and has entered me and is dancing me to an incredible height. She's here—it's unmistakable. I know her too well. I'm slightly shocked and awed and my feelings are raw. But I'm going to this audition.

I dance in that audition at a level so far beyond my current skill; The possibility of me. I'm elated at the end of the experience, something like the ghost of Christmas Future showing me my fate and it's impressive. And as dance has always been in my life, it's a physical focus, no matter what I'm feeling. I can shift into work and give myself up to the task at hand.

Shortly after, Trisha calls me herself and says quietly, in the tone she has that takes you into her confidence, into her inner circle, allowing you to feel the pleasure of her intimacy and attention: "Well, Stephen, I really enjoyed your dancing and would like to work with you. Can you start in August?" In that one call my life shifts forever.

The first male in Trisha's company, I remain for seven years (1979–86). A sweating, snorting bull in the china shop alongside one of the most intelligent and silky bodies on the planet, I am duly challenged. Fortunately, Trisha has a kind of alchemic effect on me from the beginning. (I'm not alone in this respect.) She continually asks me to think and dance beyond my grasp. More often than not, and to my great surprise, I would find myself doing it.

Trisha's technique is more on your feet than the Contact work that led me to her, but it has that same alert openness, the same malleable continuum. Fluid. It's more willful but something like bodysurfing in gentle, rolling heaves or riding on swift, soft jets of air. Surprising. Unpredictable. Muscle tone is relaxed, alert to signal deeply folding joints through fluid calligraphic journeys.

The company in those days is filled with heady ambitious individuals and Trisha reigns over it masterfully. I come from working-class Italian roots but she works harder than anyone I had ever seen did. When she is after something in the studio, she is relentless, patient and works with a curious calm. She creates an environment of trust, humor and ownership. Each dancer feels the realness of contributing to creation.

The language she built is methodically written yet maddeningly elusive. She then couples it with improvisational problems that demand each dancer employ that language on a primary creative level. This is a dancer's dream challenge. We work hard and laugh loudly through creative periods (*Opal Loop, Son of Gone Fishin'* and, most notoriously, *Set and Reset*). I vividly recall lingering in a kind of feverishly creative state throughout the rehearsals for *Set and Reset* and well after, into the night, only to wake up and jump back in the next day. It was sheer bliss for a twenty-five-year-old to go to work and find himself dancing next to a woman in the fullness of her creative power, and to be making something with her that we all sensed was momentously potent. Dancing with her always seemed like an endless series of doors. If you were up to the challenge of walking through them, the benefits were huge.

Trisha is generous and open on so many levels, from the way she makes work, to the intimate environment she fosters in the studio, to the friends and collaborators to whom she introduces us, to the consistent encouragement with which she supports my own earliest attempts at dance making. Trisha arranges for me to have the enormous basement of her building as a workspace for next to nothing, and it was in this space that my first dances are made and performed. She looks at those works, speaks with me about them when she can (she never rolled her eyes when I was looking), and always comes with her family, friends and supporters to see what I am up to.

Trisha smashes the mold both artistically and personally to forge a new movement model that is her own. It is a spherical, snaking and elusive language, more subtle than any before it. During my years in her company, my eye was trained to see the intelligent invention that the body is capable of. Now, years later, a choreographer with my own company, I walk into her theater and am amazed again and again by the inventions she continues to unearth.

Photo: (c) Estate of Jack Mitchell. *Set and Rest* (1984), Choreographey: Trisha Brown. Dancers: Trisha Brown and Stephen Petronio

Rauschenberg: I have to look him up and in those days (1979), it's no Google, it's a trip to St. Mark's Bookshop. I'm in Trisha's company fifteen minutes and she tells me we're going round to his place for cocktails. I have no idea who he is or what I'm in for. That ignorance is the foundation for a relatively real friendship with him. When I see his art up close I know immediately that it will change my life and I begin asking him endless questions about it and how he makes it. Everyone around Bob defers constantly, letting him drone on and not seeming to treat him all that authentically. I just keep plowing forward, refusing to be a passive audience to his one-man Jack Daniel's Revue. I simply talk to him in a direct curious way, engage him, ask questions when I don't know what he's talking about, call him out when I think he's talking crap. I'm smitten, excited, inspired, irrevocably changed by his art and the scale of his personality. And we share a common love for inebriation. I often collide with him at the bar at the constant parade of art world events I find myself inhabiting by coincidence or related to one of Trisha's productions.

His work is kinetic, piercingly rhythmic to me, the way layers of images move with/against each other, the space, depth and motion between them creating dynamic motion on a still canvas. It really is a kind of choreography to me, and he indeed loves dance with a passion. Bob expects a lot from people but he gives just as much. He's over-the-top generous with all the dancers around him, frequently inviting Trisha's company to his house on Lafayette Street for some occasion or another, four floors of art and booze and Rocky the turtle, turtling around. Bob often has some homemade soup on the stove and he loves to entertain, perform, feed the dancers who are poverty stricken compared to him; he tries to rectify it every chance he can. Many gatherings end up with the dancers in the basement and Bob requiring that we all choose one of the numerous prints he lays out in anticipation of the opportunity to send us home with some piece of his affection and generosity.

During the making of Trisha's work *Set and Reset*, we're all invited over and there is a lineup of seven original collage works, one for each cast member, printed on fabric with images Bob's using in the dance's projected décor. I'm beside myself when I see that I'm in the one he's made for me, along with some of the iconic images that he uses as shorthand in his visual world: wrought-iron hearts and tufts of desert grass. After many drinks he uncharacteristically begins to elaborate on their meaning to him, then catches himself when he starts to get a little sentimental and *verklempt*. It's then that I glimpse a bit of how these images function for Bob, how they catch meaning, then swirl and shift in his eye, creating an intimate and alive world in two dimensions.

I continue my friendship with Bob beyond the Trisha years though while I'm still in the boyish chapters of my life. He's so gregariously entertaining, showing me his latest project—or just drunken or sordid or chatty.

He's always fun, never mean, to me at least. A boy with an amazing sense of wonder and scale, he surrounds himself with a mountain of his work. We're on our way out the door one night and pass by the most exquisitely beautiful, gossamer work on the entrance wall. When I stop to admire it, he casually snatches it down, folds it and puts it under my coat, demanding that I don't tell anyone or he would be in trouble. "They hate it when I give stuff away."

Even postmodernism has its *Primas* and Eva Karczag was one of Brown's. A Hungarian refugee transplanted to Australia, where she emerged as a talent in both ballet and postmodern circles, Eva has it all. She rejects the strictures of ballet but retains the lines and carries that purity of form into the energetic fluidity that is becoming central to the softer released techniques being forged in the 1970s and so instrumental in Trisha's work. I'm still the company puppy and she's a queen, but in a bait-and switch room assignment on tour to Jacob's Pillow Dance Festival in Lee, Massachusetts, I end up in a rustic one-room cabin with Eva as a roommate. It seems she needs a puppy.

Before long we're lovers in a relationship based on a deep curiosity about movement, dance and alternative bodywork. It's framed by the intense life of dancing and touring the world with TBC. As the relationship unfolds playfully, there is a naïveté about emotional commitment and what it takes, coupled with a more focused understanding of what she and I need on a practical level.

Eva doesn't have a green card that would allow her to continue working in the U.S., meaning no viable way to continue on in the company. Concurrently, my mother is in the last stages of cancer. The thought of sending Lorraine off less worried about me seemed like a compelling enough reason to marry, whether it was that conscious or not. We do it at City Hall with Trisha and her husband, Burt Barr, as witnesses.

I'm still an emotional infant at this point, simply reacting to stimuli as it hits me. I have no perspective, am not particularly rational and respond immediately to warmth, comfort, sexual urges and love. I need love, or what I think it is. Eva brought a sweet and confusing mix of the above. And there was the Australian accent. Not to mention my family is overjoyed, their secret worry that I was irreparably damaged by Eleanor's death alleviated. While sleeping with Eva was *charged*, the marriage license we obtain is a bucket of cold water tossed on my desire. Commitment phobia is almost instantaneous. She's organic white cotton and I am skintight black leather. The polarity attraction devolves to repulsion. Within the year, the marriage is on the rocks, divorce imminent. We manage to be fairly civil to each other while continuing to dance for Trisha and are fiery stage partners during Eva's remaining years there. But personally it's bitters on ice.

Oddly, my second marriage, ten years later, was to another Australian, Rebecca Hilton, who danced in my company for the several years we remained husband and wife. Ever the parrot, I still like to repeat everything twice.

Shortly after the breakup with Eva, I'm out at a local gay bar called **The Last Resort** on First Avenue and 9th Street, just around the corner from my apartment on St. Mark's. I'm with a casual friend passing time at a low-key, non-trendy watering hole, working on raising my Blood Alcohol Level. In walks a flat-topped, square-jawed, cartoon colt. He's prep-in-training with a twist, full of Italian good looks and charm. His gangly movement and ultra-long lashes are irresistible. We hit it off, proceed to flirt and drink till the room starts to warp. I've never seen a boy quite like this and he *is* just a boy. In fact, this night is his eighteenth birthday. I'm a cut-loose twenty-five-year-old on the prowl. Around about the time the room starts to full-on spin, I lean in and whisper in his ear, "I want to fuck you." He looks back at me with a smile and we're off to my place to do just that till the sun comes up. An electric night turns out to be the first one of a seven-year relationship with Justin Terzi.

Justin's an advertising design student at FIT and he vibrates at a high frequency. He loves the surface of things, a refreshing contrast to the world I'm dancing in. I fight valiantly to win him from the assortment of Mercedes-driving Southampton prospects around him. He's also dallying with visual artist **Kenny Scharf** (punk Jetsons and Flintstones paintings) at the time, which drives me nuts. The second I meet Justin, I irrationally want him for myself. I was never interested in monogamy before, but with him it's an obsession. Though he's younger than me, our cultural references are aligned. Lower-middle-class Italian-American, with the sprawling families to match; same taste in food and a shared obsession with fashion. He looks like he could be a cousin and I'm on familiar and tantalizing turf.

By the time he moves into 95 St. Mark's Place with me, we've achieved commitment and monogamy. It's 1981 and in a year or so people start to disappear from the neighborhood with odd abruptness. East Village celebrity **Klaus Nomi** is one of the first to go missing. Klaus, a German punk-opera countertenor is a daily sight on my block for years. *Zap!* After a few weeks of absence, the worrisome rumors kick in.

In an unthinkable rush, the news of AIDS is everywhere and no one really knows what's going on. Whatever drove me to the sudden need for monogamy with Justin, and however difficult it was for an eighteen-year-old student from FIT to accept, it may very well be this restriction that saved us from a similar fate.

In 1983 I'm reaching a peak in my dancing with Trisha Brown. She's just begun a momentous collaboration with Laurie Anderson that will eventually become *Set and Reset*, and she has a three-minute study completed to a new Anderson song called "Sweaters." It's an exciting start but way short, so she decides to bring back one of her earlier equipment pieces as a prelude to it. *Man Walking Down the Side of a Building* (1971) is just that: a man, me in this case, harnessed into simple mountaineering ropes/belay system, stands at the top edge of a building, feet planted, facing out, and leans forward into space and shifts planes to achieve a perpendicular relationship to the building (tipped 90 degrees).

We practice on her roof in SoHo off a four-foot wall. The riggers don't seem certain about the mechanics of it all. There are no real records, just the twenty-year-old memory and this is not really mountain climbing—we are not scaling a wall in the usual face-to-the-wall orientation. But the group assembled is an intelligent group of experts tackling a problem with excitement. The wall is on T's roof but it's only four feet high, and I am off on the fact that I am the first to do this since the early '70s and I'm not really worried. I'm eventually anchored to the building from behind and there will be a dancer lying at the bottom of my descent to belay my rope. We do it easily in two attempts, and I am good to go.

We arrive in the south of France where the venue is the high-walled courtyard of a fourteenth-century monastery, Cloitre du Cimetiere Chartreuse de Villeneuve-Lez-Avignon. In the corner looms the four-story turreted tower that is my challenge. In the flesh it's suddenly real—and four stories is HIGH.

At rehearsal we climb up to the turret and suss out the situation; we decide to anchor me to one of the turrets at the edge of the tower. The anchor will be the source of support for my weight on the way down. I tie in and hop up onto the turret in preparation to lean out. Just then T suggests we test the stability of the turret. I jump back down and T, another dancer (**Randy Warshaw**) and I shoulder up against the massive stone and on 1, 2, 3 we push. Shockingly we lift it gently off its base then drop it with a thud. My anchor is adrift! Through nervous laughter we reboot and decide to tie me off to the entire tower. Final curtain averted, we move on.

The moment of leaning out for the first time at that height becomes one of those peak "Am I doing this?" moments of my young career. Theoretically it's not a question and I give no consideration to any possible risk. But at the actual moment, several stories up and hanging my life on a string, it hits me full force. Up on the edge of a massive turret, heart pounding, spotlight blaring to call me down (no turning back), I lean out in the slowest-motion dive into the abyss. Now perpendicular to the tower, my world shifts. T's instructions: "Walk normally down the side of the tower in a casual manner until you reach the ground." It lasts a matter of minutes.

The Mother's Day Game

It's Mother's Day and I'm home for a holiday visit. Dinner is the usual mid-afternoon pasta feast: *gavadeal* with gravy (cavatelli and tomato sauce to you), iceberg, cucumber and tomato salad. We do the gift and cards with pineapple cream-cheese cake and coffee, after which, my father recedes with the predictability of the tide to watch the game on television. I'm not sure which game because there's an endless stream of them every Sunday of every season on every TV in every house in America. I could care less which game. Just THE GAME.

I hang out with Mom to chat in the dinette. It's Italian-American tasteful with white-on-white textured fleur-de-lys wallpaper and hanging sconces, and it opens out from the kitchen. It's the center in our home. Yes, a space to eat but its primary function is social. This is my mother's domain, her stage, and the place of power where her magic is worked. Her specialty is listening, supporting, communicating, prodding, face-to-face interaction with all people in her home and usually over all kinds of food or just coffee and.... The dinette is where secrets are told, advice is given, gossip is shared, and futures are planned. It is our hub. This is the same dinette that we all flocked to instinctively after her funeral, unable to be away from her table, needing to be in her world, to eat and drink and just *be* where she served us so lovingly and so well. It's where most of our family life played out for all our lives with her orchestrating.

Pepe, our black miniature toy poodle, pulls on his leash, straining toward us from the kitchen stove where he's fastened, inching exactly up the gold metal strip that separates the '80s beige pebble-in-resin patterned linoleum floor from the beige wall-to-wall carpet of the dinette. He will ride that line his whole life but never cross it for fear of reaping the "wrath of Mom." But he wants so badly to be at the table and on her lap.

The conversation continues between us, the usual back-and-forth, her curiosity about everything and scolding/goading/laughing at whatever I tell her, me goading/ flirting/pushing gently on the boundary of what she can handle. I push much like Pepe, except I cross the line continually with her, having learned to do so long ago to hold her attention, rile her, keep her engaged in my life. I love this tango between us. It's our dance.

I decide the ultimate honor for this Mother's Day is another kind of game. I plan to "officially" come out to her, gifting her with my honesty. She always wants to know everything and I'm twenty-five and have been with Justin a year now, my first serious male relationship. Not telling is so obviously lying and it feels wretched in the culture my family has fostered, especially given the ongoing health battles that send her in and out of remission and treatment.

The conversation kind of rambles and in my adrenalized state I can't really be in it anymore. I watch our mouths move in a long shot, not hearing words but noticing posture, hers easy, mine overly erect, newly learned. Unable to hold back any longer, I spill: "I want to tell you something."

Familiar lead-in.

"OK."

Familiar response.

"I'm gay and Justin is my boyfriend, not my roommate."

And 1, 2, 3 and 4

"Don't fool around," she says.

And "For real," I say.

Silence, 2, 3, 4, ...

"No, you're not." Awkward face. "Really?"

"Really."

Silence (unmeasured).

"Are you sure?" she returns.

"I'm sure," I volley.

Longer silence.

"I don't know what to say (tight mouth) but...so...OK..."

Pause.

"But...just don't tell your father whatever you do!" she blurts in stress, the instinctive maternal motor taking over.

"Why?" I slam back.

"He can't handle it. I don't know, just don't!"

And the shock ("really?") and contingency plan of action ends the conversation.

I pack up some leftovers and prepare to return back to sodomite central on St. Mark's Place where J and I are living above Yaffa Cafe. I arrive home an hour or two later, feeling rather footloose, and as I'm opening the door, the phone is ringing—this is pre-cellular America—and when I pick it up my father says, "Stephen?"

"Hi, Dad."

"Your mother told me," my father says.

Silence.

"What a surprise," I respond.

"So really?"

"Really," I say.

Silence....

"You're a...*cornholer*?"

The word slips out like unexpected gas. There is an accompanying farmyard graphic with it involving a handsome blond farmhand, work boots in the air, a ring toss game and a happy golden ear of corn on the cob. I love this term I've never heard but understand intuitively.

"Yup, Dad, I am."

"I just want to know one thing," he says.

"What?" I say.

"Do you do it to him or does he do it to you?"

Silence...

There are absolute roles in this particular relationship but I won't divulge details on principle. I won't give him the satisfaction, the graphic he desires.

113

"It's not really up for discussion, Dad. I'm just glad you know now," I say.

In the back of my mind I wonder how he would feel if I asked him what he and my mother's preferred position was, or what was the thing that never failed to make him come.

More silence.

"Justin is really very handsome so I can sort of understand," he says.

I almost drop the phone, but drop my jaw instead. I hang on long enough to hear him say that I'm his son and he loves me no matter what. "But whatever you do, just don't tell your brother." Bad-a-bum.... He pleads like the predictably repetitive pattern on the dinette wallpaper.

There's this crazy instinctive reflex that comes in response to my aberrant sexual disclosure and that is to continue to conceal it. It's something like the blue wall of silence that governs police behavior. We can do anything as long as we huddle round in protective fraternal silence. It isn't really happening if we don't speak about it; theories can't be offered, blame can't be assigned, nothing is admitted, and it's not really there.

Take Flight!

After dancing with Trisha for six years I'm straining for more. Several years earlier she had mentioned she would like to do a solo for me, and I wait as patiently as an Aries with blind ambition can. I petition quietly in those last years. Somewhere during the making of *Set and Reset*, she calls my number.

It's a perfect moment. I'm at the height of my dancing with her, completly committed and deeply engaged in the work that seems to be careening to its place in history as a touchstone in postmodern dance. We can feel its import in the studio and our lives. She arranges for me to come back to rehearsal in the evenings, outside company hours, Trisha and me alone in the studio, relieved of the social confines of group behavior in the company. It doesn't take more than three weeks at an hour a day, but this small pocket of time-out with *La Brown* changes my world for good. Three weeks of following her lead anywhere, of submission and seeing just how far we can go. I'm full of impulses to offer but completely happy to be told what to do, a state that I often bridle against. So much interesting movement falls by the wayside, golden moments that are exhilarating but wrong for our trajectory. I marvel at her ability to see the larger picture of what is essentially an unknown proposition. Unsure of what's guiding her choices, I go on with the sheer joy of going, for the sake of going with *her*.

When it's finally completed, it's thirty-eight seconds long—a joke of idiosyncratic puzzles or a solo to take out into the world as a precious nugget of invention?

In the weeks that follow, I struggle desperately with the material, unable to fill the edges of the research that's so full and amazing when originally unearthed, unable to get back to the golden state that is my time alone with one of the most inventive dance makers on the planet. What is it that we did, where did it go? Why did it seem so right at the moment and so illusive now?

The improvised moment can be perfect—a 100 percent parcel of rightness that, when wrangled and broken down to choreography (like a wild colt tamed for service), loses a certain percent of its perfection. This is an assumed risk. The goal is to bring home enough of the genius of the moment to make it worthwhile. It can be successful or end up like the dream where you capture the solution to that most meaningful problem—it's right there in your hands. Then you wake up tangled in sheets and sweat to find that you're merely holding your pillow.

A week before the premiere at Brooklyn Academy of Music there's a showing in the studio and all of Trisha's team is there, including family, friends, supporters and the collaborators, Laurie Anderson (music) and Robert Rauschenberg (costumes and decor). We perform the work and when I attempt the solo placed near the pinnacle of the piece, it's a balloon deflating before the eyes of those who matter most. I'm mortified by the classic freeze-up. I call for greatness and a knot of half-realized missteps answers.

This happens in the process of building something new. What was full in research can misfire the first few times out; not yet fully in the bones, it hasn't become what it *might*. Transitions evaporate and the pathways that were carved deeply in the long hours of full-bodied rehearsal, executed a million times in a row, can atrophy in the precious seconds they are allotted in the actual performance of the dance. Not to mention nerves, the great destroyer of all natural instinct and coordination. My experience has proven that often when a new work has its first showing for a live audience, it's only then that it rises up to become its full self. The act of a performer meeting the collective gaze of the audience seals the creation.

Later that day, Trisha calls me into her office: "Where did it go? It's just not there anymore," she asks and proposes cutting out the solo from the dance. I try not to crumble. I ask her to give me the weekend to recover the prize. She agrees and I go down into the basement studio that I rent from her at 541 Broadway and work nonstop through Sunday, obsessively visiting and revisiting the slippery magic we devised. It grows, but still I question if my desire is bigger than my ability. On Monday in rehearsal, enough of the solo is recovered and Trisha decides to extend some trust: It makes it into the final work.

But it's on opening night at BAM that it happens. In those seconds before the solo begins and I hear my introductory notes played live for the first time, I see the spiky top of Laurie Anderson's complex and beckoning head and the bow of her violin arc up in motion with piercing sound. In that instant, my world is transformed. The music, the moment and the movement call me into a space I've not yet occupied and I go forth with more power than I know I possess. The thirty-eight seconds of motion stretch out like a bird lifting off in flight and expand to a solo of immense proportions. When I come off stage I know something has happened to me and I was prepared, lucky enough to be there and hungry enough to accept its challenge.

Bloodlines

So much battle and work and sweat and you think, "Look what I've done, how far I've come!" But in the end you get it from your mother, the family and friends, the bent, proclivities and patterns, the posture and movements are all there in your genetic code like some time-based kaleidoscope waiting to unfold.

I am the bastard child of Steve Paxton and Trisha Brown. My surrogate parents in dance, they instill in me a deep love of pure physics in motion. Their renegade minds are linked with the minimalism of the New York visual art world of the '70s—the delights of abstraction and purity of form over the histrionics of theatrical dance.

Steve is some kind of postmodern Hermes, a wing-ed messenger who delivers me tumbling into Contact Improvisation in my first year of dance at the tender age of eighteen; then on to Trisha, mercurial force who agrees to let a mortal boy into her inner circle of sophisticated female calligraphy. Along with the cerebral Yvonne Rainer, who anchored the Judson group in theory and manifesto, these were my pillars, my early gods of motion, and they were open with their gifts.

Hanging with giants has its advantages to a mind in formation. So much of the real work transpires socially, at parties and elaborate dinners with labyrinthine conversations about the finer details of the minimalist theory that was fueling the dance world's postmodern shift, fetishizing the nuts-and-bolts characteristics of weight, momentum, energetic pathways and volume, never content or motivation. Their world is populated with the details of physical fact and the process of gathering them. Of physics and untethered action, everyday/pedestrian moves. But their fate is not mine. The treasures of their doctrines are so rewarding but I want something else. My generation wants a face.

What possesses me to join in the mission of dragging modern dance into the twenty-first century? Why do I think it so urgent to build a language of movement that feels like the world I live in (fast, chemically fueled and extravagant), the way my body works, my mind races and spins, the music I am listening to, from **Grandmaster Flash** ("The Message"), **The Sex Pistols** ("Anarchy in the U.K.") and **Bow Wow Wow** ("C30 C60 C90 Go!" or "I Want Candy") to **Talking Heads** ("Psycho Killer") to media (MTV begins) and art I look at (**Robert Rauschenberg, Andy Warhol, Jean-Michel Basquiat, Julian Schnabel, graffiti**) the fashion I love (**Commes des Garcon, Parachute, Gaultier,** *anything* vintage)? What can I be thinking when I decide to bring the things that are my cultural needs into an art world of physics and stripped-down minimalism?

It's the '80s now and for me in those days it often comes back to sex: Sexual is the backbeat in my life and so too in my dance. The zeitgeist was asking me to bring forward my sexuality and the civil injustice surrounding it and I was ripe to do so. All with a heightened sense of ME, ME, ME! ("Express Yourself" by Madonna and "Every Breath You Take" by the Police are anthems of these days.)

Why do I think a moving model of a realistically blurred gender is something that would be of interest? What can I be thinking when I decided to bring issues centered around my cultural passions and needs into a cool and abstract new world? That the impact of men behaving as virtuosic athletes in adrenalized, tender or erotic ways, as objects even; that women in functional and subjective action are important to weave into the fabric of my dances as a given (not an over-theatricalized thesis)? Why are these models important to pursue?

120

Sex is on my mind a lot at the time and I want it embedded in my work, but I do so on the wings of a love of form that's so deeply imbedded in my... dancing body.

It's been on my mind as long as I can remember—a full-time occupation. It's not a big stretch to see why it's present in my dance. Why am I bent on bringing my sexuality to my dance? I just can't understand why it *wasn't* in the dance I was seeing to begin with. Such an obvious exclusion seems coercive. Why do I spend so much time thinking, dreaming, anguishing and stewing about sex?

My running joke about men in the audience at any given dance performance is that they are: a) currently sleeping with one of the performers, b) used to sleep with one of the performers, c) are dreaming about sleeping with one of the performers. Ask around next time you are in the lobby at intermission of a dance performance. It's law.

Fucking is an act of affirmation. It's one of the most instinctive animal and creative things humans do on a regular basis. It keeps one fresh and tuned; joins the base physical and metaphysical realms. Ever notice how horny everyone is at funerals or times of trauma and distress? I'm not surprised by the comment Billy Forsythe made to me after his home theater, the Frankfurt Opera, burned to the ground. "The house was burning before our eyes and everyone seemed to want to just go home and screw." Or when Eleanor was killed suddenly, hit by the side of the road by a drunk driver, I was uneasy, broken to the core, inconsolable, but when friends embraced me in condolence, I was oddly aroused. It was a physical response I couldn't control, my body on some instinctual animal program to couple, to affirm through copulation that I was alive and still viable. When I moved to New York in the late '70s everybody dancing downtown was sleeping with everybody who was dancing downtown. We lived and worked below 14th Street but our bodies were the playgrounds—and we played. A lot.

❖ ❖ ❖

Motion is my medium on every level. Inertia my friend and foe, not naturally grounded but gravity always steals the show. It happens often when I'm moving through space on foot, or while driving on the open highway by car or, traveling by train or plane; a heart-pumping metabolic lift. The rush of propelling forward through space trips my mental switch on to a mode labeled "intuition," and the thinking animal takes over and I am most at home. Dance, then, is the obvious choice, the action of swimming in multidirectional spherical space, touching places with polyrhythmic bliss, places where I am most alive.

It is the most glamorous possibility I could imagine—a life of continual transit, touring from city to city and country to country, loading in a show, checking into a hotel and finding the unknown treasures of a new place. I love the antiseptic anonymity of a hotel in a city that is a clean slate for me. Having to decipher the language, the best little local to eat in, the seductive strangers waiting around the next bend.

The platinum-haired GI from Texas stationed in Wiesbaden, Germany, with broad chest and insatiable tongue. He's my steady for the four days that I'm in Frankfurt. Then the Belgian James Dean named Gui whom I meet backstage after a show who comes along to dinner and on...later turning up in Paris to my shock and odd disdain. He is piping hot, but has broken some rule of transitory eroticism, so the magic is gone. When he mentions in partial English that he wants to move to NYC with me, all the oxygen is sucked out of the room.

Or in Milan, blonde Lara with the tiny waist, pointy tits and erupting laugh. "Dai Stephen!" (Come on), she prompts, her sexy voice goading me forward. That's just her way and I almost do go.

And the handsome, manly L who was straight, young, built like a statue, long, sweet foreskin. "But why everyone want to make sex with me?" as he eyes my grappa-drunken lips, his stiff rod stabbing through his pants. We go on like triathletes for hours in the dark luxury of his parents' queen-size bed. What he lacks in experience he makes up for in earnestness—he swallows hungrily but slips out of bed before dawn to prepare a breakfast of digestive biscuits crushed into a bowl of coffee. I can't coax him back to bed in the light of morning no matter how I try. The moment had passed.

Or the stagehands, still in school, or young marrieds with new babies and French or Italian accents that all seem to ride motorcycles. The harshness of their red wine and tobacco breath, the European-cut underpants (slips), the gruff casualness of their hunger for sex. Foreskinned, straight and willing—then move on like it was a dream. It's an existential, erotic pilgrimage that permeates my performing life.

I'm twenty-one and on my first European tour as a dancer. There's a break in the tour, a yawning five-day space with no employment, and a potential roadblock to the success of the season. Management scrambles to find a solution. A dance friend of the company is installed at a private school in southern England and he offers up his home for some of the dancers to spend the period in repose in the countryside.

We arrive and our host is a mirage in the flesh to me, a hero, a leader, a warrior in motion. We're distributed among the rooms of his modest accommodations. Space is limited, so it's casually decided that I'll bunk with him and the women double into the remaining rooms. I can hardly believe my fortune. I've ached for him on such a deep existential level since I met him a few years back, but my young mind can hardly articulate, let alone admit this. But this is social, casual, and I'm cool in the understanding that the circumstantial twist of fate is just a sleeping arrangement.

Dinner is homey and conversation lively and relaxed. When we retire I'm exhausted. I'm an innocent twenty-one, and he is in full leonine prime at thirty-five. I feel very cared for, safe and thrilled at the prospect of the unimaginable prize of resting beside my mentor for these nights. We climb in and turn back-to-back, expecting sleep. Of course it won't come...it won't come...it still won't come...and I lay there like a trap waiting to spring, suspended in an arc of desire that stretches out into some distant future.

The quiet is voluble. Interminable. He turns to me with an effortless roll and I respond deftly in kind, the fronts of our naked bodies blend in a flash. I fall deeply into him and I can't tell what's pressing into me most. He's leading with every part at once: His chest and cock beat into me in light counterpoint pleasure. Skin alert and highly charged, our bodies blend in a long and tumbling conversation, speaking on a level that's understood but undeciphered until that moment. We're at it for hours and hours, my tongue digging deeply into him searching for his core and it only seems to find more void, delicious and vast. We're everywhere on each other, tumbling and tangling with no end in sight. An elemental purpose is on me, ravenous. I try finally to push into him with saliva but he winces back away and we continue on with no orgasm in sight. We tumble and press for hours and eventually he suggests we let it rest. My train of desire drags me into the bathroom where I instinctively find some body oil and I'm back on him in a flash. Now slicker, we glide into each other with ease, at last coming in huge, happy spurts. We're asleep in each other's arms by sunrise. I can't contain myself.

If you've spent the day in the ocean, whole body bobbing in the up and down and repetitive roll, the uncontrolled lift and drop of your body riding in the surf, you know the delight of "after-burn" in your muscles, the lingering motor memory, the rock and sequence and float that continues on the beach as you lie down breathless and exhilarated.

The next morning that's the experience as my mind replays the night before over and over in passionate loops that accompany the mundane tasks of the day, splitting my screen of awareness in the most delightful way. Here now is my conversation over coffee, spliced with close-ups of his nipples in my teeth, or the meeting about rehearsal goals that includes an unstoppable mental jack-in the box with his cock springing to life, the noticeable pulse beating continuously in my hand throughout my activities. And the day passes somewhat jarringly like this until I get him in my arms again that night.

It started as a "thickness" at the underside of her right breast. Not a definable something, a lump with shape, perimeter or warning, but a vague thickness that inhabited my mother's assets like a cloud on a sunny day. By the time it was discovered, it was too late. A cancer- producing mechanism took charge of her and used eighteen of her lymph nodes to transmit its skewed message throughout her body like a feature story on the Voice of America. The diagnosis, the waiting, the fear and ignorance of THE BIG C back in the early '80s.

Mastectomy 1.

Mastectomy 2.

Chemo-bald illness.

Radiation transformed my meek mother to an Annie Sprinkle of disease. Annie is a performance artist best known as the prostitute and porn star turned sex educator. (I saw one amazing show where the audience was invited to peek into her speculum-opened vagina to glimpse her cervix.) My mother is prone to lifting her shirt frequently and at the most pointedly of social moments, dinner, for example, on Sunday, over ravioli and meatballs. She needed to perform the things that were happening to her, a way to wrest control of the process that was consuming her. In many ways her need to show, to bear witness, was the most empowering relationship she ever had with her body, a body that she struggled with in accepting its many stages, the onus of womanhood, the beauty and litheness of her youth, the conjugal bliss of her sexuality with my father, the childbirth and numerous miscarriages she underwent, her resultant struggle with weight, effects of DES, the hormonal treatments (now banned as carcinogenic) that her trusted doctor since birth fed her to strengthen her pregnancies. And fed her again later to "hold" her womanhood when her body began to shift into premature menopause in her late thirties. Heaven forbid she become devalued by an inability to produce offspring, even though after two sons and numerous miscarriages, she was done and frazzled from the effort of it all.

Now she would take solace in revealing the experimental treatments and harsh results that were carving and branding her body like some medieval canvas placed on exhibit. J, my boyfriend at the time, was revolted on that Sunday afternoon while seated at our pasta dinner, the moment that my mother picked up her smock to show us her scarred flesh canvas and told us there was a foul odor coming from her radium-cooked flesh as well. I was secretly proud of her bravery and willingness to command control and not let it all defeat her in silence.

With Annie Sprinkle and Michael Clark at her performance at the Kitchen in New York (1990).

LAUNCH

These are the women who surround me,
Angel food cake light on wings that wrap and lift me into a flight of motion:
Here are Lorraine and Marie together again, now the aunts: Anita, Pearl,
Norma, Aggie, Phyllis and Gen, the cabal of female spirits that nudge and
look after and come round more often than one would think.

Lorraine never got to see my success. She and my father came to all
the rundown lofts and basement shows where their car was towed for
illegal parking, or his tools were stolen out of the trunk while they were
watching me do things they did not try to comprehend. She got to cringe
in my roach-infested walk-up on Lafayette and Grand and help paint the
burnt-out blackened shell on St. Mark's Place before seeing me roll around
on the floor with an underworld of downtown dancers.

The last show she came to was *Apollo Object.* It was performed in The
Basement, at 112 Mercer Street. This is the space that Trisha Brown convinced her co-op to rent to me: 5,000 square feet of open subterranean
space that stretched from Mercer Street to Broadway, where I could work
24/7, my own studio/theater. I named it, cleaned it out, sanded the floors

127

and it was good to go, all mine. It was a base where I could rehearse, workshop new dances, teach, build sets and install shows for as long as it took to get them done. And it was a coveted space to perform outside the treadmill of possible producer-driven venues whose decrees dictated what was hot and what was not. *Independence.*

This space jump-started my company and at $100 per month it was a miraculous luxury. The shows began to draw publicity, crowds and critics and were always followed by fabulous after-parties. When the building figured out I was illegally jacked into the Con Ed source on its dime, the writing was on the wall. First the space was split and I had to share it with a high-strung florist from Long Island. As SoHo gentrified, I was eventually booted out and The Basement was subdivided into many tiny cubicles and rented to individual craftspeople—art to commerce. It only lasted a few years but they were salad days, unfettered and unpressured research time, the days that set me off and running.

Apollo object ((ə'päl·ō 'äb·jikt) (*astronomy*): any asteroid that crosses the Earth's orbit. *Apollo Object* is in collaboration with my boyfriend Justin Terzi. We are focused on art, fashion, clubbing, junk collecting, dumpster diving, construction sites and Ecstasy.

The dance floor in The Basement is in the middle of the open space and J devises a rectangle of floor-to-ceiling plastic walls to surround it, making a huge plastic box. He paints these walls with white vertical stripes (to match the space's columns) alternating with the natural opaque plastic. Inside the space is our performing arena. The audience occupies one single row of folding chairs (eighty-five per show) outside the plastic, facing in and up against the box. At face level J cuts out 12-inch by 12-inch holes for viewers to poke their heads in to watch the event. Around the inside of the room, the audience's faces are beautifully framed and appear "hung" on the plastic wall, a line of living portraits that acted as living decor for the work.

Inside there are various activities: my six dancers, all women, shifting through moves I make for them based on my interest of the moment. At that point I am obsessively collecting photographs that I would drop into my fluid movement continuum in order to anchor or interrupt its natural flow. There is always a wealth of Xeroxed Greek Olympians lying around during the making of *Apollo Object*.

This period is a formative one in that I am still in the process of deciding if I'll actually pursue the making of movement as an artistic motor. Late '70s/early '80s is very much a Performance Art moment: **Laurie Anderson, Tim Miller** and Klaus Nomi. As a result, *Apollo Object* does have dance, the hard-core dancing that is just beginning to get onto its feet as a Petronio language; however, I am very interested in performance activity outside of what I considered formal dancing. Day-Glo–sprayed plates are smashed on stage, real-time haircuts in silhouette, circular saws buzz and Justin and I dance with life-size cardboard cutouts of ourselves and with various graphic and text props like exclamation marks and quotations. Objectification, self proclamation/promotion, distortion, and the fabrication of originality are the interests. Most prominently there are the three bodybuilders (small, medium and large), fabricated masculine signs contained in gold-wrapped boxes that they circular-saw themselves out of for a static and sexy alphabet of Greek-inspired postures. Justin's sister Bobby sings an aria and Ray Rudd (a Nutley High friend who was an extraordinarily talented musician involved with **The Who**) improvises harp throughout the show. Grapes are served. It's 1981.

Stencils, T-shirts, guerilla-flyering, poster-plastering, word-of-mouth: These are our marketing techniques and Justin's interest in advertising helps immensely. We considered the marketing as a performance in itself, and treated all our activities as such. Half the fun is meeting afterhours at The Basement with whoever is game, to stencil and poster throughout SoHo and the East Village. **Samo** (a graffiti tagger associated with artist Jean-Michel Basquiat and friends in the late '70s/early '80s) is bombing actively then, so we have to be sly to avoid the police on high graffiti alert. Subway stairs are our specialty, though the most dangerous target. We never get caught (though I dumped many a spray can just in the nick of time), if you don't count the time I was bringing mega-speakers into The Basement, and was detained because the police were sure we were robbing one of the non-artist lofts that were springing up like weeds all over the neighborhood during SoHo's well-documented gentrification.

Trisha is always on me to find a loft in SoHo: "You're young, energetic and driven. What are you waiting for?"

She purchased her loft in the late '60s for under 20K. By the time I'm looking there are still possibilities for under 100K but I can't even get a credit card at that point. I wasn't raised to understand capital and can't crack the mystery. Later in my life, when my five-year-old daughter, Bella, asked me innocently, "How do you get money, Dad?" I admired the perception of the question but still had no revelatory answer for her.

I make a few other evening-length works before that at The Basement with Justin: *Deconstruction, Wistful Vistas, City of Homes* (with my first wife Eva Karczag) and finally *Adrift (with Clifford Arnell).*

Apollo Object (1983).

With Justin Terzi in The Basement during the making of *Apollo Object (1983)*.

Deconstruction is conceived right before I begin delving into French literary theory and semiotics. We are hanging out at construction sites at night and the word just pops into my head. When I announce the performance to a friend of Trisha's, Yvonne Rainer (one of the founders of Judson Dance Theater), she asks me what Deconstructionists I'm reading and I look back at her blankly. The next day I leave St. Mark's Bookshop with an armload of **Baudrillard, Derrida** and **Barthes**. Everything begins to change. Semiotex(t) Publishers become my best friend. Physicalizing critical theory becomes my private form of amusement and gives me a focus that holds my interest, in a way that current compositional trends from the minimalist art world can't. Not the most likely source of inspiration for a dance back then. Colleague Randy Warshaw presses me when he sees my bookshelf: "Oh, you read that elitist propaganda?" I do. My reading of Baudrillard et al. shifts my understanding of artifice in the way it can for a guy from New

Jersey who knows nothing about art and ends up getting smashed with art world giants. Nothing seems real to me anyway. All was artifice, and when you start with nothing, isn't it a simulation of real until it's not? That's how I read these forays into French literary theory. The trompe l'oeil of reality is completely compelling to my young mind and gives me free rein to jump into things, without what I perceived as the proper pedigree, experience or knowledge, all of which I think I lack. It was punk DIY (Do-It-Yourself) aesthetic but for smarty-pants theorists and I run to the street with it like a bandit. Permission to go anywhere.

The stage is preset for *Deconstruction* with a mass of cardboard boxes painted white from floor to ceiling, creating a giant back wall to the performance space. While the audience comes in we are spray-painting our outlines caught mid-motion in Day-Glo paint, to build vibrating friezes across the wall. Paint is atomized in the air. When the performance proper begins I sneak around the back of the wall and crouch in a central box on the floor.

I'm folded like a jack-in-the-box ready to spring, sweating in the buried-alive dark of a small square performance coffin. It's cramped and I have to pee of course. There is a light bulb at the top of the box and when it turns on it's the cue for me to begin sawing the outline of my head painted on the front inside wall of the box. I'm cutting my way out till I push through and slink out of the head-shaped hole (a cartoon birth) to dance in black suit pants (vintage), a dress shirt spray-painted thick crusted electric blue, thin yellow Egyptian print tie and my trademark ridge-soled black dress shoes (no socks). OMD's (Orchestral Manoeuvers in the Dark) song "Souvenir" kicks in:

It's my direction
It's my proposal
It's so hard
It's leading me astray

My obsession
It's my creation
You'll understand
It's not important now

In conversation
In combination
I tell the truth
My feelings still remain

All I need is
Co-ordination
I can't imagine
My destination
My intention
Ask my opinion
But no excuse
My feelings still remain
My feelings still remain.

And I mean it—I'm sincere.

The wall comes tumbling down and is rebuilt in shifting configurations that shape the space for various segments of the show. Our fluorescent-painted outlines are deconstructed and our parts scrambled and rearranged in the process.

There's lots of attention around these shows and after *Apollo Object*. **Cynthia Hedstrom**, longtime friend and the curator of Danspace Project at the time, one of the few downtown NY dance-presenting organizations, taps me to create an evening for her performance series. It's my first invitation from a presenter. She tells me it's time. I make *Adrift (with Arnell)*.

Adrift begins on a walk home from the optometrist where I just got my new black-framed Clark Kent glasses called "Arnell's." This very hot home-boy comes up behind me and starts in: "Hi, Clifford. How are you today, Clifford? Where you off to, Clifford?"

It is instantaneous. **Clifford Arnell** is born. I had been crystallizing this nerdy persona, an awkward bookworm, "out of his body" and detached from the smoothness that was embodied by the world of dance. I had only been dancing a matter of a few years when I was tagged as this silky vir-tuoso. I knew it was too short a trip from the clumsy guy from NJ to this NY dancer. Clifford was always there. He just needed to be made more self-aware than he already was.

I begin to develop Clifford and put him in the dance but don't want to do a traditional "character study" dance solely about this persona, so I multiply him by thirty and create a living set of Cliffords to inhabit the dance space of the work. By this point I realize that I have a talent for making movement that's original and complex and I decide to go for it full force. It's what I understand intuitively and with passion, but I'm conflicted about what it means to construct and reproduce movement, to physicalize mental states and fix them into motion. I've remained conflicted through much of my career.

Clifford frames and contextualizes the slicker Petronio language in progress and is a graphic way to polarize the two extremes in me. Clifford necessitates that there are *books* everywhere, piled in corners, often car-ried through shifting scenes, with other identifying props like glasses of milk and loose change pouring from pockets. Each Clifford builds a per-sonality on a private history of clumsiness and carries mementoes from that history into the performance. He's *silent* for the most part, with large banks of projected text; non sequitur letters (greeking) as substitute for his thoughts or narrative. The one point when Clifford speaks (this particular Clifford played by downtown choreographer **Vicky Shick**) he told stories about his grandmother in Hungarian. The Hungarians in the audience get it, everyone else gets something else: another layer of foreign texture for his identity.

I am fixed on the jumbling incomprehensible crossword of signs, sym-bols and meanings in dance while working on *Adrift*. I use words, speech, "character" and presence to underline the emptiness of the narrative vessel and the disjointed loss of meaning in the reality of our contemporary collective mind.

And juxtaposed to the boxy-suited, bespectacled Clifford who swarmed the space in Berkeley-esque lines and stoic frames, there emerge pockets of hyper-rolling "pure motion" dance passages all set to a score for horns by Lenny Pickett (longtime bandleader for *Saturday Night Live*).

So much in the beginning is about artifice. My career began as an adult, so it often seemed awkward and artificial: "Am I faking this?" There's no personal history or deep wealth of training to refer to so how can I be real/authentic? I'm self-consciously aware of everything as I'm doing it, of going through the stages of becoming a dancer, then a choreographer. Where are my tools?

I revel in two-dimensional sources as a springboard for action. Photos, film, TV and paintings: I love film techniques, panning, zooming in and out, fading in and out, quick jump-cutting. I have no traditional dance composition training, but film is deeply embedded in my life. They become my frames of reference.

And language. From as soon as I could read I did so voraciously and it is natural that I turn to the rules of grammar and syntax to build my compositions. Noun-Verb-Noun structure applies to the logical principles of movement. Plié—jump—land—turn would follow the natural laws of physics then cry out to be rearranged to fight the usual and expected flow. *Jump—up—up—turn—plié—fall.* It is a kind of cut-and-paste literary technique but for movement that operates outside the natural rules of physics that govern these movements.

Interruption of flow and rearranging of natural grammar of movement becomes a passion. If I am not going to speak the language of classicism or modernism, I will take a buzz saw to it and then build a new context step by step, word for word, until I can uncover the principles that governed these constructs as they develop and fall apart.

After I lose The Basement and am being produced aboveground, I find my way into the system at Dance Theater Workshop (DTW) in Chelsea. David White reigns at this theater, one of the three smaller downtown performing venues. It is a black box with ninety-five seats, which, along with The Kitchen in SoHo and Danspace, are the prime games in town.

For an early season at DTW, I create a work called *Walk-In* with composer **David Linton**, a downtown punk percussionist and electronic wizard. (We went on to build a large and substantial body of work together over the '80s and '90s.) Décor is by Justin Terzi and costumes by the young Korean designer Yonson Pak. I'm just turning thirty and *Walk-In* is a runaway hit. That week **Michel Guy**, the director of Festival d'Automne in Paris, attends. After the show he sweeps backstage, his coat thrown over his shoulders and swirling behind him as he kisses both my cheeks and tells me: "I must have you *à Paris maintenant* (at once)."

I see these moments in movies and of course witnessed Trisha's cultural star shoot across the continents, but I didn't expect to be watching this scene with me in it so quickly. It is with curators like Michel and **Val Bourne** from London, where I would open prior to Paris, that I learn there's nothing logical or predicable about a career. Or fair. Solitary people with a particular vision are responsible for making things happen. And that's just how it is.

The title *Walk-In* comes from a book I am reading about spirits that hover around waiting for humans to reach the near-death moment then slip into their bodies and take over the lives of the schlemiels that were the previous tenant. The walk-ins are supposedly much more highly evolved so it's all good. This is a perfect pop-spiritual premise to contain my use of found visual material, photographs and drawings, and then reconstitute them with new life. Walk-ins are an interesting metaphor that dovetails nicely with processes of for composing (cut and paste and reconstitution of found photos) that I'm already employing.

Tony Whitfield from the Lower Manhattan Cultural Council gives me my first residency at his space on Broadway above Canal. I have this box of photos, negatives, cut-out snippets of text that I would scatter out across the floor, and with my dancer Kristen Borg (the blonde tornado who ended up as my assistant for fifteen years) I would improvise, absorbing the image or parts of it, as I would dance by. Or in keeping with a theme, I'd put a photo on the floor and close my eyes until I inexplicably exploded in shape or motion. It's an engaging anchor and provides an unexpected direction to the movement invention. It is all in the selection of the photos: accidents, sports competitions, statuary, animals and on and on.

I'm crossing First Avenue at St. Mark's, early a.m., heading west to rehearsal for Walk-In. I'm not so awake when I step off the curb to cross and hear in my left ear a long metallic painful SCREEEEEECH KABOOM! Instinctively I freeze and restrain myself from turning toward the sound that's most definitely a car's impact with flesh. At the same time I see in my left peripheral vision a body arcing up in space and it's all too clear what I am witnessing with the edge of my sight. Life is arcing away for someone right now, in split-second slow-motion. I continue on steadily to my rehearsal. That person's arcing exit is sewn into Walk-In that afternoon. Hurling bodies remain crucial to me to this day.

The works of this period always start with a title that will serve as the filter or file for it, a word or group of words that form an evolving worldview for the work. I am never an artist who sets out to make a thing that is preconceived in a determinate way. My works start as a sense of something and the title, a frame for related material that might inform the work. I never know where they'll end up and hope the ride is a lively and interesting one.

In 1986 I receive a Bessie (a New York Dance and Performance Award, akin to an Oscar or Tony) for *Walk-In*. I'm also newly single after seven years with Justin Terzi and enjoying it. I spend a lot of time training at the gym on Broadway and Houston (named Pineapple or Raspberry or some fruit). I'm in the sauna and **Mark Morris** walks in so naturally we buck-naked chat. We're eyeing each other sideways, as men are wont to do in these situations, and I sense he thinks I look good but I play it cool and let it slide. He is Mark Morris, and we all know by now how quickly I respond to attention. Plus, I think it's kind of funny. We are so opposite. I fancy myself a superhero diametrically opposed to him. How could I resist.

I first meet Mark in Seattle where I'm performing at On The Boards back in the early '80s. He started his company there and knows some of my dancers, so he pays a social visit to the bar of my hotel. He is incredibly welcoming and sweet, famously funny in the "it's hard to get a word in edgewise" way, but his charm is not lost on me. He's not staying in Seattle for our performances but sends his fabulous mother to the show, and she makes sure to come backstage to introduce herself. I love her immediately.

I'm cognizant of "the pull of Mark" and have found him revelatory: The giant sweep of large communal groups is a particular thrill. I'm aware that he is one of the biggest talents coming on in modern dance. In 1986 he's poised for it; it's only a matter of time. He has all the right boxes checked. But in many ways he makes my life miserable.

His relationship to music can be beautiful and infuriating: the big exquisite compositions plucked from the classical pantheon of great music that he has the balls to choreograph, often with an incredible but rigid physicalization of the structure of that music. It leads the viewer on a time-honored tradition that is so very satisfying and comes to be expected. It can make other kinds of investigations with or without music seem lesser and even invalid by comparison.

And when his work starts winking at a certain brand of New York cafe society, all in on the same jokes, I just flat-out can't for the life of me see the humor. I bridle at the way he deftly railroads an audience, keeping them on his track, making the stops and destinations he wants. How he repeats a movement once, then twice, just because, and then a third time just to make sure every single person in the house sees it. Is this a lack of faith in the audience's abilities to focus, a ploy to force the eye to not look away? If it does, no worries. It'll still be there when you return from your slumber.

The need for retro-worlds remodeled anew irks my punk heart. I need to annihilate the past in search of freedom in order discover something I suspect is "the possibility of new." But what do I know? He's breaking B-I-G in America while I am blazing around Europe. I can barely get arrested in my home country at this point. And he *is* so incredibly funny.

A few weeks after our naked meeting in the sauna I get a Guggenheim Award and I'm at the Billiard Hall in Chelsea. Mark's there and we're both drinking vodka martinis (so dry) and he congratulates me (he got the award the year before). He asks me to dinner and I figure "why not? It'll be fun." Am I now in some invisible club that I suspect but am not sure of?

He suggests dinner and attending a **Paul Taylor** performance. Dinner is extremely entertaining, and Mark is bubbling charm personified. There's a lot of animated conversation and laughter, then on to City Center where Paul is holding his annual season.

Paul Taylor is one of the grand masters of American Modern Dance. He danced for the source of it all, Martha Graham. She was radical in her day but Paul keeps on her track of narrative and interpretive exposition. Locked into the music. He is the reverse image of Cunningham, who cracked open the contemporary mind and put dance on a decentralized abstract grid. Taylor portrays things in a theatrical and artifice-driven sense; Cunningham just does things. Mark is clearly in Paul's camp, I in Merce's.

I dislike the performance with a passion that only an arrogant young artist can, and in a way it equals Mark's passionate love for it. He giggles on like a schoolboy about two-dimensional friezes taken from Greek vases put into lines of bare-chested men. It's pure camp to me. And the audience is fancy night out and digging it in a "This is serious, I'm in on it it so I'm sophisticated" way that makes me an outsider again.

He takes me backstage to meet Paul. I'm young and brash enough to find it unremarkable, definitely not starstruck, although Lorraine raised me to be very polite in situations of this nature. Everything about Paul—his sensibility, his use of music, his relationship to narrative, his reinforcement of ideals and expectations—is at the epicenter of my young distain for modern dance. Not that Paul's not a good soul; my young sensibilities favor disorientation and new forms and I need an "enemy" to push against at this point in my evolution.

I hoped a peek at our opposing worlds might be fun, but this date is not going well at all. Mark invites me back up to his apartment and we chat while he shows me lots of treasured memorabilia and knickknacks. I can't stop feeling still married to Justin though it's been over for months. I'm breaking a sweat. He excuses himself and returns wearing a sarong. We exchange a few innocent kisses and I'm stiffening up and not in a good way. He offers to crack my neck and I get horizontal to let him. I'm starting to relax... *Kaboom* is the sound of a shotgun snap. It's shockingly loud. I'm open but not this open. Shortly after my adjustment I excuse myself, telling Mark I'm just not ready to rock so soon after my recent breakup. Sleeping with the enemy was not on the menu, and I quickly slip out and disappear into the cold, artless night.

Restless Aries has a deep need for motion, to be set free traveling forward in motion, in space. I'm claustrophobic on a deep level, happiest in flight. Tossing, turning, pacing, walking, swimming, rolling, running, always moving even in the roiling litany of small physical adjustments in my pedestrian routines.

Wind hitting my face and slicing into space, catapulting forward, meeting it head on. Fast and giddy, I slice into it and it washes back at me, cleansing away social grace and restraint, freeing me to open up into space and thought. The act of space hitting my body ignites my brain and imagination, tripping me on and forward and on. Forward motion precipitates forward mental motion.

DREAM GIRL

I'm a dreamer who loves family. The crazy-loud emotional blurry one that I come from has its ups and downs, but it is a net that I can count on to catch me at any time. Unquestionably. Forming a dance company is part of that thing I want and need to function in life. I'm a social being and forming a company is social by definition. If people are waiting for me, expecting the goods, I show up. I'm prone to deliver. I know deep down that in a family I could flourish, a family that speaks the same body language, my language; a family that makes and breaks things together, blood-related or not. With lovers I recreate this paradigm and always need them fully integrated into my blood *famiglia*. If the family objects? Tough shit. They raised me to be open so here it comes. And I'd long wanted the whole Italian dream, the love, partner in life, humongous wedding and *kids*. I even loved the late '60s show *The Courtship of Eddie's Father*, with preppy-cute Bill Bixby as a single father raising a cute miniature version of himself. OK, no wife, but I can do it solo if pressed and want it badly.

During my term away from Hampshire I start studying with body repair genius Susan Klein in NYC. In the late '70s she had a forward-thinking ballet studio with a partner in Midtown. There she pioneered a deep and integrating technique aimed at connecting the body to the world in a very practical and powerful way through stretching and ballet. Susan moved downtown on her own a year or so later and formulated the Klein Technique, and I continue having private sessions and classes with her

141

throughout this period. She offers essential maintenance, continued development and sees me through any problem or injury I ever have. Her hands are absolutely thermal and could move mountains of blocked tension or set the multiple damages of the trade back on the path to healing.

In 1979, I'm mourning the death of Eleanor while Susan's going through a nasty breakup. We start dating, two souls consoling each other through a rough patch. The relationship ultimately doesn't last long but we need that moment together. Afterward, our friendship deepens into a strong one, free of attachment. And separately we both become much clearer about being queer. Or queerer.

We see each other at least weekly when I am not on tour. Somewhere in the mid-'80s we go out for dinner and come home with something more. That night, over rounds of Cuervo Gold Supreme Grand Marnier margaritas, we decide to try to have a child together. Our friendship is strong enough, jealousy absent, and we're both anxious to love some new flesh in the world. We etch our basic plan of action and we are off.

This is the dark ages in relation to what we really know about HIV or of gay men fathering children at all. The social discourse is being forged at that moment: the extent of involvement, of a father's parenting rights and responsibilities, healthcare protocol. It is all new territory and we are happy to be in the first wave of people hashing it out.

Of course the assumption is that my lifestyle of multiple male sexual partners doesn't bode well for any of us involved. Susan is relentless and thorough about researching what she feels is the safest protocol for us to proceed. She amazes me with her understanding of the latest firsthand research into the behavior and parameters of HIV. It is her body, along with that of a future child she is protecting, so she leaves nothing to chance and does exactly what she feels confident doing, based on the most current research she can find to support her decisions. She's in full mother-protective mode. And obsessed.

And so we begin the long journey with multiple doctors, charts of sexual history surveys, HIV tests, waiting periods and retests. One visit to an internist, Dr. Sharon L, is a stereotypical nightmare. I arrive at the office with a cold and go through a seemingly thorough exam and interview with the good doctor. No blood tests as yet, but still a good physical exam. At the end she calls in Susan and proclaims that after examining me, hearing my sexual history (without inquiring as to the actual activities I engaged in) and detecting swollen glands in my neck (yes, I have a cold), she feels I would most certainly test HIV-positive. The test would be a formality, but she cannot in good faith advise moving forward with our plans. (Hey, but no moral judgment here!)

My jaw drops. She's a doctor, she should know, I think in guilt and panic. "Bullshit," I say.

I have been meticulously careful in terms of safer sex but am trying hard to stave off the guilt that my fallen Catholic mind might be subconsciously harboring about casual sex and queerness in general. I am active and proud, but the jury is still out about a more complete picture of HIV transmission. We are undone by the glitch in our journey and we insist on a test anyway, sentenced to wait the two torturous weeks it took back then for the results. It comes back at last: negative. Weeks later the retest is negative, and six months later, negative again. After I stop the by now perpetual palpitations I've developed while waiting to find out if I could father a child without viral risk to it or Susan, and indeed, if I might escape a fate that I worried deeply about through the early '80s desert of misinformation, we proceed.

On our second attempt Susan gets pregnant, and in 1989 Bella Elizabeth Naomi Klein is born. But she's another story.

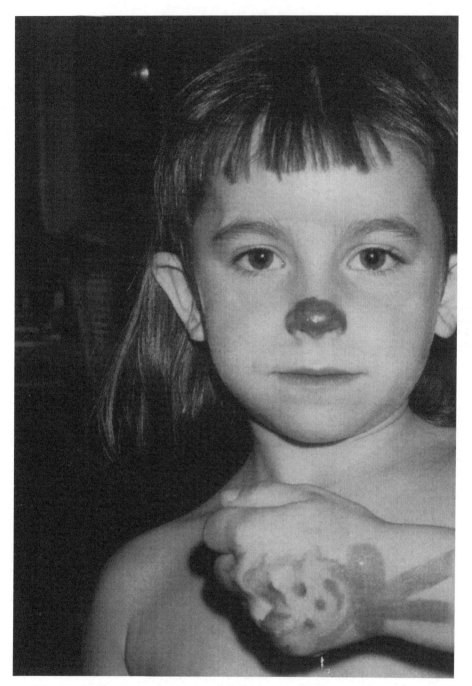

Bella (1991).

London Calling

"I thought being an artist meant you had to do anything for the experience." —Eileen Myles

"Steeepheen."

I know. I know. That call, so...familiar. That's me walking on the chilled damp streets of Glasgow, May 1989. I hear it again, a distinctly stretched rendition of my name:

"Steeephen!" I turn around to see two figures swathed in black, one short, gray, sturdy, the other tall with a big, fuzzy earflap hat framing a pale moon face. Zoom in on Michael Clark and his mum, Bessie.

I never met him before though we'd seen each other's work. I note his comfortable assumption calling me by first name, familiarity of fame, recognition that we are members of some club. In London everyone is first-name-only *if* you're in the club, the ruling-art class. Clark is the ballet prodigy gone punk choreographer with pop-star status in Britain. The rep is well-known: country bumpkin, Scottish folk dancer to Royal Ballet School poised for greatness, the rejection of it, the meteoric entrance into the worlds of culture/fashion/music/drugs. Aka "Boy Wonder" shook up the world of British dance.

He ignites dance for young underground London, slams it on the cultural map in a way that it has never been before and firmly installs himself as the dance world's Prince of Punk. Clark is a cultural force in motion, riding on the wave of fame alongside collaborators **The Fall**, British speed-punk rockers, as well as the designs of performance artist and cultural provocateur **Leigh Bowery**. By all accounts he's trouble and looking him in the face on the street here in Glasgow, he looks quite good to me.

He makes small talk about my photo splashed across the front page of the arts section in that morning paper. I'm the headliner at the Mayfest Dance Festival opening in Glasgow the next evening, and I invite him to come along. He does and finds his way to dinner with us afterward.

Our host is Val Bourne, presenter from Dance Umbrella, and an avid supporter of both of ours, so it's not out of place. Michael is positioned at the far end of our table, an elongated pale, sweaty presence in the distance. His smile is sweet, his look the most twisted take on post-punk fag I've seen: head shaved, apart from the too-tightly coiled Hasidic spit curls resting on either temple, held in place by Mum's setting clips. He has proper posture and his demeanor has him suspended in some out-of-time substrate that pronounces his movements in a slowed-down kind of dream.

I cannot be rude, nor can I resist. After the meal I go down to his end of the table to chat art. He's sweet and curious about everything he saw. There's an idea floating that we're American and British counterparts, and we're both interested in finding out what our counterparts are like.

We end up at a club together afterward, and I witness for the first time his star power in the real world: drinks sent to us from all directions, teeny-bopper girls asking me breathily if I was really with Michael, and who was I by the way?

The competition is instantaneous, exhilarating. We match each other drink for drink, both quite bottomless in that respect. I'm not yet attracted to him as much as...intrigued. There's the rush of notoriety, of dance worldliness and industry interest mixed in with a faint sense of challenge. Copious drinks and mountains of fags and hours later we end up scraping and grinding across his hotel room floor, completely off our faces and in each other's business. When bells go off, he calls out, "Oh, David!" (David Holla of Bodymap, his recent ex), and I chuckle, not at all offended or surprised, but I take note. He's somewhat broken and extravagantly in some other zone.

I sneak away afterward, just before the crack of dawn, while he's passed out. We're both left with knee burns from the grimy hotel room rug as a remembrance. I toss his phone number in the bin at reception on the way out of the hotel and file him away under "interesting research," but not really wanting to see daylight with my British counterpart. It's a fun night though, and a good story. I go back to my hotel for a nap and wake up in my bed around 10 a.m. to the phone ringing. I pick it up and there it is: "Steeephen...."

He comes over that afternoon wearing a red mesh baseball cap, white tee with a single giant red poppy on the front and red knee-length Vivienne Westwood shorts. He brings me a Xerox collage of his private parts. The courtship has begun.

He heads back to London and I go on to Portugal. He phones regularly, incessantly, and we chat several hours through the night while he shoots coke. We get acquainted quickly. He's predatory with me and it's a bit shocking. He's nudging into my usual role as hunter and although I'm unsure of how to trust it, I find it intriguing. He threatens often to return, and after a few days he finally just shows up in Lisbon, chiffon scarves flying, and that's it. We're together, plunging into a deep affair.

Perhaps each of us wants what the other has. I admire his unmatched style, the heaving fame, and I find London irresistibly attractive. He admires my bent on pure speed and motion, and New York is necessary to secure any Western choreographer's reputation. There's a lot to be said for our match in these respects, plus the sex is unusually hot. I've never been with anyone like him. He's brazenly flamboyant and serious at once. Compelling. Addictive. The attraction of opposites is classic and genuine. Once in his orbit I don't want to be out. And he's a Gemini, always irresistible to me. The Twin sign offers my single-minded Ram two for the price of one, and even if the price is high, I crave change.

There's a kind of perfect storm between us. The attention we garner because of our professional status is a powerful tool, and we both silently know we will go as far as we can with whatever we do together. No discussion of limits. And not only is the impact on our art-making potentially drastic, the effect of our unabashed public love is equally exciting. I understand that we might sacrifice the private stability of our bond but it's a political stance we both seem willing and adamant about. We jump at the chance to take that risk for the incremental social gain that might result, even if it's inching the cause of gender equality in small ways. It seems well worth it. And natural. Neither of us could conceive of it any other way. M and I are lovers, subversively loud and clear, and we use every public opportunity to flaunt our open happiness. It's practically a mandate.

My dance company is up and running full speed, and Michael's just disbanded his. He's weary of the grind and devotes himself with characteristic discipline and passion to a spiraling addiction. I provide an excellent structure for him to exist in. He simply travels with us on tour, watching the shows and lavishing me with a slavish attention, the likes of which I've never known. When the sweet side of this Gemini is present, there's no one more loving and engaging—he's utterly irresistible. Though I hear rumors that he can turn on a dime, I don't see the dark side for that first year at all. When I'm not touring, I fly to London and dive into an insulated cocoon of romance, drugs and a fraternity of pop stars and street thugs. He returns to New York with me when I have to work, visiting friends, watching rehearsals, attending to my needs and swimming through a constant stream of underworld celebutants... **Susanne Bartsch** (nightclub entrepreneur), **Neneh Cherry** (singer/ pop star), **Connie Girl** (transgender stylist), **Leigh Bowery, Pearl** (master corset maker), **Charlie Atlas** (filmmaker), **Victoria Bartlett** (fashion designer), **Dancenoise** (performance duo**), Michael Alig** (nightclub promoter/"Party Monster") to name a few. It's crazily fun and unusual in that early stage. There's a freedom and glamour to our joined forces that's not hard to take. I haven't heard the word "codependence" yet, but the idea of merging into each other and disappearing into something new is magnetic for both of us. We speak of working together under a single nom de plume. Nothing seems more fun and ideal than disappearing into an identity of our own fabrication.

We take it all in copious amounts: oral, nasal, intravenous and it usually ends in triathlons of shagging, his face shifting quickly through many identities, a multi-headed pagan idol. He's several boyfriends in one; his ability to merge and transform matches and fuels my need for new. The mutual ability to disappear into each other is deep. It is definitely a psycho "Sybil" sexual experience and I'm hooked.

To Bed

"The jab from prick to a needle, straight to betrayal and disgrace, conscience showing not a trace." —*Lou Reed*, "The Raven"

June 6, 1989. It's Mike's twenty-ninth birthday so we go around to Mack and Rosie's for a celebration, i.e., lots and lots of Charlie. The evening's under way, long crazy loops of revelatory (or not) conversation about everything imaginable and in great detail, sworn kinships between us and current sexual tidbits and like intimacies, all punctuated with jacking more Charlie: the ritual and the gear required, the anticipation of the next hit, the pinprick puncture and flash-hot rush, the swift, nonchalant trips to the loo to vomit the surprisingly pleasant, thick oatmeal vomit, as a matter of course. And so the night goes, gets more intense and cryptic until Rosie comes out of the kitchen with a white-cream birthday cake adorned with twenty-nine syringes to mark the momentous day. "'Appy Birthday Mike! Wi luv ya."

151

Michael is invited by **Anthony d'Offay** to perform at his prestigious gallery in the first months of our relationship. At this point the gallery is on fire, the home to the incredible **Joseph Beuys, Gerhard Richter, Richard Long, Anselm Kiefer, Jeff Koons** and other art world luminaries. It's a major moment, especially considering Michael has stopped his high-profile company and is not producing work.

He conceives an installation called *Heterospective* and asks me to dance with him as part of the evening. We make a few attempts to dance "collaboratively" together in the studio and the results are dismal. He won't lead, and when he does I won't follow. I realize after some bruising sessions that our approach is wrong. And we can't force some new, desired model in a few rehearsals under the kind of scrutiny this show will receive. There's a lot of hubbub about us right now, and our first dance outing requires special consideration.

I try to beg out but Michael is persistent. I insist that we perform the only real thing that we have a serious daily practice in: sex. We devise *Bed Piece*, a reimagining of John and Yoko doing PA announcements for peace and love from their double bed. *Bed Piece* is an improvised sexual encounter in one of the three gallery spaces that the show inhabits. We are in bed in-progress when the audience comes into the gallery, and over the two weeks we perform, not one public viewer is brave enough to enter that back gallery. Many peek into the doorway as Michael and I move through the fifteen allotted minutes of naked/erotic rambunctiousness on a raised platform pedestal bed in the middle of the room. It ends with a rendition of Liz Taylor singing "Send in the Clowns," and serves as a prelude to the rest of the evening of choreography and antics devised by Michael. But *Bed Piece* is ours, and perhaps the most real thing we could do, did do, in our time together. It's not choreographed, not theatrical, not simulated. It's the real deal, "of the body" and prohibited by law in Britain.

The show runs for two weeks and on certain days there would be a mystery call warning that The Law was coming to close us down for lewd behavior and whatever else it could. On those days Anthony, the consummate supporter and gentleman, might come to the back of the gallery to the walk-in closet that we moved into as our living quarters for the duration of the engagement, and casually mention that although he loved the incredible formal investigations that were taking place in *Bed Piece*, we might want to tone down the graphic exposure here and there for this performance.

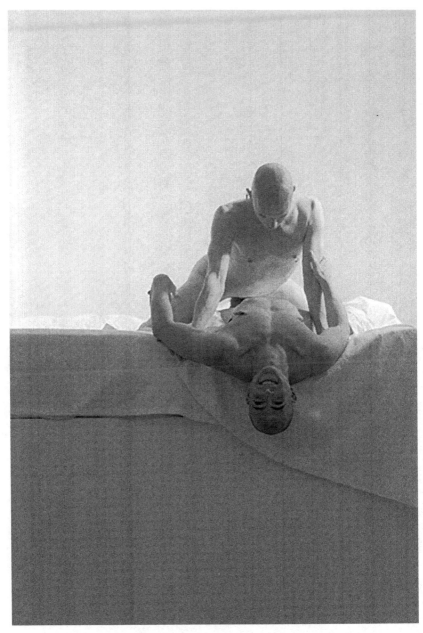

Photo: Hugo Glendenning. w/Michael Clark
(during rehearsal for *Bed Piece*, London (1989).

Photo: w/Clark from
his *Heterospective*. London (1989).

One weekend in Shepherd's Bush we start on something called "Ice," having no experience with it, but the usual eagerness and gusto for something fresh. Sonic rush forward and it is three days later: I'm in the back room making a collage of photos I have, when the paper I've been working with suddenly has the most amazingly fluid nature. I'm intrigued and go to the front of the flat to discuss it with Michael and he mumbles, "Get real, you're hallucinating. It's normal paper."

He, on the other hand is more concerned with adult things like the undercover officers parked outside "watching the flat." His paranoia runs deep during this period and is predictable enough to set my watch by. I look and see nothing, telling him in turn to "get real and get a grip". He continues on and on. After a while, I peek out the flat window, note two suited men walking by and I'm sucked rapidly into his movie. It really doesn't take too much. Now that I too am convinced we're being watched, we wind each other up exponentially. We fret and debate and eventually form a plan to "do a runner," leave the flat and check in to a hotel. We pack our clothes in a trunk and a backpack then spend precious loudly ticking time deciding where to hide any incriminating evidence, most prominently, our works. We settle eventually on a plastic bottle of some Liquid Plumber–like product, and jam it all into the muck and return it back under the sink in the loo. We take a deep breath and venture out into the sunny possibility of arrest or freedom and bolt for the safety of the Hilton, not far away. Paranoid beyond belief a day later, we are still high as kites and on a plane out of London. We head for Spirit Square in Charleston, South Carolina, where I am to be a resident artist for a few weeks. We hide in our hotel when we arrive, coming down a few days later, scratching our heads and wondering if any of that escapade should be filed under fiction or non.

My company joins me in a few days and it's here, in the post paranoia of our "Holiday on Ice," amid the shining hospitality of the well-mannered sweet South, with buttermilk pancakes and grits for breakfast every morning, that I lay down the first steps of the dance that will eventually become *MiddleSexGorge*.

❖ ❖ ❖

MIDDLESEXGORGE

The phone rings at the flat in Shepherd's Bush in the summer of 1989. Val from Dance Umbrella asks if I would do a photo shoot for them, as I'll be appearing there with my company the following fall. I don't have a costume (there are none yet), so I rummage through my things and find a corset I am thinking about using, and complete the look by sewing some silk flowers from the Shepherd's Bush market onto my knickers. It works so well in the photos that I begin to develop movement around it that eventually becomes *MiddleSexGorge*.

In the fall of 1988, before I met Michael, I got arrested repeatedly in NYC with ACT UP in civil demonstrations against New York City's non-existent AIDS policies. Being lifted into the police van by a group of NYC cops within the context of a massive demonstration leaves a searing, visceral impression. Could I build my sexually charged anger into a dance that has as much meaning to me as these moments?

It hits me that my work might be more engaged if I try to build the most sensual and abandoned part of my nature into the movement language I'm making then, so I begin to push my pelvis forward off my leg and into the face of the audience, hips and head rolling, carving arcs, arm and legs slashing out through space. All of the impetus in partnering is about the gain and loss of control, giving up to or taking over the trajectory of one's weight. Then I meet Michael and my sexuality is in the public domain full tilt. Personal and artistic collide and blur further.

The score for this work is originally supposed to be written by an arty, New York duo who shall remain unnamed. Their music is interesting but the flashy half of the band is an insincere mess and his album in progress along with his drug habit take precedence over his work for me. I've naïvely paid in full in advance and have to walk away empty-handed when I hear the excuse he offers as a final mix. I need help and Michael calls **Bruce Gilbert** from **Wire**.

When **Graham Lewis** and Bruce agree to do the score for *MSG*, they're in London and I'm in New York. There is no time or money to get together for rehearsal so I chose one of their three-minute songs I've been listening to a lot, "The Ideal Copy." I ask them to make a twenty-four-minute remix, suggesting only that they begin the mix with the original song first. They just go to town. I'm almost done with the dance when they start, and since they can't see rehearsals we hope for the best. The tapes are late arriving for my last rehearsal before the premiere in Lyon, France. Graham ends up playing the mix into my answering machine so that I can get in some rehearsal. It works shockingly well with almost no adjustments. The actual show disc arrives the day of the premiere, and that's how it all happens.

MSG goes on to London and after the premiere South Bank Center's Queen Elizabeth Hall, we all go out for dinner. Michael's mum, Bessie, Bruce and Graham and a few mates are with us. We're the last patrons in the restaurant and are getting the full attention of the staff, feeling fabulous after conquering London, and Michael and I are giving the usual public display. Men snogging (kissing) in public is still illegal in Britain in the early '90s, though I generally feel the immunity that results from naiveté or the privilege of notoriety. A skinny weed of a waiter starts giving me shit about it when I'm on my way to the loo. I quietly tell him let's take it outside if he has a problem and he disappears. I don't give it another thought.

We spill outside after dinner in giddy laughter when a full posse of waiters ambushes our group. They deftly trap us inside a circle and our fab crew of dancers, punk icons and mother are hostage to their bigot minds. The smallest one springs at me and fires off a punch to the back of my head before Bessie's screaming and Bruce's forthright intercession of logic breaks the spell of violent anger. In my peripheral mind I note the handsomely swaggering Graham in the background and I am impressed and grateful for Bruce's quick-witted action. The schism between the success of the night and the harsh reality of its sexually empowered theme is surreal.

Photo: Chris Nash. Stephen Petronio from *MiddleSexGorge* (1989).

Back in New York, a few weeks before Christmas, Michael and I go up to the Dakota with **Robert Tracy** for tea at Rudolf Nureyev's. Robert is a prolific writer about modern dance and ballet. He is also Rudolf's longtime companion and a new friend of ours. The apartment is legendary, filled with romantic nudes jammed frame to frame on the walls, and that fabulous velvet settee that formerly supported the buttocks of Maria Callas (who owned it before Rudolf). There we sit, waiting for Rudolf to finish the bath he was in the middle of when we arrive. He makes his entrance to welcome us dripping wet in nothing but a towel, providing the seductive performance he can't restrain himself from giving. Despite his age and in what must be very compromised health at that point, he's rather stunning. His body is creamy-smooth, not unlike many of the paintings he is surrounded by. He pours champagne, flirts a bit, tries to gain some signs of encouragement from Michael, whom he is clearly drawn to, and apparently has been since those first days, when they met in Paris.

We are there because of the friendship forged with, and the lust he harbors for Michael. They met a few years earlier when Rudolf commissioned him to make a new ballet while he was director of the Paris Opera Ballet. Rudolf is rather dismissive of me at first: "Why are you here?" is darting from his eyes, as I am an obstacle in his path to Michael. How can a modern choreographer trump Nureyev's star? I'm completely secure in my place in Michael's life and just don't engage on that level. R gets it quickly. Before long he opens up as the fabulously warm and generous man he is. We talk art and fashion and the charm of his curious mind is irresistible. He just wants to know everything about what we're doing, and if and how he might get involved. He fancies himself still very able to dance and hints at ways he might fit into projects we're involved with. It's inspiring and unsettling at once. Very hard to say what's still possible for him, but on the settee in his towel he appears perfectly able.

He eventually dresses and we continue chatting about dance, then on to *The King and I*, which he is currently touring in one of his last ill-advised performance ventures. He's keenly curious about my upcoming NY season a few weeks away. R then casually mentions that Jackie and **Maurice Templeton**, her diamond-dealing companion, are stopping by to say hello.

If I weren't already champagne high I might be shocked, but very little really surprises me at this point in my life. Still, **Jackie O**...

She arrives quietly and politely and we all sit around chatting, Jackie on one end of the couch and I on the other (with Michael and Rudolf between us, Maurice on a chair opposite Jackie), a social ordering for sure. (Where would Maria C park herself? The irony of the triangulated derrieres that have been on this sofa is not lost on me. I suppose **Mr. Onassis** sat here too at some point in time.) She is speechlessly elegant and chic, fresh from a little facial touch-up according to Robert, her skin taut, immobile and ravishing. They speak of their plans for the coming holidays and general catching-up, inquiries about our work, and it's all casual and light. Maurice is instantly likeable—present and relaxed in his skin even though his appearance is strictly aging business magnate in contrast to Jackie's radiant star. The warmth between them is obvious.

Michael and I rise to leave at the designated moment, exchanging polite kisses and saying our good-byes (kiss a cultural icon: check). We go out into the hallway to don our coats and there, Jackie's coat and scarf hang, too. It's simply and utterly irresistible. We try it on just to be in *her* coat. It is black cashmere with a high, tight black mink collar and it feels insanely luxe. Walk a mile in that. When I speak to Robert the next day he mentions that Jackie is intrigued and smitten by the two bald dancers and wants to see us dance.

January 16, 1990, is, among other things, the night that *MiddleSexGorge* premieres in New York at the Joyce Theater. It is also the date that the United States begins a war, a Gulf War. As I am warming up onstage, bombs are sailing down in the Persian Gulf. The premiere of *MiddleSexGorge* is so personally linked in my mind with the force of physical power, freedom and control and is about to be born into a world where people continue to die for the ownership of oil. Suddenly we are in the movie where a struggling Irving Berlin is opening a musical on Broadway when one of the great wars breaks out, the news of it spinning into the frame as a headline in the *New York Times*.

Rudolf and Robert are coming to the opening with Jackie and Maurice. We've known for days and as the curtain draws near and the bombing begins, all of us at the theater are waiting to decide how to reconcile a historically bloodied moment with a dance premiere, and the possible attendance of a former first lady and cultural icon.

They *are* coming. They aren't coming. They reconsider and the curtain is held in anticipation. **Martin Wechsler** from The Joyce Theater reports that they are all waiting in their limo out front until the crowd settles down. In the end, at 8:15, Rudolf, Robert, Jackie and Maurice slip down the aisle and into their seats as the curtain rises. We dance for our lives that night as personal, cultural and political moments merge and history is sealed.

The review that week in the *New York Times* has an uncanny similarity to the "Suzy Says" social column in the *Post*. By its counts, *MSG* is a hit; Petronio and Clark are a sensation "not to be missed"; and "Rudolf and Jackie and Merce (Cunningham)" are in the house.

When I first meet Michael, he's stopped his company and is floating. He began traveling with us, then dances for me in my work. I make a solo for him and a duet for us in *MSG*; love and dance are blending incredibly. When he's ready to begin making work again we discuss merging companies. It becomes an obsessive megalomaniacal dream. We want to tour a show that consists of some of his work, some of mine, and a collaborative work with our individual dancers plus some shared. We plan a version of *The Rite of Spring* called *Wrong Wrong*, as in two wrongs don't make a Rite. Haha.

There are problems all over the idea. Half my dancers want no part of him, and his are not necessarily thrilled with me. The collaborative version of *Rite* alternates sections of the score and we also try a few sections where we simply merge what we've made in the same space. It is a spectacularly flawed idea and we end up simply alternating. I do Section 1, he does 2; I do 3 and so on 'till the end. Leigh Bowery does costumes and **Charlie Atlas** lights, so it's his team. We shop the project until a presenter at the Centre National de Danse Conteporaine (CNDC), in Angers takes the bait and we all ship off to a creative residency. After a year of planning, the entire crew of dancers and designers arrives to live and work together for a two-month creative period. Living and working together is by turns incredible and insane.

We are realizing an unlikely dream but we are certainly not one big, happy family. The dancers are wary, the shared ones overwrought; creative pressure and the wear of abundant alcohol/substance begin to show and the foundation of our relationship starts to crack. The creative process can be a rough one, even though incredibly satisfying. Digging in and down to find authentic material to make physical: It's not all fun and games, even at the best of times. And now there are two of us with loads on the line. Temperaments are on edge and insecurities and power struggles flare between us.

Eventually, a vicious battle erupts between Michael and me in the dancers' residence. It progresses from a screaming match to a high-speed chase through the building and lands in the communal kitchen with fly-ing dishes and glasses smashing across the floor, then swells to a throttled embrace that careens around the room, bouncing from wall to wall. It peaks with him holding me bent over backward out of the fourth-story kitchen window. And in that rage-filled moment of physical extremity it hits me full force—I'm arched back again in time to the igloo fight on Briar Lane, the fight for domination on my childhood block, for power and control. But this time it's not Kenny K, my childhood rival, but Michael, my lover, the man I'm most intimate and unguarded with, the man I've gone further with than anyone into dark and disorienting places, the man I'm risking it all with both artistically and personally, going to places that have hardly been ventured in public between two men. And now I'm bent back out a window in Angers in the throes of mortal anger, in a deeply dipped arch, romantic, dangerous, lethal fighting for some kind of power in a relation-ship wildly out of control. The sting of adrenaline and defeat rages across the surface of my skin.

Though more than glass shattered that day, somehow we hobble it all together and bring the show to Paris. But the trouble mushrooms when crit-ics begin to pit our work against one another's. We had both separately been well-touted in Paris up till this moment. But for the most part, critics decree our collaborative work *Wrong Wrong* to be "le flop." Emotions are raw and confounded by the disappointment and the fact that M and I are not in complete control of our work in the way we are used to being on our own.

When we head to South America for the next part of our tour, we make a huge splash: São Paulo goes for my work and Rio prefers M's. We walk off the plane in Rio to a Hollywood-like press and photo deluge. We end up on the front page of the main papers and when we walk into the hotspot restaurants people actually applaud. It's an unimaginable dance mania by U.S. terms and despite the rift between us all, the coke-fueled fights and incredible love and passion, the sobbing dancers backstage unable to cope with the strain of two directors, the danger and excitement of the beaches and clubs at night, it is amazing fun.

Our show proceeds on to Bogotá and Medellín while the War on Drugs declared by Bush is in full swing, despite strict travel advisories issued by the U.S. Embassy. American tourists are disappearing en route to their destinations and many never turn up again. When we check into our five-star hotel there is a knock on our door and someone connected to the theater enters with a covered silver tray. When she removes the cover there is a mountain of coke that rocks our world. (There is so much that we actually have to dump some out of the windows of our van a few days later on the way to the airport. Try as we do, we can't possibly consume another grain.) I demand an armed bodyguard as a condition for going on this tour, and my incredulous sponsor agrees. We are supplied with Jorge, a cute young blond from Bogotá with a large *pistola*. He follows Michael and me everywhere, and stands outside our door while we sleep. In transit between a distant mountain restaurant and our theater, the company is actually stopped by hostile police, at least that's what they said they were. It seems like the middle of nowhere and hard to tell where they came from but Jorge springs into action, flying off the bus and chatting up a storm with the group. Seems like a tense forever, but eventually he gets back on the bus quietly perspiring and we continue on. I maintain that Jorge is the only reason I'm still here to tell this story.

In London Michael and I often eat at the The Zen Oriental Kensington at the Hilton in Holland Park. The sushi is superior, and in 1989 the options are limited. There is the kebob shop, the chippy, the Indian down the road for a good vindaloo or The Zen. It's frequently a scene there, a wide array of upscale business guests of the hotel and the young and fabulous of London. Random evenings include **David** and **Iman, Merce** and **John, Mark E. Smith (The Fall), Neneh Cherry, Lizzie Tier, Jake** and **Josie (Big Hard Excellent Fish)** Leigh Bowery (performance art/fashion) and Pearl (master corset maker) for meetings, **Bananarama** (OK, OK, but the food is very good and it's practically walking distance from our flat in Shepherd's Bush).

It's Saturday night and we stop in for some quick sushi on the way to the midnight premiere of *Twin Peaks* at a theater somewhere in Nottingham Hill. Over dinner, musician **Bryan** "(Everything I Do) I Do It for You" **Adams** stops by to say hello and "I think you two have something great going on" (we're apparently the queer couple of the moment).

Next **Rifat Ozbek** (fashion designer) plus three others sit down for a drink. Random chatter, clanking of dishes and egos. At some point someone gives me a bubble-wrapped sleeve of Rohypnol (sleeping pill/date rape drug). As soon as they go, Michael and I slosh down two each with the already copious amounts of sake and the ride begins to blur...

By the time we reach the theater and find seats it's officially incomprehensible. Michael disappears (we *never* leave each other's sight in those days, especially in public).

Alarms go off.

I wait as long as I can before I go outside to ride out the earthquake illogic that's the warped screen I can't make sense of. When it's over Michael is still MIA. Panicked, I check all the possible friends, then bars on the way home—home to a hollow codependent nightmare.

Hours go by with no sign and I begin to hit a rage that causes serious damage.

I am dumped.

I am dumped and in a city that's not mine.

I am dumped in a city that's not mine, in an empty flat.

I am dumped in a city that's not mine, in an empty flat in Shepherd's Bush.

I am dumped in a city that's not mine, in an empty flat, in Shepherd's Bush and I am alone.

I smash everything that isn't anchored down and carve the wallpaper with morbid epitaphs. Somewhere near dawn I gather my belongings to evacuate and begin to drag my rolling case to the tube station as M pulls up into our lane. He coaxes me back. When he sees the flat he says, "I'm home."

The next morning the sunlight underscores the Charlie Manson–esque twist to my decorating esthetic. We don't discuss this but silently agree to leave it like that for the rest of our days together. It's not till the random visitor stops by that I really appreciate my knack for interior design.

Rosie Takes A Dive

August 1992. Michael, Mack, Rosie and I are at Mack's house enjoying a night on H(heroin). I am sitting in the couch next to Rosie, whom I adore. She's a sarcastic Liverpudlian with the meanest Scouse accent around, a chic chignoned-blonde and loyal friend. Mack, her East End boyfriend, is a sexy, compact stud. He's a sweet lug/minor thug, an endless source of whatever we require, whenever the moment arises. He sleeps with a bat next to his bed. We love them to pieces. We hang with them often and know each other intimately, i.e., we do lots of downtime together and take lots of drugs in each other's company—mostly Charlie and Ecstasy, some H, though that's a substance that doesn't really have much appeal to me, never really grabs hold of me. Luckily for me it's just not in my temperament.

So we're hanging out on one of my rare H-excursions with these two, and Rosie and I are on the couch. Michael and Mack are somewhere else in the room, their voices a muted drone that's unintelligible but comforting. We're listening to a single that Rosie and Mack are working on that's just about to be released, and just generally in the mood, and I turn to Rosie, who's now closed her eyes and looking so very beautiful tonight in a head-back, relaxed way. She has the slightest tinge of celestial blue to her skin and lips. I'm thinking how underwater lovely that color is when it begins to dawn on me in the slowest motion. I s s h e b r e e a a a a t h i n n n n n g ? She's turning blue! Bluer! She is going out! My voice struggles to the surface to sound an alarm when Mack streams horizontally across the room like a Jedi and lands on top of her, calling and slapping, while we're all fretting about what we'll have to do if she doesn't start breathing. All the while he's shaking and slapping and suddenly she vacuums in a deep breath. Her eyelids pop up like muffins in a toaster, with a look on her face like "what's up?" The three of us decline to reveal particulars of that "blackout" conversation to Rosie until a few days pass and all's back to normal. But it dawns on me the night that Rosie takes a dive: I've lost my way. In the briefest of instants, a night of recreation escalated to an epic OD saga with all the full-blown gruesome details—luck, circumstance, vomit, possible police involvement—and back again so very easily. It's just too easy, too casual. Shortly after that night I began to mentally pack my bags.

I'd been so in love, obsessed with Michael, practically disappearing inside our codependent world, a world of fun, glamour, fame, creative and social challenge, civil sexual rights and empowerment, that the thought of leaving was unbearable. Excruciating. Void. But in the end I couldn't trust what was between us. Who knew what either of us really felt, or for that matter who we really were. We were too high to decipher.

A year or so later we've worn ourselves out. The thought of waking up next to a cold blue boyfriend becomes just too much in my fragile state. On a trip to Berlin to discuss a triple bill evening with Michael, Bill T. Jones and me at the Deutsche Oper Berlin, I announce my departure. Though it drags on for several painful months, the final wall began to go up in Berlin.

There's No Place Like Home

Touching down in a new foreign city makes me desperately needy. I'm tired, disoriented, lonely, hungry and usually urgently frisky. I paint the globe in motion, touring the world to perform modern dance. I travel in the stratosphere as an artist of note and I ache for intimacy. I need to see this new landscape, taste it, know some of its secrets and make love with its people. I grow extremely attached to my compulsions; this one allows me to believe I belong in this new place. Often I eventually do.

I drop into a jet-lagged sleep far from home....

My eyes pop open and register the neutral white ceiling and nondescript beiges of everything else. "Hotel room...again. Where?...remember!!!" comes the command.

The ceiling glares back down at me, offering no clues. I sweat out the seconds it takes me to remember. I'm on tour I know but...stiff and supine, I register the familiar pressure in my stomach, "aching organs" that translates as "bursting for a pee." My weight is liquid, too, and I gently slosh it over to the left side of my body. "Paris. I'm in Paris." The motion jogs my memory. Locates me. When I tip into a slow roll, weight pours into the bowl of my pelvis and with a push though my extending left arm I'm sitting up. This is me. Wincing. In Paris. I can tell I'm awake by the pinching hot pain in my sacrum, hard and brittle as ice but burning. New York City dance critic Deborah Jowitt once described me in a review of one of my dances as "the Master of Melt." Well, this is how that master begins the task of getting out of bed every morning.

I often feel that the rapid hypermobility I achieve in the studio is akin to driving a Porsche over an obstacle course that it's simply not designed for. Or like making that Porsche sprout wings and fly. The body's just not supposed to do what I ask of it. I get it done and it is thrilling, but a Porsche is not really built to lift off the ground and fly. The reality of what it takes to rise in the morning is the price.

This morning is worse than usual. From sitting, I slip down to all fours, then lie on the floor, roll to my back slowly pull my knees up, first one... than the other... to touch the crown of my head. I strain forward toward my knees and gently emulate a rocking horse to pump synovial fluid up and down my spine. Eventually the ice melts, the pain dissipates, and I'm good to go. This is my life sentence: a life in motion. Can't sit still, can't stop, still hurts, so move I must. I'm locked in.

I often think that Advil, Motrin or Tylenol should sponsor the Stephen Petronio Company. So many dancers consume one, or the other of these products regularly in the thick of the working/performing process. I've known them all of my adult life and no matter what style or class, that's something we all have in common. Pain.

I love that scene in the film *Invictus* (2009), where Matt Damon as Francois Pienaar, captain of the South African rugby team, meets with Morgan Freeman's Nelson Mandela for the first time. Mandela breaks the ice by asking how Pienaar's recently injured ankle is and if it's back to 100 percent. The reply comes back quietly, something to the effect of "When are we ever at 100 percent?" It's so telling for anyone whose instrument is the body. There's always *something* and it usually involves pain. We are always nursing a tightness, pull, sprain, tear, misalignment. That's just part of the territory.

You see the dancer leap and bound, defy gravity and press the boundaries of human movement possibility, yet the mechanics and sensations of these efforts are for the most part concealed. In the mainstream forms of dance, artists often paint a smile over the top of Herculean efforts, but their soul is gritting and grimacing for dear life. The dancer has come to represent the ethereal, outside the laws of physics, but we live on the earth and the pull of gravity is definitive. We work with it, attempt to defy it, and yes, we eat real food, pant, smoke, drink, eliminate, copulate, get married, divorced, addicted and healed. We are human. We sometimes break. And it all hurts at some point or another. And we all do something to deal with that pain. Some more than others.

After Michael, I'm gutted by love and spend five years adamantly solo, continuing on in Williamsburg where I moved us to get away from the East Village life. It occurs to me that I haven't been on my own for most of my adult life. Now I'm slightly uneasy, empty on my own, but unfettered by a companion and all the accoutrements that come with that. I've lived through a series of contiguous partners and here is a rare opportunity to dive into myself and see what I might see.

It's 1992 and I'm still the only artist visible on Lorimer Street. I find one of those improbable summer cottages that were built behind apartment buildings in Williamsburg. I have a large single-story two-bedroom, with basement, a back porch and vast backyard. It's plopped down in the middle of the back gardens of the surrounding apartment complexes, a little Shangri-La filled with windows and light. I never even lock the door. There is no access from any street and I have to walk through an apartment building and down a private high-walled alley to enter into the exclusive courtyard that holds my house. It is perfect and about $600 per month. The neighborhood is a triple intersection of Polish, Italian and Puerto Rican. The weekends are overrun by alcohol (Polish), gambling (Italian) and crack (Puerto Rican), all according to where your gene pool landed you. The Italian ladies all around adopt me instantly, offer me food and keep track of my comings and goings. When **Nashom Wooden**, the fierce performer/singer/drag personality **Mona Foot** and later singer/songwriter of **The Ones**, comes home to spend the night one weekend, curiosity is immediately piqued, the ladies probing to decipher whether or not my Italian white ass has taken an African roommate or lover. "We're just so curious about your friend that was here this weekend..."

Bigoted or not, this nosey enclave is what I grew up in and I know how to handle it. I'm at home being the freak surrogate son on the block and embraced despite my open nature. By the end of the conversation and my deft marketing pitch of Nashom, they're chiding me because they didn't get to meet him.

I've been around some of the greatest visual artists in New York and although I love dance with a passion, I'm envious of the plastic arts that produce a product that you can touch or see whenever you want. Dance doesn't produce a product you can possess. My art disappears and that's its blessing and curse. My gift is in my body and not in my hands; I have no dexterity or patience for supplies and instruments. But I am alone now and begin to dabble, working with visual elements, acrylics, oils and found images, using my walls for canvases that turn into vast confessional collages of obsession and worship. I joke that "to exhibit I will have to saw out chunks of Sheetrock from my walls," but this is all play.

I operate from this fortress with complete privacy. I dance all week from Monday through Thursday, up at the crack of dawn, onto the LL line to **Crunch** on Lafayette Street in Manhattan, where I work out rigorously for two hours daily, sculpting myself into whatever I decide is the right form for me at the moment. I like to think of my body as a costume in those days and pride myself on an ability to change my physique like it is one. One moment mesomorph buff, one moment lean and mean, one moment ultra-thin "Bowie on smack." I juice organic vegetables and eat low-fat, high-protein, sugar/salt free. It's all about fuel for efficient motion and control of the shape I'm chasing. I'm unbending, obsessively strict with this regime.

Thursday afternoons I come undone. After work I score some coke, pick up a bottle of vodka and head back to the fortress and by Thursday evening I am off and running. There's a pattern that emerges during these marathons of disappearing. It starts with music blaring while I clean my apartment from the ground up, laundry at the Laundromat down the street, and then the evening alternates between choreography, drawing, painting and collage. I'm alone and free to dance in a way that I never do in the studio and I treasure this trip to the desert. Those previous years, my addiction took a back seat to Michael's—I perceived his as larger. Now my own is front and center.

I made *The King Is Dead* during this period, set to Ravel's *Bolero*, unfurled in thirty-second cycles that turn into convoluted circles in the body, building to a giant swirl in space. That music would blare and loop all night, me in the center of the living room casting pathways and vectors of energy that locate me like a compass in space to mark my journey.

Night turns into day and I barrel on. At some point on Friday night the obsession shifts from dance and art to sex. I hunt partners by phone and Internet and bars and I hook into a strata of similarly driven souls and screw half out of my mind from Friday to Sunday, with breaks for art in between. I'm drinking and getting high on coke the whole time, alternating the snorting of drugs with the tempering by alcohol with the smoking of cigarette after cigarette. Furniture gets moved and returned, steps get traced and notated and varied like a kaleidoscope, and sex is reveled in. I see multiple partners as a necessary communing with the souls of strangers. I want to know no one's last name. This is a spiritual quest and recognition of identity is interference.

My partners in the neighborhood are thugged-out or blue-collars on the DL: the welders and bodega boys, oil deliverymen and cab drivers, the hardware stockmen and the occasional policemen. Guys from the hood and if they pack a gun it's a plus. But they're men who don't want entanglement and I'm drawn to that aspect of their agenda. The sex is usually without discussion, animal hot.

Or later in that period I fall into an ongoing circuit of sex parties thrown by elite New York hustlers who spend their after-hours recreational time honing vocational skills until the sun shuts the parties down. Without question, it's always unquestionably safe. I'm well trained by my pro-sex, safety first ACT UP years and there's still basic agreement in these days that if you are playing, it's by those rules.

This life blossoms over several years and I function at a high level all week, then drop out for weekends. This duality seems to be workable for the most part. I see my work and private life as research, and although I don't discuss it with anyone, I see it as relatively normal. Weekends are long, sleepless marathons of substance-fueled perpetual motion, in my haven in Williamsburg and out on to the streets. It seems like I walk all of New York by night on the weekends, a need to keep moving and searching for...something. These walks go on and on, punctuated by pit stops at bars and encounters that are random and veiled and continue on until sunrise drives me back home. Typically somewhere around Sunday a.m., when I begin to see faces in every architectural detail I study, or the molecular structure of physical objects begins to become all too apparent, I finally consume something solid and slow down to sleep, at last falling backward into my floor-level bed, in deliciously suspended motion. Blackout.

I wake early Monday fresh and ready to begin the week again.

At year four of the Williamsburg Period, around my fortieth birthday, I begin to show signs of wear. It occurs to me that my unwillingness to speak about my current social life is lying, and I begin to perceive that life as *not social* at all. Language is missing and this renders it seriously null and void. My dealers begin to slip crystal meth into my coke and I'm getting blurry, speech slurry on the weekends. I hear myself not quite forming the words I want to as fast as I need to. And it always needs to be fast.

One night in the spring of 1995, I almost sleep through a benefit performance I'm scheduled to perform at an event in homage to Merce Cunningham, who will also be present at the dinner. I pride myself on never missing, always compulsively early, always fresh, always well pre-pared. This near-tragedy is a sudden and monumental crack in the foun-dation of my illusory world. Luckily my manager at this juncture, Janet Stapleton, notices that I haven't arrived early for my preparations, as is my habit. She knows I just got in from Europe days before and begins to worry. She has the presence of mind to cab out to Williamsburg and rap on my door until I stumble awake and make it to the show in time for the pre-cocktail reception and performance. She saves my skin but it's deeply worrisome.

And I'm beginning to fall into erratic depressions, the spiritual/sexual mission of touching the souls of a multitude of men becomes draining and suddenly seems deeply empty when reaffirming and egoless fulfillment was the aim. My knees begin to hurt constantly, dehydrated by the overdrive I've been living.

I suppose in the end, the cycle of destruction just seems transparently that. Destructive. And sad. I'm so worn it doesn't take much but listening to my body. My body always knows before my brain. It's finished with all this before my mind processes it. I simply burn out on it all and stop. Full Stop.

Aries is the child, the stubborn, impulsive and instigating sign that will crash through walls to reach a goal, not perceiving or considering an easier, smarter path if it is longer.

Spring ahead first day of spring, Zero Degrees Aries, on the cusp of Pisces, between the end and the beginning of the Zodiac

Pisces rules the feet, Aries the head! My body seems to know first, intuition propelling me into unpredictable unpremeditated action. My body understands what my mind has not yet formed. My body does not lie.

Getting Flack

And when I finally do stop I seem to be all there, perhaps a bit frayed but the essentials are intact. Miraculously.

It's 1996 and I turn 40. I'm hitting a physical peak, finished with "the journey inward" and ready to face the outside world with a clear mind. I decide it's time to let people closer to me again, to have relationships in real time. My disciplined nature doesn't mandate rehab. I ignore the possibility of delving into the underpinnings of my addiction, esteem issues, obvious need to succeed and travel at top speed, to be loved and desired, respected, to feel my worth. Instead, I just white-knuckle myself off all recreational drugs. They've lost their purpose and allure. I am still drinking, but casually, and my physical training routine kicks into overdrive without the hindrance of sleepless debauched weekends. My new dance, *Drawn That Way*, has its premiere at the Joyce Theater, and is a success. Andy Teirstein's score is written for a live youth orchestra and chorus, my first foray into teen collaborations.

I feel cleansed and childlike and make a note to allow myself to start dating again. There are a few practice runs, including one with Joseph Stachowitz, a Herculean but somewhat fastidious interior designer and painter, whom I meet at Crunch on Lafayette. It ends badly when I prove to be too much for him. In truth I treat him quite horribly and think, "OK, just testing the wheels. Don't fret!" Then on to a brief period with interior design czar Robert Couturier that starts as a blind date, set up by a friend who thought we might hit it off. Robert is charmingly sweet, talented, stable, well connected and well heeled. He's all that a guy could wish for. But that "something" is missing for me.

Now that I am on the market, everyone is suddenly a *shadchan*. When Camille Gargiso, a board member of my company, hosts a Sunday dinner party for friends she wants to introduce me to, there is vague mention of some guy she wants me to have a look at. I bridle at another "match" and when I walk into her apartment on West 13th Street, I slide by the intended without noticing. My eye does, however, zoom in across the crowded room like a heat-seeking missile with only one place to land: the alluring **Jean-Marc Flack**. He's low-key and unassuming, dressed in sand-colored baby cords and a white cotton long-sleeve T-shirt, his tattoos peeking out of the back of the neckline and the wrists. His hair is in a regulation-tight buzz cut.

I'm caught off balance. He is most certainly not my type, but my type usually has a wife, child or gun attached. This is a new moment and I readjust. I ask Camille who he is, and she relates that he is a co-owner of **Showroom Seven** and immersed in fashion; his partner is **Karen Erickson**, who also is a wild creative force behind **Erickson Beamon** Jewelry.

Camille doesn't think Jean-Marc is for me and tries again to steer me in her intended direction. It's too late. Her voice seems distant as she makes her case; I'm already pulled into Jean-Marc's orbit and linger there a good deal of the night. Is there ever logic in these matters? I don't particularly think he is "handsome" (as it later turns out he is stunningly so, but I'm not looking with those eyes). I can only say that for the first time in years, I feel infinitely better simply because I'm standing next to Jean-Marc Flack.

During the course of our conversation I begin to go into some altered courting state; obviously smitten open, not aggressive but I'm bold. At one point in our conversation I touch his face and ask, "Did you shave tonight?" Incredibly forward to do to someone I've just met—but I can't help myself and have to make contact, a body connection to mark him with my touch. He doesn't flinch.

We eventually end up cross-legged on the floor and my clothes zoom into focus. The Westwood summer-weight-wool bondage pants, V-neck tee and black ankle boots that I suddenly hate with a passion. I can't stop them from enlarging to huge proportions in the room as we chat and I think, "I would never speak to him for this long if he were wearing these boots." I will him not to see them.

I've had some great and significant loves in my life and at forty feel lucky about that. Most people never find one. I'm thinking that I'm done and have no qualms about it. Perhaps a quiet friendship would be nice at this point. I even ventured to a girlfriend (Lara from Milan) before I met JM, reasoning that if there is not a man whom I can get interested in, maybe it's a woman I need. And then JM.

He's there with **Stephen Jones**, British milliner, a friend and client of his from London. I learn later that Stephen has warned him to steer clear of me because my high-profile London antics have preceded me. "Stephen Petronio is trouble" he later tells Jean-Marc. He has no idea...

I leave that night without his number but for the first time in five years I have to know someone better. I call Camille and ask for his number. She thinks it only proper to check with JM and when he consents I call him immediately and ask him to dinner later that week.

We meet at Orologio, an Italian hipster restaurant with decent food on Avenue A in the East Village. I arrive early, as usual, in pink peach jeans printed with da Vinci reproductions of cherubs kissing and a champagne-beige down puffer coat. I'm carrying my practice gear, notebooks and the new edition of the *Village Voice* in a plastic greengrocer bag, as is my wont during this period. I have a distain for backpacks and male carry bags at this stage and the greengrocer is a a look I like. But I laugh to my self when suddenly I wonder if I seem too much like a homeless waif from this perspective of a suitor. I hope so.

JM arrives in a white T-shirt, black down Northface puffer and custom leather jeans that I am certain he has to lie down to get into. He's ridiculously calm and now I see that he is also ridiculously handsome. He opens dinner with the edict "Let's not talk about your work tonight."

He doesn't say why, and my megalomania winds me up and drives me to assume he must hate it. (Fourteen years later I learned that because he loved it he didn't want the night to be all about me.) I don't skip a beat and we go on to have a lively and interesting conversation, including my work and life in dance, his showroom and stuff we're reading, movies we are seeing and normal "warm-up things" like that. It turns out he has also seen me around the gym, but embarrassingly I haven't noticed. We split the check and when we get up to go, my disheveled plastic bag crinkles extra loudly. I walk him down Avenue A and 6th Street and we are at his door, the moment looming to say good-bye. I lean in for the briefest kiss (cheek) and disappear into the subway back to Williamsburg.

I'm totally smitten by his cool reserve but the fleeting peck leads me to believe this is disappointingly a bust. My impression is that he is underwhelmed by my considerable charm.

When I get home I call Camille and report the bad news and she commiserates with me, then I putter about the loft preparing for tomorrow's rehearsal. A half hour later she calls back and reports that she just got off the phone with JM and he thought the date was "one of the best he ever had." I'm reminded that my speed and intuition often outpace others. We have another date at **Nan Goldin**'s retrospective at the Modern. It's formative. A month later I'm living on Avenue A with Jean-Marc.

Photo: Christian Witkin. With un-named dancer. New York (2006).

This is my body

My kingdom, the jungle of my flesh

Vine-y limbs swing over rivers splashing along the runnel of my spine,

Twisting, torqueing, reaching out amongst the dark mysterious bulrushes.

I climb interior space made visible in time and place. This is not a flat world but dimensional, filled with passion volume and peculiar curves.

This is my body with flesh and bones and blood that takes me out into the world for better or worse.

My body soft and young and caught between its inheritance and my desire for this life

This is my body that carries forward, the stream of family past,

twist, blend, surge forward to my present skin—

A journal of family and experience that weld me into the thing I am:

the slouch of my shoulder, the swing of my arms, the rhythm of my gait as I gallop through the world.

This is my body, tentative, cautious or fearless as it dives headlong into the desire

my feet cannot keep pace keep pace keep pace with—

The leap for joy pulling all that I am with me,

my will and ungoverned intent,

stretching me into a place in space that I just thought not

possible to be in, could be, can be. Can be.

This is my body, stooped in sorrow, deflated with loss,

of love, friendship or success that disappears like weather shifts

Into mist

This is my body, my costume, my friend.

It carries me forward into a future that I am built to live and challenged to supersede.

This is my body, walking, carrying, in repose,

with habits that keep me bound to a past that is well known but forgotten,

A past right there on the surface, yet so deeply burrowed beneath the bone.

This is my body, mindful of its skin but stretching into points impossible, unimagined, unknown.

Photo: Sarah Silver. Stephen Petronio Company *Underland (2009)*.
Dancers: Reed Luplau and Natalie Mackessy.

Regular Or High Test

The glamour of touring is an illusion. I've traveled the world so many times, so many inspiring places, beautiful strangers, exotic meals, famous mugs and posh accommodations. Every city has a flavor, its people, cuisine, architecture and museums, but I'm there to do a job. I am there to do an amazing job, so the focus is all around that, and usually on a very tight, economically frugal schedule.

And when you are dancing, you only have a few hours of sightseeing in your legs before they fatigue. And the flights, trains and busses do a number on your body that is debilitating and unexpected even after all these years. What is that thing that happens to your neck and back, that sharp-as-a-knife thing where your spine inserts into your pelvis down in your sacrum, after sitting on a plane from LA to Sydney? Why does it feel like shattered glass is in my trapezius when all I did was sit on a train?

In the end, it is a job of motion and transience, where relationships are short stories together, vivid and alive for a brief moment then gone in a puff of smoke. Some of these stick and become longer friendships, but more often than not they are one-night stands. Those back home come to know you in a different but equally fleeting way—in weeklong stretches separated by monthlong absences, long-distance calls discussing petty slights at work or what you had for lunch. Transatlantic bonding includes no physical contact. When you are home for longer, there is the readjustment of daily life together, of not living with a ghost partner; earlier alone and free to do whatever you want to but with the invisible link to a partner absent, but now having to embrace the reality of the partner in the flesh.

Everything seems calmer and less pressing in the cities I visit and revisit. And when the shows are over for a night, if you don't have friends in the audience, or they choose not to come backstage because they don't want to bother you or had other plans or God forbid didn't like the show, you are alone for the night, unless you choose your coworkers. Often I don't. After 25 years of touring, interests on the road shift. The book I'm reading is more pressing than a night out and I'm miserable about keeping any but the deepest friendships alive on tour in host cities. So when the lights go out and the makeup is off, I walk from the theater alone and quietly find my way back to my home of the moment.

When morning comes, it's in this slightly sad, lost in the middle of a glamorous world state that I head out in Metz to see a few sights and visit a few galleries. I surrender to a crowded street packed with Germans and French, neither of which I speak, save for the basics that keep me fed and oriented, pressing along with the traffic flow in the Saturday afternoon crush, where I find comfort in releasing into the proximity of strangers and the aimless path I take. I stumble into a gallery and am confronted by a superb work by **Cindy Sherman** and it hits me in a way that is inexorably linked to my own drifting persona.

COLLABORATIONS

Cindy Sherman is a New York artist whose medium is the photograph; unique in that she largely uses herself as the subject in elaborate disguise or rather constructed identity. She is theatrical and funny and crazily over the top, and I see her art as performance in two dimensions that springs to life upon viewing, works that haunt me long after I move away from standing in front of them. Her subjects so vivid to me I'm certain I can hear their accents, what they're about to say, the thought lingering behind their eyes.

I'm looking at a particular piece that is a historical portrait based on the old masters. The work reaches into my eye and lingers, offering the pleasure of its artifice, conjures its reference and comments bluntly on it, offers vulgar irreverence and crude erotic beauty, how it speaks of a picture of woman-ness and how its viewer sees it. Assumes it, owns its subject through viewing.

I've loved Cindy's work for ages and as I'm standing in front of this one, it hits me. I've been waiting for something to happen to me and instead I can precipitate the action I crave. I decide on the spot to call Cindy and invite her to collaborate. She's the artist who inspires me most passionately and I can't believe I would consider settling for less. Why am I waiting?

When I return to New York I find her number and call. Surprisingly, she answers the phone herself and we begin a conversation that leads to other calls and meetings and eventually our first collaboration, *The King Is Dead* (1994).

She arrives at rehearsal on Avenue A where Movement Research used to reside. She is petite and beautiful with long blondish-red hair and a lithe, athletic figure that gives her the appearance that she's really arrived to audition for a place in the company. I have a crush immediately. This is her first look at what I'm doing and she sits intently on the floor in the corner without saying a word. She says she'd like to come back the next day and she does.

After the second rehearsal we adjourn to a bar on Avenue A and 2nd Street where we sit down to drinks to discuss it. She asks about the process of building the movement, of intent and thematic interests. I offer her the title and begin to associate mental oxbows springing from the words. I discuss my interest in moving away from the pelvis-forward thrust of my latest works, masculine and aggressive, to a focus on retreating the pelvis away from the eye in a kind of "death of the masculine push." She's quiet, listens thoughtfully, and I'm happy that she hasn't bolted for the door yet. A few weeks later the set begins to take form as a series of images of wrapped or mummified body parts that will float over the dance in diptych frames. *The King Is Dead.*

Fifteen years and three collaborations later (*The Island of Misfit Toys* and *I Drink the Air Before Me*), we are still friends and her work continues to rock me like few others. I love so much about working together but paramount is the quiet calm meeting, casual discussions, intimate little conversations that are as drained of drama and eruption as her work is packed with those weapons. It's comforting to know there are great artists in the world that can also be sweet, so generous, polite, easy to be around. I'd go a long way to do *anything* with Cindy.

And dances *are* made like anything. You start somewhere and end up somewhere else. Thought becomes action built step by step. There is no formula per se. Just a process that turns into a result, then shaped to an end. The mystery understands that the unknown is essential and knowable.

Photo: Sarah Silver, The Island of Misfit Toys (2003). Performers Amanda Wells and Shila Tirabassi.

I have no formal compositional training so I have little idea how any-body else does it. I'm self-taught and come out of the world of improvisa-tion so I know how to generate movement; I am bossy and know how to drive a group forward. The rest is taste, how to make choices and run with them.

A sense, an impression bathes in my mind and eventually crystallizes into a direction that finds a word or phrase that becomes a title. Finding these words is instrumental to me and the words become a guiding force. They're a focus, which becomes a place to assemble shards of information, a pile of photos, visual or literary references that will drive the work.

When I go into the studio, all this research has been germinating in my mind, sometimes for months, sometimes overnight, or sometimes it's just something connected that caught my eye in the paper that morning, and this drives the improvisational research through which I make move-ment. I work to move these far beyond the illustration of an idea, further down into the marrow of my bones and fashion movement that is far past illustration or narration.

While making *MiddleSexGorge* for example, sexuality and power were my motor for the work. If the natural body and principles of efficient motion rely on a posture that is vertical, the body's core at a 90-degree relationship to the earth, much of modern dance has been about tipping off that vertical, i.e., falling through space. The dance material generated in *MSG* pushed the sexual center, the pelvis, the tail and pubic bone forward *off* the legs, leading the action into the eye of the audience. If vertical is a plumb line, *MSG* pushes the sexual center forward and out of line with the head and feet. This simple discovery led to a rich source of movement invention, a physical problem that challenged the notion of efficient move-ment and eventually an important part of the basis of my style.

Dances come one step at a time like words grouped into sentences—but the rules of grammar are replaced with rules of motion and similarly can be bent in any fashion as long as physics complies. Sometimes, and especially in the early days of my career, I work alone, fighting to lose my orienta-tion, to let go of logic and judgment and to discover something new and unusual, then fight like hell, repeating it and its variations to bring it home to a quantifiable form that I can repeat, then access.

It's like hacking a path through the jungle—you know you can go but not where and when. You lean out into the unknown, expand to meet a space previously unimagined. Intention expands your pathway into an unknown place and a new pathway is forged.

The pleasure of this practice is that it's repeatable. Once you understand the process of extending your boundary you begin to trust that it is possible every time you hit a wall and you can say "No" to the fear of a lack new possibilities. And you can practically smell the possibility of the rewards.

So much of my training and creation has been turned away from the mirror, working from sensation and intuition rather than a picture of perfection. Most dance studios are equipped with mirrors, dancers facing them, using their refection to tell them what's right. I want disorientation, not completion of a goal or reaching a goal. *I want to disappear.* Shadows cast on walls or translucent ghost reflections in a studio window, the blank, cold screen of a TV that's turned off in the studio are more my speed. Those phantom-smudged hints of dancing with my shadow give me enough sense of what I'm doing and enough freedom from "goal" and perfection to pursue the unknown without judging too severely along the way. And when you're not looking outward at your image, you're feeling action from the inside, your kinesthetic sense.

I used to believe that it was imperative that I choreograph every step, and as if every dance were my last. And this lent a certain edge to the dances from that period. Now everything seems somehow set in motion before I begin. I am an entity that's already rolling, Petronio the choreographer has a mind of his own and I show up and work hard, but there is something chemical in progress—when I look away and it's all still going. Sometimes I do something "wrong", or what I see as irrelevant or something perfunctory to just get to another place, and the next day it's a thing that's right and magical, somehow done overnight and embedded perfectly in the dance when no one's looking. This is an advantage of the long haul, of so many years of history, its momentum impels creation forward and I love it when the dance becomes a living, breathing entity that wants me to step back and allow it to shape itself.

At this current stage in my art making, I work with the dancers at inception, improvising in front of them, then have them follow and capture my ruminations. Their attempts, their hits and misses in reproducing me get shaped into the final product of that movement. My torso combines with Gino's legs with Julian's head with Shila's arms, and in this way the end result becomes a collective journal of response to a sought-after moment, the best of our physical worlds. These "combines" become motion that one body could just not do, and are more precious for their unlikelihood.

Movement phrases culled from improvisational research become the building blocks of a dance, much the same as the colors a painter mixes in anticipation of a new canvas. We practice these phrases together, a communal language that we achieve fluency in. This takes as long as required by the dictates of each new phase and I put off the actual building of the final work until the language becomes so known and doable that it's reflexive. When this state is achieved, the composition of the dance begins.

Sometimes these phrases are dropped into the actual dance verbatim, a demonstration of the language and direct communication with the audience of that language. More often, I will devise a situation for the dancers to interact in, using the phrases as a springboard. For example, one dancer will perform verbatim the base phrase we are working with, while several others will be instructed to "swarm and circle that 'source dancer' like a pack of hungry dogs," or to only do the arms of the base phrase or to perform the "negative space of the phrase" or to perform it "as if there were an earthquake in the room and the floor was crumbling or shifting beneath your feet," or "lazy and without interest" or some other more ridiculous prospect. So it is an improvisation, but the dancer improvising is a gun loaded with very specific ammunition to draw from, a common language to access and vary from, and is behaving instinctively in a tightly structured situation. Then the results are memorized.

My goal has often been to disorient the dancer to the point of reflexive unconscious response, to bring out the unconscious reaction to a situation. There is nothing sexier in my mind than watching these highly skilled and sophisticated bodies disoriented and solving problems from an intuitive place. It brings out the animal in them. Intelligent animals. That creates a drama like no other.

All these physical responses get memorized and reproduced, and I begin the process of selecting, shaping, editing and joining them together into the final composition that makes it into the dance.

I simply have to work with **Yoko Ono**. Mythological Yoko. Avant-garde artist, composer and renegade feminist, she's the woman who takes the hit for breaking up the Beatles (what nerve, what power!!). The mainstream cringes and Yoko howls! How she grates Middle America, which only wants to hum "She Loves You" into its old age.

The first time I see her perform, I'm still in high school. It's 1972 and she and the **Plastic Ono Band** are opening for **John Lennon** at Madison Square Garden. The concert is called *One to One*, a benefit for kids with learning challenges. I'm bordering on too young to be there and this is part of the buzz. Everyone I'm with is older: my brother and cousins Michele (years later she gives birth to a son **Michael Volpe** who will become hip hop experimentalist **Clams Casino**), Joanne and a few of their hippest friends. (Joanne was the president of the New Jersey Chapter of the Beatles fan club in the '60s, The Beatle Bobbies. She's been at most of the Beatles New York "moments," including Shea Stadium.) I'm poised to hate Yoko as passionately as these young women adore John. I'm clueless about her music and my record-buying prowess hasn't taken me underground yet. I still feed off the top of the music world chain, consuming what the general public is being fed.

All I know of Yoko is what most people know—my perception of her is filtered through the media. Although I am suspicious of the image being splashed around, she is essentially kind of a cartoon to me. I am really there, like everybody else, to hear John.

But when she breaks into her song "Open Your Box," it is disorienting. Here is this tiny figure in the BIG spotlight with a lot against her. She is wailing and screeching a song about her vagina and her mind through music that's enraged and thrilling. I've heard nothing like it before and I'm pretty sure no one else has either. The crowd seems torn, a massive question in the room, not sure if they should be into it at all. There is no shortage of dissenting, derisive laughter, but I could not believe my ears. I am marked by the possibilities she presents that night.

In 1993 Hillary Clinton is waging a massive public relations campaign for feminism, promoting the "Year of the Woman" as part of it. The collaboration with Yoko has to happen in this moment. Robert Tracy arranges for me to collaborate with her, as they are friends through Nureyev. She decides that she can't write new music for me so we negotiate songs from her catalogue of greatness. She agrees to my selections and is startlingly generous, simply giving me her music.

I conceive of a work called *She Says* that plays with the image of Yoko, and uses what I think is a challenging and danceable arc through four recordings from her catalogue. *She Says* opens with a quiet, simple vocal, a phone message from her (ring... ring...ring.... Click..."Hello? This is Yoko"), then breaks into "Nobody Sees Me Like You Do," "Open Your Box" and ends in the amazing anthem "Woman Power." This work is definitely not for everyone. I give it full-on contrapuntal punch and high-kicking thrust. The movement is sophisticated, intentionally virtuosic and complex enough to keep my interest, but I want it to reek of visual pleasure to counteract the automatic Yoko-haters. It's still one of my favorites.

I finally meet Yoko face to face on opening night at the Joyce Theater after the show. She comes down the hall to my dressing room as I'm heading for the showers. Post-performance, still sweating, I wear nothing but a towel and a grin. Am I finally exposed enough? While she approaches me, my initial thought is: "She looks just like Yoko Ono."

She's incredibly soft-spoken and gracious. She tells me she enjoyed the dance and seeing my vision set to her music. It's performed on a program with *The King Is Dead* and she's intrigued by it and Cindy's set as well. When she says good-bye and turns to leave I remain motionless in my towel and watch her walk quietly down the hall. I couldn't have dreamed a better moment.

Much of the time, a life in dance can seem glamorous and alluring from the outside. Especially when the details are vague in the public's eye. Just what is the moment-to-moment of a life anyway? A string of things to do, habits, feelings, perceptions, necessities, consumptions, compulsions, gifts adding up to being, breathing and navigating through a day. The frame of distance is deceptively intriguing. Glamorous to you is a day at the mines to me.

Glamorous and mundane by turns. I chose so wisely when I chose a life in dance, a life that puts the pursuit of the unattainable, the intangible, at its center. So every day I wake up, and begin the ritual that takes me to a practice that is the pursuit of ether, of inspiration, of the invisible puzzles of our existence in physics.

I spend the day training for and building to physical moments that can reach inside a viewer and touch her/him with something felt or sensed. The pursuit of the unknown is an interesting trade. And I do happen to do this in the most comfortable clothes possible to facilitate speed and articulation, and I am barefoot and oh, yes, I am generally surrounded by some of the most talented, intelligent and sexy twenty-two-year-olds that one can hope for.

It's 1982 and Laurie Anderson is performing *O Superman* at the Ritz on 11th Street in Manhattan. She is on her way to No. 1 on the British charts and she is riding a massive wave up. She has caught the moment perfectly in her song; it sounds subconscious and filled with sharp, conspiratorial truth and the New York art world feels part of her journey. She's one of New York's own.

I'm with Justin Terzi standing in the middle of the floor. The room is packed and hot and the night has been long and winding to this moment. I'm in orbit on E and riveted on the stage. Laurie bounds out, so diminutive and strong in an all-black suit and signature spiky blonde hair, dimples deep and visible clear across the room. Her movements are deliberate and flat in the vertical plane, announcing her posture of power and strength. She is foreboding as she lifts her right arm and shapes a right angle, her bicep flexing slowly and she sings, "O superman. O Judge. O mom and dad...." She continues on in the most frighteningly seductive voice, sweeping us up in her ominous tale. The crowd is dead hushed and she stares out into the sea of blackness before her, her eyes like a hot laser hitting their mark. She makes visual contact with that blackness and she is staring straight at me, burning through me, as I'm sure every fan in the room feels. I'm pinned by that stare, learning a prime lesson in performing through it. Without warning the room fades to black. The weekend has caught up with me and I hit the floor with a thud. I'm out cold. Justin quickly yanks me up and carries me over to the side bar that's a bit cooler. He's irate that we had to leave the room but I catch my breath, rebound and finish the performance out in shaky bliss.

Shortly after, I meet Laurie when she collaborates with Trisha Brown on *Set and Reset*, which launches Trisha into a new stratosphere of respect and fame. I'm over the moon the entire working period and happy to get to know Laurie a little. When she conjures up the opening notes of my solo in this work we can see each other from where she is in the pit and I sense that she is playing for me.

Jump ahead twenty years to post-9/11 New York and I'm home with my company, our world rocked to pieces by the attacks on New York. Life as we know it is changed and we are all holding on. There's a generosity and humbleness in the usually dog eat dog New York air, people staying home with friends for quiet dinners, not sleeping through the night if they ever did, people holding doors for each other, offering each other their seats on the subway, going out of their way to be human again. The abruptness and suddenness of the shift catches all of us off guard and the city is new.

Touring collapses this year, so we are in New York without reprieve and nothing is certain for the dance world. People are hesitant to travel and Presenters to book companies. Everything seems suspended, a collective holding of breath.

My reaction is one of severe loyalty to the city that's the backstory to my creative birth and life. I suddenly begin creating furiously from the place where I began my career—a deep need to create, to mark my moment and the world around me. The creative impulse is primal, something like the urge to fuck after funerals, devastating fires and similar catastrophic events. Where there is death and destruction, human spirit seems to call forth a pro-creative response.

I become obsessed by the notion of small, fleeting glimpses of lives on the streets of New York, and I begin focusing on character studies, collections of traits that point to iconic beings with an archetypal New York bent. There is an angelic hobo, a forthright sailor, a threadbare burlesque dancer, an unhinged street guy, a raging woman and so forth. These characters are not meant to be part of a logical narrative line but more of an exposition of traits that hang in the space of the dance, interacting together.

I'm working for months without music and writing about these archetypes, using words as the creative motor. I listen to an enormous amount of music and composers and nothing seems just right. The whole time I am listening for pleasure to the new tracks that Laurie has just released in a collection called *Life on a String*. She captures vivid and quiet pictures of New York in these emotional songs and they rivet me. Listening to them frequently, I think about calling Laurie but resist for some reason, perhaps because *Set and Reset* was such a major work for my mentor Trisha Brown and I don't want to brush up against that history. Still the songs perfectly catch the mood I am in and am projecting on the city at large.

Finally one night when I am reviewing the day's rehearsal rushes on video, Jean-Marc sneakily puts on *Life on a String* and it works miraculously with the movement I'm building. I call Laurie the next day and we agree to work on it together. She very much likes the portrait idea and I cautiously hand over my written character sketches:

Photo: Sarah Silver. Stephen Petronio Company
City of Twist (2003). Dancers: Jimena Paz
w/Gino Grenek in background

Smoke (dancer Jimena Paz): Broken-down stripper is all smoldering rings of smoke curling through the space. In fact, her spatial pattern was built on curling smoke. Something 1940s about her, noir in stockings and heels and naïve in some way but unselfconscious and confident, neon sign flashing somewhere in the distance. The phone is ringing while she's off-stage dressing and she breezes in to answer, half put together. She misses the caller but she doesn't care.

Metal (Gino Grenek): Young, military precise and metallic cool, slightly tense. Very vertical, he's a stand-up kind of guy, forthright and clean. You can count on him.

Fire (Ashleigh Leite): Raggedy Ashleigh, the image here is a rag doll, angry and used, but not beaten. There is an aggressive jangle to her personality. Along with the discoveries based on this image, I'm trying to tread as close as I can to referencing the doll cliché without losing the battle to it. I keep thinking I want to get up close to the cliché as I can with Ashleigh but I need to feel her real defeat and rage in every molecule as she careens through space.

It's late summer and sweltering hot in the city and Laurie is here and not overly busy. She begins to come to rehearsal regularly, and sits wrapped up in the corner writing in a large notebook. I have no idea what she writes—perhaps she is paying her electric bill or working on something unrelated. But she is surprisingly there a good deal. About a month before the performance, I am getting itchy and ask Laurie for music so she invites me to her studio where she plays many short clips of sounds, shards of things really, asking me what I like or not. This goes on for an hour until L indicates it's time for me to go. As I go out into the afternoon heat, I think, "That was interesting," but have no idea what direction she will take. I am grateful, however, for the intimate moment together.

Photo: Christian Witkin. Stephen Petronio Company City of Twist (2003).
Dancer: Ashleigh Leite.

To my surprise Laurie calls the next day and asks me to come back and I do. And we continue to meet frequently in the coming weeks, working in her studio together on the evolution of the mix. She's recorded music during the process and has it and various sounds/instruments loaded into her mixer, but she works alone for the most part doing everything herself, from mixing to equipment repairs. She is composing to a rehearsal video of the dance as it stands at the moment and it's inspiring to watch her, a diminutive and agile form scrambling over mountains of massive electronic equipment that produces the sounds that eventually become the score for *City of Twist*.

Lou Reed. Velvet Underground. Andy Warhol. Edie Sedgwick. Nico. Pop Art, the epicenter of New York underground drug-fueled breakthrough rock and roll cool. "Venus in Furs," "Sweet Jane," "Walk on the Wild Side," "Metal Machine Music." These names are bold-face to me.

I was just finishing up an amazingly satisfying collaboration with Laurie. We made *City of Twist* together, a thirty-minute work riffing on iconic New York character studies and we are both quite pleased with how it's all going. As this work is half of a program I ask Laurie whom she might like to see her work next to in the upcoming collaboration I need to plan. She answers quickly: "Why don't you ask Lou? I think he might enjoy something like that." Subconsciously I am praying for that answer and I just as quickly ask her to put us together.

As open and easy Laurie is to speak to, Lou is the opposite. I know they are a couple but I've known Laurie for years and have never met Lou. He is legend and kind of frightening by reputation. Laurie sets a meeting in motion and after a series of third-party phone arrangements a call time is arranged.

I'm in the bedroom of my Windsor Terrace townhouse, our recent retreat from Avenue A after 9/11. I'm dressing for an event for some foundation in the Meatpacking District and running late. The phone rings exactly on time and when Lou asks for me by name I find it difficult to fathom that I'm on the line with him. After all these years and travels I still soften reflexively at the sound of his voice. He mentions that we can meet and he would like to speak further and gives me a number to call. I hang up still trying to fathom his interest in dance and head out the door.

I show up at the event and as I am walking in with Janet Stapleton, former manager and now longtime friend and publicist, Laurie and Lou are walking out. Kismet! We stop on the sidewalk for introductions and within sixty minutes of my call from Lou we're face to face. He's charming and handsomely weathered, very playful with me as we chat, then they take their leave.

After an interminable volley between my agent and his about meeting times and conditions (I must come alone, his address will be given to me right before the meeting, and so forth), I head to a designated neighborhood in the West Village. When I approach the neighborhood I call a number as instructed, the apartment number is released, and I am on the elevator up to meet him.

He opens the door without a smile and grumbles; "Hi, take your shoes off." (I like this and require the same of my guests, despite the protestations of the fashionistas in my life who live from shoe to shoe. Asking them to remove their footwear is akin to asking them to remove their leg.)

I walk in and Lou seems prickly, immediately announcing, "I know nothing about modern dance, don't really have an interest in it and I'm seeing you because Laurie suggested it."

"OK, that's clear, don't despair, at least you're in Lou Reed's kitchen," I think. The slate floor is pumping radiant heat and feels deluxe after the cold walk, so I soldier on.

I tell him about what Laurie and I did, and that she thought he might like to make the companion piece and that of course he would have absolute free rein to proceed in any way he might choose. I explain the range of ways I've worked with music (I follow you, you follow me, back and forth and so on) and that anything was possible. Lou tells me that he is hesitant to write something new but has an enormous catalogue of music and we move to the living room. We're both still stiff and formal with each other.

Then we sit cross-legged on the floor across from each other and begin to chat about his music. He mentions that he would love me to use *Metal Machine Music*, the legendary hour of piercing feedback like a typhoon of sound that makes the ears bleed. That if I chose it, I indeed would win his respect. He proceeds to pull out other music from his long and triumphant reign as a rock innovator: disc, reel to reel and vinyl from vastly different periods. When he gets his hands on the materials he transforms visibly. Suddenly he is a laughing, soaring, animated artist filled with excitement and passion for the project. He turns to some things he is currently working on based on Edgar Allan Poe. The Poe tracks are stunning and unpublished and the privilege of our meeting reasserts itself. (They will later become the compilation *The Raven*.) Mutual friends are on several tracks, **Kate Valk** and **Willem Dafoe**, at that point still working together in The Wooster Group. It is too good to pass up but how could I choose one thing? I want it all. As we dig deeper Lou becomes more engaged, beginning to offer movement and costuming ideas for particular tracks, what he might like to see in movement or its theatrical location. His artistry is infectious and I couldn't be happier when he sends me home with lots of raw material to mull over and permission to do what I please with it. His generosity and its contrast with the first minutes of our meeting bowls me over.

I listen to it all constantly and with great excitement for a few weeks and lay out plans for a dance called *The Island of Misfit Toys* set to twelve tracks that Lou gave me spanning his entire career. I see him regularly at Sunday brunches at Time Café on Lafayette St, where we both seem to be regulars during that period, and we discuss direction and progress. Cindy Sherman joins the collaborative team shortly after Lou, along with **Tara Subkoff (Imitation of Christ)**. I continue to update him right up to the premiere. He is always encouraging, always interested and basically leaves me to my own devices. Ours is another kind of perfect collaboration, in some ways the antithesis of my experience with Laurie. When I arrive in London where the work is to premiere, Lou can't be there but a bottle of Dom appears at my dressing room before the show with a note: "Best wishes from Lou."

At the New York premiere of *Island*, it hits me that one of Lou's songs in the show, "I'm a Little Balloon," is sung by the formidable Canadian singer-songwriter **Kate McGarrigle**, mother to singer-songwriter/gay icon **Rufus Wainwright**. What have I been thinking? I call Rufus that afternoon, introduce myself and mention that there's a song of Lou's sung by Kate in the show and that I would love to have him come by. And he does. At the after-party I ask him if he would consider writing for dance and he says sure, and that's the way it starts.

In numerous phone calls and a few rendezvous during various one-night-stand tour stops around the world in our zigzagging schedules, we eventually devise a plan. Rufus's star is really rising at the time we meet and it makes everything more complex. I'm afraid to tell him that I'm hoping for a choral work as I'm determined to bring my new love, The Young People's Chorus of New York (YPC), into this mix. When I finally tell Rufus that this is where I want to go it becomes the very reason that he commits to the project in the end. He was a chorister himself in his youth and loves the idea. We both fix on the poetry of Emily Dickinson as a point of interest. Eventually I add Walt Whitman into the mix and Rufus begins work on an almost exclusively vocal score using the text of "Unseen Buds" and "Of Thee I Sing", by Whitman followed by the pièce de résistance by the Belle of Amherst: "Hope is the thing with feathers." It's devised as a forty-part recorded vocal for Rufus with live choir and is sung in New York by YPC and all over the country and Europe by local choirs taught for our performance. Rufus is amazing to watch with the choir, demanding and charming as he builds his score. Later, touring life takes a new and unexpected turn, as I become rehearsal director/mentor to young singers in each city, all of whom are excited by the music and the unusual situation of participating in a dance performance. In fact, this experience is many of the singers' introduction to modern dance. My experience of life on the road grows into something more connected to my host city and the artists who live there. Seems like a step.

Jean-Marc and Karen have already introduced me to Tara Subkoff: starlet, actress, designer and maker of things that catch the sense of the moment with uncanny accuracy. She is the consummate IT girl, fabulously beautiful and her eye for trends is spot on. Her line of clothes is a "social experiment" called Imitation of Christ founded with Matthew Danhave. Really it is an art project, a critique of the industry that the fashion world in New York goes wild for. Almost all their clothes are found or thrift-shopped, then reconfigured or framed in some way, brought back to life illuminating a different aspect of their already impressive nature. And Tara loves dance with fierce passion and understands it intuitively

The first time she comes to see a show of ours, she rushes back to say that the work touches her immediately and deeply, that she needs to work with me. She has an idea that she believes will help people embrace my essentially abstract, expressive world more eagerly. It's a simple idea, and so obvious that it's almost funny. "Let me dress the dancers as people," she offers.

And I did and that was the first of six collaborations that were some of the most lively and successful works in the company's history: *Prelude*, dressed in black rags; *City of Twist*, straitjacket white shirts and tighty-whiteys for men, black burlesque/cocktail dresses for women; *Broken Man*, deconstructed men's suit; *Bud*, a duet in a divided men's jacked strapped onto each dancer; *The Island of Misfit Toys*, in cartoon graphic pj's; *UNDERLAND*, in a range of looks suitable for an existential Goth trip from darkness to light, which had just under eighty costumes for twenty dancers over the course of a full evening. And the more specifically I dug into the notion of character, the more specific Tara got. She effortlessly made bold choices that I might have shied away from, like using simple Army fatigues to transform the dancers in *The Weeping Song* into soldiers crying for the sins of man; or the performers in *Carney* into broken-down ballerinas and carnival freaks; or in *The Ship Song*, invoking castaways from different periods of time shipwrecked together on the little island of their dance. Or making the men in *City of Twist* escaped inmates of an institution by removing their pants and turning their white shirts backward. Simple, yet loony in a French cinema kind of way. Perfect.

Photo: Sarah Silver. Stephen Petronio Company, Bud (2005).
Dancers: Michael Badger and Gino Grenek.

Photo: Sarah Silver for Stephen Petronio Company. Shoot for *City of Twist* (2003) Performers: Michael Badger, Todd Williams, Ashleigh Leite, Jimena Paz Stephen Petronio, Anna Gonzalas, Kristina Isabelle, Gino Grenek and Gabby Malone.

I've learned to melt into the slumped musical ledges, the most difficult landmarks and rhythmic shifts. My mergers are intuitive. I don't read music or rarely count its structure. I can live around or on the beat, on the slimmest musical ledge.

This can frustrate some of my collaborators from the more traditionally or classically trained worlds, like **Michael Nyman** or **Nico Muhly**, whose constructs are counted elaborately, on massive grids. But I can dance a twenty-minute passage with my stealth dancers within a count or two of the music's life. Once, in Portugal, the speakers cut out mid-dance and we kept going, unsure of what would happen. We always have a second CD running simultaneously for just such occasions and it took about three full minutes to identify the glitch and switch over, but when the backup track kicked in, there we were, exactly where we should be. I wasn't surprised.

Before I know him, I obsess on Nico Muhly for weeks, listening to his music and thinking, "I HAVE to call him." I walk into my gym locker room one morning and there he is, in all his nakedness. Without skipping a beat, I move into his orbit and introduce myself, still fully clothed. Dancers are essays in ease with their bodies and nudity, stripping in front of each other to change into practice clothes, in a multitude of situations. Undressing is akin to a violist taking his instrument out of its case. But musicians are different animals. They have an uncomfortable thing with their bodies, perhaps because they spend so much time orchestrating the minutiae, small motor actions, brain to fingers...I just know they hold body weirdness. I have the advantage here and I press my advantage. I like Nico exposed on our first meeting—it leaves an impression. Plus, he's cute in a mad genius kind of way. We exchange numbers and plan to meet later in that week to begin our collaboration.

Nico is a generation younger than me but number age is the grand illusion, and I fancy I'm a much younger vessel than my numerical equivalent. I always feel younger than everyone, maybe because of my position in my family, maybe because I'm the eternal youth, Aries, the baby of the cosmos, but I just do. This posture is a weapon when approaching a new problem and a hindrance when I just won't grow up.

Here it is between Nico and me. A generation. The power of his music is all I feel. I don't question if it's driven by age or...I just know I have to meet it. Still, generations need each other, the dialogue essential to balancing the respective territories that come with youth and age. For me the power that comes from the generations behind me is pure fuel to fly on, and Nico brings it in in spades.

I've chosen extreme weather as the jumping off place for *I Drink the Air Before Me*, the hourlong work we will eventually make (the title comes from Ariel in Shakespeare's *The Tempest* and is a reference to speed of action), so I've been scouring the available literature, researching weather graphs and graphics, fire and ice storms. I'm obsessed with the recent greenhouse debates that are still absurdly taking place in America's political spheres. And there's those giant Weather Channel hurricane spirals every August that track the bird's eye view of the impending storms of the century, of Katrina (and soon to come Irene and Sandy). Nico jumps on the idea of storm as score and at an early meeting over coffee pulls out a pad and draws a graph curve from the lower left edge of a sheet of paper to the upper right hand corner and hands it over. "That's our dramatic arc," he pronounces. A year later we arrive at a tumultuous brooding composition played by an amazing group of New York musicians that I've placed floating above the dance at the rear of the stage like a menacing cloud.

Photo: Sarah Silver for Stephen Petronio Company *I Drink the Air Before Me* (2009). Dancer: Gino Grenek

And Nico Muhly didn't skip a beat when I asked him for a suggestion for someone who could work on something related to Romeo and Juliet and the classical music of Prokofiev, but modern. "Call my home girl Ryan," he responded. **Ryan Lott** aka **Son Lux** is the perfect storm of classical training and electronic rock sensibility. He sings like a sad angel and between 2008 and 2012 we make four works: *Tragic Love* (Ballet De Lorraine in Nancy, France); *By Singing Light* (National Dance Company of Wales, UK); *The Social Band* (Other Shore, NYC) and *Like Lazarus Did* (SPC/NYC). Each of these projects is such a different assignment, from the Prokofiev-laced look at modern love as seen through a compilation of letters by star-crossed partners (an idea that originated from *Letters to Juliet*, a book by **Lise Friedman** and **Ceil Friedman**), to setting the riveting poetry of **Dylan Thomas** for the National Dance Company of Wales, to the use of a book of American slave spiritual songs for *Like Lazarus Did (LLD)* and *The Social Band*. Ryan is fearless and inventive in any context I toss him into, especially when anchored to a historical reference. Plus he's hysterically goofy. And bite-size cute.

There are so many other collaborations along the way: the visual design by landscape master and longtime friend Stephen Hannock (*Not Garden*), Anish Kapoor (*Strange Attractors*), composers Michael Nymam (*Strange Attractors*) and the incredible Diamanda Galas (*Not Garden*), James LaValle/UNKLE (*Strange Attractors*), Atticus Ross (*Water Stories* for the National Nance Company Wales) fashion designers Yonson Pak, Manolo (with whom I made a significant body of early and adventurous work), Tanya Sarne (*Strange Attractors*) and Jillian Lewis (*Ghostown*), and collaborators who have created with me over the longer haul making formative contributions to a larger body of the company's work. Composer David Linton (*Surrender, Surrender II, Walk-In, Simulacrum Reels, Simulacrum Court, Close Your Eyes and Think of England, Lareigne, Cherry, House of Magnet* and others) and visual/lighting designer and confidant Ken Tabachnick, with whom I've collaborated on every work I've ever made save one or two. And others who are onstage and behind the scenes in technical capacities that are no less artistic or significant:

Stan Pressner, Collette Barni, James Latzel, Tal Yarden, Christopher Plant, Burke Wilmore, Lynda Erbs and a host of other talent who make the work live. The managers (Janet Stapleton, Trisha Pierson, June Poster, Craig Hensala) and press agents and photographers who propel it into another form in print: Annie Leibovitz, Sarah Silvers, Tom Brazil, Paula Court, Beatriz Schiller, Johan Elbers, Ken Probst....

But in the beginning there are the dancers. The heroically rigorous souls who sweat, toil, laugh, stretch, think and venture with me hour by hour and day by day over months and years through the march toward fulfillment in their lives. The legion of dancers who bring years of training and effort with them, artists who have offered their whole beings to help carve out a language that has come to be known as Petronio. Artists who have honored me with their trust, personal histories and perceptions in the generous desire to contribute to something bigger in the world than themselves, ourselves and our small needs or selfish desires. These are the dancers, artists, athletes and heroes of the highest order, the first collaborators on whom I've written my works, my style, my world. They are where it all begins. Over thirty years—I can't name them all and there's a brave new crop germinating now—but I must mention the significant talents who remain visible to this day, resurrected daily through the mark they've made in movement: **Kristen Borg** (the Blond Tornado, my first assistant for the fifteen years), **Jeremy Nelson**, **Gerald Casel**, **Rebecca Hilton**, **Mia Lawrence**, **Ori Flomin**, **Ashleigh Leite**, **Todd Williams**, **Jimena Paz**, **Michael Badger**, **Shila Tirabassi** and my current assistant, the incomparable **Gino Grenek**.

SPC on tour in1999. The beach at Mauna Kea Resort, The Big Island, Hawaii. L to R with Kristen Borg, Steven Fetherhuff, Todd Williams, Ashleigh Leite, Ori Flomin and Ana Gonzalez.

The Marquee at the Joyce Theater, New York City, where SPC has had almost twenty performance seasons to date.

Photo: Sarah Silver. Stephen Petronio Company. Dancer: Davalois Fearon (2010).

Ghostown

Oh, every day gestures that mark my life

Unnoticed action, discarded thought,

Unconscious gesture with my speech, ticked off automatically as in my sleep,

And phantom limbs gone but deeply felt

The twist of a neck, unconscious swipe, half-hearted reach

A touch without attention, an uneven gait,

the press of my torso against yours.

And come again mother, brother

you so deep within me,

fingers V'd as we share a cigarette out on the porch in the cold

bonded in smoke and ash, head nods in question, disbelief and boredom...

Lust, shape me and move me into something, somehow new.

Hello continuum of actions that are my body's motor—

to which a second thought is rarely paid.

You are the kingdom of my daily way,

the gesture, posture and path of me,

the ghosts left behind and brought back to life,

the memories and future moments that take me over again

and define the quietly, constantly ticking litany of action that amounts to me and women and men at the end of the day.

Nuts And Bolts Of Magic

What it feels like to perform, to be on the wild intuitive moment of abandon: Letting go into a score of movement that is so deep in your muscles it needs no conscious thought but is like some invisible guide moving you through the dance and moving through your body which has surrendered to it. It's like being completely lost to yourself but sensing exactly where you are in space and where you must go.

Sometimes inspired
Sometime mundane
Two versions of the same dance on different nights:
1) My arm is moving like no other in history, no other has moved quite like this ever before. I am invisibly carrying forward some unknown mythical narrative, some cosmic whole that gives a deepest sense of meaning to this stroke of my arm. This movement and audience are joined together and we can hear each other at last.

2) I am moving my arm, how humiliating that all can see my mechanical artifice, arbitrary choice unconnected to an organic sense of whole. "No, not that old trick again, how transparent, how mundane, what does any of this mean?" This self-serving masturbatory movement is cut off from the world and embarrassingly trite.

Sometimes inspired
Sometime mundane

Sometimes I think my dances are like passing ships that require I board them with just the right equipment and luggage at just the right moment. Some works sail before I get it right and sometimes it's all there.

Typical me: Sleep has never been my strong suit so I wake up around 4:00 every morning and write or read, think about my current dance or waste time on the Internet, have a bowl of cereal and either fall back to sleep for an hour or continue on to the sunrise. I feed the animals (four sphinx cats) and the fish, make strong coffee, answer e-mails, clean litter boxes, shower, shave, dress and head into Manhattan for the day. I speak to June, my manager, about the specifics of the day outside of rehearsal (the tours or planned projects, contracts, grants or private funding we are in constant dialogue about), hit the gym around 9:30, where I do weight training and cardio work till 11:30, then shower again and head for a quick bite (salad with protein), then off to rehearsal.

Rehearse 12:00–4:00, Monday through Thursday, because these 4 hours four days per week oases are all the time my company can support. I love to brag that we do in sixteen hours what other companies do in forty, but that's an incomplete truth. We're pressured, overworked and have little time to waste. It is an unforgivingly small period to build worlds in. Then again, I've seen miracles take place in the shortest period of time, a magic five minutes, the result of meandering research that comes to a head in an instant that is "the breakthrough moment". These moments drop out from the continuum of time and stretch in all directions, into a three-dimensional five minutes that's spherical and vast, filled with information. But this is the result of treating your art like a practice.

You go in to train, forms you know by rote, a routine to offer the body, a sound and dependable architectural and energetic home base that can be counted on. These are exercises focused on grounding the body, releasing external muscular tension that inhibits the action of the joints, which activate its full power and open it to the fluid and conscious direction of energy any way I might choose. All my body parts are stacked up in an efficient relationship to the basic laws and the properties of physics: Feet are directly under my hip sockets, my hips on top of my legs, my torso released gently forward and up into space, my spine long and activated both out my tail and up through my atlas (first vertebrae), my neck with an easy S-curve and my head in a "curious" active state, moving forward and up into the space above it.

When this process heats up and moves toward the creative moment, routine falls away and there is liftoff, the you that was just the ordinary you training your way through a through a well-known, physically chattering being—it all falls away and transformation occurs. You shift into that space that is vaguely familiar but totally unknown, improvising with an intuitive and intelligent mind, a mind of the body that takes over and moves you forward. All the familiar boring preparation, the tedious repetition of physical forms you've been tracing for twenty years becomes "a possibility of revelation," of a moment that seems new and right, a moment that has been waiting patiently all this time for you to arrive.

Everything is ordinary. My body's clunking around the room, an awkward and unlikely instrument. Where is the pain today? What's tight and immobile or vaguely throbbing? When I walk in, there's an undercurrent of stiff, solid, blocky. Not warm. The clock ticks, the room is cold, a collection of external facts, the floor hard and uninviting. There's chatter in my mind, an incessant litany of wants, sensations, desires, who I want to call or what I need or don't have or who I want to see today. I'm hungry or fed, chilly or hot, worried or cheerful, expectant or needy about some prospect "out there." It all feels familiar: me entangled with external details.

I settle down to standing on one place on the floor and breathe awhile—in/deep and out/slow. I round over from the top of my head, vertebra by vertebra, till I'm folded in half at the waist, creased at the hips, deep and soft feet, connected to the floor through their soles, while my head hangs heavily to the floor as well. I focus in and begin to scan down my body, checking inward, to the details of all my parts: head/neck/shoulders/arms/ spine/ass/legs/feet, feel where it all is today. Then I start to watch my breath.

Deep breath in, slowly down to the bowl of my pelvis, widening into the space between my pubic bone and my tailbone (coccyx), widening the left and right halves of my pelvis away from each other. Then breathe out, softening all these parts gently back toward each other. Then again, sending breath down to push against my perineum, ballooning out, then relaxing it all on the exhale. The minute I start to notice this thing that I do continually/involuntarily, second by second, minute, hour, day, the most basic thing, breathing in and out, my world begins to shift.

Breath becomes deeper and slower, and as I watch the expansion and release of my body, the leaden lumbering sack that seems like a limit just a short while before, like a carton holding the inanimate contents that is "me," it all softens and begins to loosen up.

Breath deepens, something stirs through my body and I begin the practice of directing energy in a more conscious way: legs bending and stretching (*demi-plié*), energy vectoring out the far (distal) end of my thighbone (femur) and into space. The bend deepens further and energy connects down my femur to the heel, into the floor, as my leg lengthens back to straight again.

This *demi-plié* activity is a slow, conscious motor awakening of mobility, the cycling of energy in my legs, expanding the range in my joints, the possibility of articulation at the knee, hip and ankle, and connecting me to the floor so that I can power down into it for the elevation and locomotion that I know will come with warmth.

And in this way it starts; the body that walked into the room earlier, a slightly awkward bundle of discordant facts, transforming into the fluid thing that I have come to know in motion, the vessel that will set me loose in space.

Photo: Sarah Silver for Stephen Petronio Company, *Beauty and the Brut* (2008). Dancers: Julian De Leon and Elena Demyanenko.

Chasing a movement down in the studio, I step out with my right foot and my knee buckles, sending a ripple sequence through my spine from the tailbone up to my head. My head starts to catch up and I sense its inevitable whip forward. Reflexively I subvert this path, interrupting its natural conclusion. Instead, I arc the top of my head around in a half circle toward

221

my right ear and finally down to my right knee. If this process sounds clinical, that's because it is. Reading this description takes twenty-five seconds; performing it takes 1.5 seconds.

I repeat this movement over and over, familiarizing myself with as much of its detail as I can. I identify the initiating impulse and initiating body part, order of events, pathway in space, amount of force and rhythmic relationship of parts to each other, emotional tone and overall whole body rhythm. This movement state is an unknown place and I determine to memorize the flavor of the newness down to the subtlest level I can. There's the gross pathway, and then there's the way your foot twists and your finger is held. There is an excitement and adrenal rush to the chase, the thrill of pursuit and discovery, of tracking something invisible. I coax it out and allow it to become knowable. I look at the variations on this movement, and become familiar with all of them and file the variations in my memory. Eventually I select the one that I will employ in the context of the "phrase" I am building.

These pathways evolve and accumulate, become fully themselves, real, energetic sculptures or pathways in space, with character and timbre and form. They are real but temporal and visible only when executed. I see them as they unfold, but they vanish as their action is complete.

The room fills up with these movement parcels as a work builds. The room gets crazily crowded with information. These movements are as real as any notes, drawings or architectural elements. They are like animals or friends, and while the act of finding, building and practicing them is a slippery process, a chasing after phantoms that might escape, there is a certain pleasure in knowing they are there if you call them forth properly and remain calm in the process.

While a hallmark of my work is its emotional intensity, the process of capturing that intensity is a methodical one. Why do I work like this? I was trained to detach my emotions from the material until it was finished. This way, you can do the most incredible or horrendous things without judgment, without being damaged by them.

Often the specificity of a movement's character is elusive in the days that follow, and what's left is a kind of postcard from the actual moment, a percentage of the original study. If the postcard holds enough of the discovery's unique flavor, it becomes a permanent part of the collection.

There have been naturally occurring "periods" in my work, defined by or related by formal or aesthetic concerns.

- Sex: The first clear period to emerge after my language was more or less on its feet was the sexual period, a conscious delving into the sensual and erotic realm that informed so much of the early work: *MiddleSexGorge*, *Close Your Eyes and Think of England*, *Surrender II* (the male duet form is a subclass in itself), *Full Half Wrong* and *Laytext*. During this period form is still a given but sex is the motor. I think of myself as a formalist with a dirty mind.

- Form: Then on to more pure form with works like *Lareigne*, *Drawn That Way* (a play on the over-sexualized cartoon character Jessica Rabbit: "I'm not bad, I'm just drawn that way"). In these works I dropped my pursuit of movement and subtext per se (with invention at the center of this interest, where the unpredictable path was followed at all costs and form was subservient to that path). I begin to choose simple steps like the "triplet" (Thank you Martha Graham, one step on a bent leg, followed by two on straight legs), steps that are locomotive, steps that can travel in space anywhere I want them to. In this way the work's invention turned to spatial and formal investigation as opposed to movement inventions.

- Contraptions: a group of works that I think of as not dances in the "Petronio speed and fierce attack in space" kind of way, but clumps of bodies, often joined together in contact, moving in "human gesture mode." Bodies moving as ordinary gesticulating people who move according to some set of simple directions or rules. Contraptions often occur in place, in lines or groups that interact but don't travel in space.

- Disintegrations: formal concerns for sure but recently I've been much more interested in more illusive forms, forms that hide, disappear and fall apart before the eye, as opposed to patterns that build and accumulate to construct an obvious choreographic power, the fireworks that give obvious and recognizable form to the stage space, the weaving and building of a feeling through bodies in space that the audience recognize quickly, allowing them to relax and take in the building up of an idea.

All Right Already

The poking, stabbing, prodding need to connect on some deeply spiritual level is prominent. I've understood the sexual act as one to help transcend the body and reach into the humanity and soul of a partner. My body is the only tool I understand to precipitate in that esoteric journey.

Then JM and Karen introduce me to Kabbalah in the mid-'90s. They've been having private lessons for a year or so by the time I meet them, but JM is ambivalent for various reasons, not the least of which is one of the psychic Kabbalists passing through New York gave him a reading telling him that he was gay because he had a female soul and needed to straighten out to correct his *tikkun* (his task to promote greatest harmony, to fix what needs to be fixed to satisfy one's purpose).

He wants to get my take on it all so he invites me to a Zohar class at the showroom (the Zohar is the spiritual interpretation of the Torah). He dangles the incentive that people like **Madonna, Sandra Bernhard or Roseanne Barr** may show up at these small insider classes held weekly in the middle of Showroom Seven, where high-end clothing and accessories are displayed. I'm amused and drawn by the idea that this spiritual study is embedded in the context of the world of fashion. The mix seems tailored to me.

So we're sitting in a circle in a class of fab people of all types, from A, B and C-list actors, to yoga gurus and financial magicians alongside small-scale manufacturing magnates. We're discussing the "desire for

225

oneself alone" the selfish desire that drives most of our small-mind actions, when the teacher, **Abe Hardoon**, pulls out the Zohar and starts to scan. We make visual contact with the Hebrew text (most of us don't read Hebrew) and the theory is that these texts are combinations of letters wrapped in energy that's released when they hit your eyeballs, only nothing is explained—we're just instructed to run our eyes over the text from right to left.

I know next to nothing about Kabbalah and am just rolling with it. After a few minutes of scanning my eyes start to feel something physical, to pull and vibrate, and I can only describe the feeling as a high-frequency buzz. I have no clue what I'm reading, don't even know if these assemblages of letters are even words (many of them are not, rather they're combinations of letters, anagrams with a specific numerical value) but I'm getting high as a kite. The experience is physical, undeniable. I turn to JM at some point and say, "Do you feel that?"

He responds, "What are you talking about? Feel what?"

At the end of the night he says, "I'm done, this does nothing for me."

I, on the other hand, am hooked by what my body is telling me, that there is some deep, mysterious energetic thing here for me. Once again my body seems to be leading me in advance of my rational mind to a place that feels new and right and I've learned by now that if I don't listen, I lose. JM's last class is my first, and it's the beginning of a seventeen-year investigation into Kabbalah.

I danced with her once in the basement of Danceteria in the days when she was just coming on. A zaftig wild child working a fishnet-layered street-urchin look, with a multitude of bangles on her wrists. She skipped across the floor like a stone across water, then stopped to work her legs in and out from the hip and rotating out in space. After a song or two, enough to trade some moves, she was gone. She left behind the ultra-blond, handsome Martin, her manager/friend whom I danced with for a long, sexy time, our arms behind our backs and pelvises slung close.

Between then and now she becomes the most famous woman in pop and at this moment she's sitting feet away from me at the Kabbalah Center in the East 40s and I'm trying to meditate on "the light," but it's Madonna. I know that down beneath the illusion of fame and desire there's a beautiful and sweet soul, one like anyone might possess, a woman just focusing on something bigger than herself, like someone making an attempt to contribute something...but I can't erase my*self*, my *chatter* or wade through all the layers to find out who is really in her diminutive and well-documented body. I watch her luminous presence push me back and I can't let go of *that* me. I want to think about dissolving my identity for a while in meditation, but I'm confronted with fame and all it drags along with it.

Or maybe it's the way her new husband **Guy** is parading around in front of the *bema* (stage for the Torah and services to be orchestrated from), owning the moment like he's a filmmaker married to an icon. And he's doting over and marshaling our Madge. On this particular Shabbat I don't want to watch this movie and don't like my uncontrollable role in it, so I disappear for a few months until I know she's back on the road. Or maybe it's all just another excuse to avoid the tough work.

The center is a place where you can pray and have lunch next to a rich stratum of curious souls, and that happens to include people like **Lucy Lui**, **Marla Maples**, **Monica Lewinsky** or **Demi Moore**. You can wrap your arms around **Ashton K** in prayer. It's the kind of place that the famous, rich and rising, or slipping, sliding, then just plain normal go to find a path to letting go of the selfish self that's driven them to be who they are. Sometimes it's just fun to watch on that level and learn from the mechanics of everyone else's process of letting go. To know that whatever illusion of rich, famous, beloved and admired one is, we all have the same work to do on the path to expanding our definition of reality beyond our own small reactions and desires.

And, yes, I'm deeply suspicious of organizations that marshal my behavior, that present the constant need to do more at, with and for the Center. And there is my lingering suspicion of any pitch for cash, which, to my surprise, never really comes into play the first year or two I'm practicing. But when a rabbi eventually calls me in to request a sizable sum in support of the Center's activities, my shock is replaced by the realization that he is doing for *his* organization precisely what I do for my own nonprofit dance company on a daily basis. Fundraising. And I realize he's also giving me an opportunity for kindness.

What *does* keep me returning to the Center, beyond all my quibbles, is the pure physical energy I feel whenever **the Rav** walks into the room. It's just that simple. When **Rabbi Philip Berg** and his wife, **Karen,** are around, everything else falls away.

We're in Queens seventeen years ago, at his brick house on the unassuming but definitely suburban tree-lined street that I drive to with Karen, **Eric** and **Mandie Erickson** (Karen and Eric's PR powerhouse daughter), Sandra Bernhard and **Lizzie Margin** (makeup artist). It's an exciting early Saturday morning trip that I'm surprised and somewhat amused to be on. A year before I just might be driving home from a dealer in Queens at this hour after a long night out. Go figure.

Part of me never wants to go: "What is this insane cult of hyper Hebrew hysteria that I'm in?" The other Stephen can't stay away because I'm feeling so incredible. Today my resistance is physical—my knees are aching with a recent injury. I do my best to wiggle out of coming, but here I sit. In walks this guy unannounced and everyone springs to attention. In a big way.

Rabbi Berg, modest and bearded, rises and starts to speak. Honestly, I can't remember one word he says, but somewhere in his speaking, I'm transported to this indefinable zone of bliss where I understand and empathize with him completely, with no rational clue as to why. And out of pain. The nagging, constant ache of ligament/cartilage strain that I know all too well from a long history of problems with both knees over the course of my career, a pain that trips off an existential dread that beelines directly to the sinking gut feeling that I CAN'T MOVE—it quietly dissipates when I'm not looking.

And I have these kind of physical experiences throughout my study: the vibrating in the scanning eyes at my first class or the time I'm sitting with my first teacher, **Yehuda Avnet**, in my apartment on Avenue A. We're chatting about the power of various anagrams with a Zohar open face-down on my lap when my legs begin to tingle in an intensely electric way ("How could he make that happen? There must be a trick..." but there is none). When I mention this he tells me simply, "Close the Zohar, you've had enough for today." Undeniable, actual real-world cues prompt me back over and over again to the practice of Kabbalah, no matter how much I might bridle at the culture and organization of the vehicle that brings me this tool.

Fallen Catholic, Buddhist, psychic mediums, Kabbalah: I've transited through some of the prominent spiritual vehicles around, wrestling with the ephemera I know in my DNA plays out in the real world. *What do I know?* This: My body doesn't lie. I choose dance. So base, so of the body, the *malchut*—but it's the physical vehicle that's so quick to set me soaring out of this world.

It's somewhere near the end of April 2008. I'm invited to the Guggenheim Awards cocktail party as a past recipient (1986). The John Simon Guggenheim Fellowship is an extremely competitive award that's given in support of projects in the humanities, arts and science. It is a high honor of recognition in one's chosen field and comes with a nice chunk of cash (currently about $35,000). My invitation is also a cold reminder that I am turning into a Grand Poobah, an elder statesman of the New York dance community. I don't know if I feel like celebrating this distinction, but a perk of this year's award is that my good friend and dancing colleague, choreographer Vicky Shick is receiving one. I always love seeing her, so I accept.

The event is held in the foundation's offices in Manhattan. At the door I am handed a nametag with the year of my award (STEPHEN PETRONIO 1986), and I flash a smile while reality kisses my illusion of youth good-bye. I make my way in. The crowd is a who's who of the NY art elite and since everybody there is in the club, spirits are high and liquid spirits are flowing fast and free. As is my custom, I am juiced within the first half hour, working the room like a house dealer and enjoying myself thoroughly. I have substantial history with many of these people, and the new ones are fresh meat to explore. Vicky and I are together for a long while, catching up and carousing in tandem. We flirt and joke with everyone, particularly with the younger straight dancers who must view me as some combination of success personified, Daddy and some ass to knock off his horse. Or God forbid, "Who are you?" I enjoy it all, have a long and overdue heart-to-heart with one of New York's best living dance critics, Deborah Jowitt. It's a great event so I continue to get plowed till the end then head off for a bite to eat and some more to drink.

Jean-Marc and I have moved out of Manhattan and up to Putnam County (north of Westchester) at this point so I hop on a late train up the Harlem Line from Grand Central and get out about an hour later, just in time to stop in at Croton Creek, a local restaurant at the train station. The owners are friends and patrons of my company, and we drink the place way past closing. By this point I have no idea just how drunk I am but around 1:30 a.m. I stagger into my 1976 300d and speed off into the night.

I need to tell you that my vintage Mercedes 300D is all-original m-i-n-t and has about 63,000 miles on it. Named Clarence for the town I found him in near Niagara Falls, this car is cherry. And even though he's the low-end diesel workhorse of the luxury models, I treat him with kid gloves. He's never been out in snow and has more regular maintenance checkups than I do. I can open him up on a clear road to ninety mph without a shimmy and it's been true love since the first time I laid eyes on him. I always feel stylish and powerful in Clarence. And safe. He's bulletproof-strong with six-inch bumpers that jut out like spears, and has a wide, low stance that takes curves in stride. He is my covert accomplice in speed. It is our late-night country road secret.

I'm plastered and roaring through the cool spring night, gulping it in, greedy and rushing on the power of the speed, not a soul on the dark country roads that wind through Putnam County. I hit a hairpin bend on Drewville Road and it happens just like that: The world spins one way and Clarence and I disagree in a blur. Tires screeching a blood-curdling full 360-degree spin on an improbably narrow stretch of road, we jolt to a stop. The quiet screams as loudly as my tires did. Clarence's beloved handsome nose is inches from a rock cliff that offers a stoic and definitive conclusion to any story. Miraculously unscathed, my heart pounds out a first thought: "Clarence is all right." I thank my angels. I sit there motionless for a spell, measuring the contrast between the speed of the "event" and the stillness of the afterburn. I blink back to earth, buck it up and roar on home. When I get there it occurs to me that my main concern was Clarence. I make a note to look into a reassessment of my self-worth and I slip into a clammy sleep.

My eyes pop open at 6 a.m. with a start, the familiar loudspeaker in my head blaring: "Stephen, up, Stephen, UP!" My ears ring as loudly as the ocean in a shell. I rev from zero to sixty instantly, still clammy but straining to start off the line. I don't understand waking slowly. I spring awake. Here is the head-pounding hangover that's so regularly present in the a.m. for so much of my adult life. This state is as familiar as a longtime lover in my bed and just how I've come to know morning.

I zip to the bathroom and a surprise guest appears: Green bile vomit lurches forth in a stomach-spasming flash and is gone just as quickly. "Unusual," I think, but not unheard of lately. "The spasms are good for the tone of my abs" floats through the haze that is my mind. I pride myself in my bottomless capacity for alcohol. Come to think of it, I pride myself in my huge capacity for everything. After all these years I still have to match the amount of food in my plate to my father's, eat the most, I have to be the best fuck, the longest, get as high as I can, take it right up till I'm dangling at the edge of no return, toes hanging off and looking out into a boundless frightening, exhilarating void to feel satisfied. For a while. This is me—my role. I can do this. I can do this for you. I can do this so you don't have to. I need to do this to feel my worth, to feel anything remotely vivid. It's what makes *me*.

By the time I hit the gym at 10 a.m. I am back to full functional normal. And this has always been the case. I can party all night and on weekends for days, then pop up early for the gym to work it out, sweat it out, or puke it out, then hit rehearsal as fresh as a bud in spring. But lately, fifty brings a dark cloud with it, hanging over the number like a tropical front waiting to break out into a hellish storm. "Always young," "late bloomer," "looks ten years younger." Fifty has brought some undeniable realities that are hard to choke down with my *four* daily Tylenol upon waking. The pain lingers longer, the eyes not so bright, skin starting to puff a bit, and is that a green tint beneath my vivacious glow? And now the hurls in the a.m.

I have been photographed constantly my entire adult life. It's just part of my working life. I've grown up in public. This year of the 5-0, I call a moratorium on all photos. I don't want this moment documented. I don't want to see it. I want it lost to history as if it is not happening. After so many years of compliance, I feel I've earned the right to a total blackout on my face and body.

Later that week I get ossified again and in the morning vomit out the window of the Range Rover on the way to the train station. High school is a long way off but here I am. A man vomiting out the car window like a kid on his way home from Six Flags. Jean-Marc looks at me but he is so quiet and never judgmental, out loud anyway. We drive on to the train as if nothing happened and the day begins.

Mid-May arrives and JM's birthday is looming. I'll be on tour in Manchester, England, on his day so Karen (Erickson) and I plan a dinner for about fifteen friends. JM hates birthday celebrations when he's the subject, is allergic to parties in general. It is an unpredictable social phobia that he wrestles with on and off. Of course he's attached himself to me, a social animal by nature and trade. Interesting. He's my opposite and would prefer to keep everything down to a maximum of four people. I want crowds. I'm surprised he's agreed to a celebration but pleased as well. We've been discussing marriage again and I've been bent on getting hitched to him since day one. It's hugely important to me, part of a larger picture of rights that I want so bad I can taste. I think his willingness to celebrate his birthday bodes well for the massive reception that I want and that he's nixed since the beginning of any of our nuptial discussions years ago.

The only glitch for JM's birthday is that May is gala month in the New York dance and art worlds. The night we choose for his dinner coincides with a gala benefit for Movement Research, a not-for-profit dance school I support and have been on the board of trustees for. Additionally, my longtime friend and colleague Val Bourne is flying in from London for the event. Val is the director of London's Dance Umbrella. This makes it mandatory. I have to attend and very much want to escort Val. I devise a plan to see Val through the cocktail hour at the Movement Research event and at the start of dinner slip away to JM's party.

I adore Val. I met her as a twenty-one-year-old dancer with Trisha Brown, on my first tour to London. We became fast friends. She was the first to bring my work overseas, and chose to do so in the middle of an international booking event that included many major European present-ers. That one date launched my European career and was the beginning of my life as an international artist. Val brought me to London every two years after that, and her curatorial care of my work has made London a second home for me, building my audience substantially over the years.

One of the bonds between us is our love of a good drink, especially wine. She can match me handily and we have raised a glass or two through-out our lives and all over the world. I'm happy to be with Val at such a fes-tive social event and the drink flows. It's time to go, and by now I've been through a few bottles of wine. When my speech begins to slur oddly, I take my leave. On the cab over to JM's dinner at Lotus in Midtown I chat up the handsome cab driver about the pros and cons of same-sex marriage and the battles currently being waged in California, where it's recently become sanctioned.

I arrive at dinner late and sit next to the love of my life, ready to party with our closest family and friends. Everything's bubbling along and in the course of conversation I seize the moment to speak about my cab ride and subsequently, our plans to marry in California. When I announce this to the table, JM asks to close any further discussion. His manner seems abrupt to me. I freak. Is he backing out again? The rest is a blur as I cross some chemical line. The combination of my crazy blood alcohol level and my adrenalized emotional response to the marriage issue sends me into a kind of blackout that is previously reserved for private performances. In full social platform, heated flashes flood over me like a tsunami. It trans-forms me into the cursing, raging Monster-From the-Depths that I can become. I lash out at our guests with vengeance, targeting victims around the table one at a time. I toss the treasured black diamond band that JM gave me for Valentine's Day across the room and try to get in a fistfight with my brother-out-law Fred. Here at last, after all my years of crazed, substance-filled glory, am I in public, possessed by some demon, careening theatrically out of control. Is it the emotional issue, the herbs I recently began taking for elevated cholesterol, age or have I just worn myself down to this moment of detonation? JM coaxes me out of the restaurant and into the car where I rage all the way up the Henry Hudson till I pass out.

My eyes pop open the next morning ("Stephen?" Yes it's me again, I'm back) and I'm instantly filled with sickening dread, mortified beyond repair. Drinker's remorse. Several of last night's guests call to chat. I meek out my apologies but when close friend **Maria Caso** calls to discuss the events of the night, she lets me have it cold. She's been through it all. She is a life coach, clearly. She begins, "OK, so obviously you have a problem. You are slipping and you have to deal." She mentions that she is on the board of Betty Ford and can get me in that day if I choose. "Or..." she measures, "I don't think you're absolutely at a point where it's imperative that you do it that way. I can coach you through sobriety if you want and we could do it one-on-one, day-by-day for ninety days."

I chose immediately. Maria. She is tough and outspoken, a street-smart Cubana who ran with the wolves in Miami before she went through rehab and moved to New York years ago. She's been involved in so many things from music to film to fashion and she is la *bruja*. She is *fuerte*. Maria is like family. She's now a life coach who pulls no punches and will not let me out of the ring. "Why are you letting yourself slide? What do you really want? Why are you gaining weight? You are a supreme athlete and you are not utilizing it. How can I look up to that?"

That afternoon I board a plane for Manchester to perform with my company at Queer Up North Festival. Maria and I began counting sober days that night. Sobriety begins for real and this is Day 1.

The unthinkable pain and embarrassment of my rock-bottom black-out performance, the public unleashing of the monster—it's humiliating beyond belief. I might have tried to laugh it off at an earlier point, but now it's enough to keep me away from alcohol without too much trouble. On Day 2 of my sobriety I'm in Manchester, so I'm distracted by travel and work. But at dinner with the company that night, the test is huge. My throat begins to itch from the inside, the itch of compulsive need. My hand reflexively reaches for the bottle on the table in front of me, but I flinch back. For my entire adult life meals were irrigated by booze or wine, so the act of dining now seems foreign and unreal. Disorienting. The social moment of dining was so programmed to include alcoholic lubrication I just don't know how to behave. "How does this thing run without fuel?" Awkward. Out of sorts. I can hear myself in conversation but the subtext ping-ponging throughout is all about liquefying my discomfort: "Just one glass! You can stop there, go ahead...STOP!"

I announce my state of drought to the dancers to add the pressure of meeting their expectations (so Catholic) and it helps. The itch wears off in a few dinners and I begin to feel the lack of drinking as something new to accomplish, obsess over. It becomes all about having the right sparkling water, the right glass, *must* have a lime, *never, never* lemon. The lime somehow makes it magically possible. And it all clicks into place, though I continue to wake up feeling hung over for weeks, months even, and it was hard to see the point of having to wake up to the pain without the pleasure the night before.

I plod forward through this early period of sobriety slightly uncomfortable in my skin; what do I do when I'm out or on my own, how did I use to behave before all this (when was that anyway?). My daily e-mails with Maria are an oasis. Nothing profound, just a short description of how the day passes, how I'm coping, how I feel about it all. And often I feel nothing, but writing about the blankness gives it some air, a bit of distance. In this way it remains doable.

Then in the third month the fog begins to lift, the headaches start to recede, and I hit a stride of renewed energy and obsessive physical activity. While out with colleagues and friends who drink, it becomes entertaining to see them begin to slide and slur into inebriation while I remain as crisp as a bell on a winter day. And there are the contact highs to boot, where I feel as loose and unleashed as the drinkers I'm with, minus the nasty bits.

In this stride the first year flies by. Then the next. I rarely have an impulse to drink and I feel just as switched on and creative as ever, newly energized in fact. Then somewhere around the third year depression begins to creep in. This third Sober Spring I begin waking up to obsessive mental blocks along with the pain associated with my compulsions. It seems that some of the reasons I might have lived in a continual state of anesthesia begin to rear their ugly heads and demand that I pay attention at this time in my clearheaded sobriety. This is definitely no fun. I thought the hard part was getting sober, but not drinking was easy compared to facing this music. I am shocked that it took three years for all this crap to surface, but here it is, undisputable phenomenological reality about myself, my history and my nature, all bound by the laws of physics. And that is annoying. Plus, it hurts like hell; it's rough and feels like nowhere to turn without the distraction of getting high but that's no longer an option. The pain is never enough to start medicating myself again, never enough to return to the old routine that seemed so inevitable before. I've dug my stubborn Aries heels into sobriety and the redundancy of the prospect is too tedious to revert to.

Everyone is addicted to something. For whatever unique convergence of reasons, innate and learned, these addictions ran wild in my life. The choice for me has become more of "What do I want to focus this part of me on?" Destructive or creative, dark or light, wearing myself out or building myself up—I don't need a Ph.D. to figure out the choices. It just comes down to making the ones that don't destroy me in the process. And then an unimagined space opens up.

HOME ON THE EDGE

These are the feet that walk to school, run to play, try on my mother's heels, and lead me to trouble, pleasure, to help a friend or stranger, march shoulder-to-shoulder in demonstration or fight or off to war or in support of some cause; the feet that lead men to men and join me to legions of souls walking forward, with purpose (or not), through time.

I make my home on the edge. The periphery. Marginal, transitional territory that is shifting physically/culturally/socially/sexually. My choices in music, clothes, food and dwelling are outsider by nature and I follow suit in terms of housing, simply by decree of my chosen profession. The artist lives on the outside for perspective, freedom, danger and lack of funds. The East Village, Chinatown, SoHo, Tribeca, Park Slope, Williamsburg, Greenpoint, Windsor Terrace, now Harlem and Bushwick, Redhook, Mott Haven and Queens. These have been places in New York to hide out under the radar and on the economic fringe. There we dwell before the real-estate market follows the artist population and carries business, trendy restaurants and lux housing, thus driving out the artists and initiating a new migration cycle to the next edge.

When I return to New York for good in 1978 I move thirteen times that first year. I start at the loft on East 13th between Avenue A and B that belongs to Brian, Hampshire alum who was the other male dancer there. I revel in my arrival and wake up that first morning to find my car gone. It's official: Welcome to New York. I am one of the few white boys on the block and in those first amazing weeks there is so much restless, unfamiliar life on the street. One late night I return home to the loft to find a group of Puerto Rican guys jamming on the stoop next to my door. They're singing and play-ing guitar in a rhythmical, sexy way so I go over to listen. The music comes to a perplexed halt and heads turn in menacing slow-motion unison to face me, laser eyes warning me away. I realize I am in a foreigner, a tiny minority of Caucasian artists east of Avenue A. I don't think much about race before this. The sting of my naiveté is tough, but I don't make that mistake again.

On to the couch in a living room on Barrow Street in the west village that I rent from a young single woman starting out in PR, then to the loft on Grand Street with eight others dancers and artists, each with our own 8-foot by 8-foot cubicle made of flimsy Sheetrock walls that don't reach the ceiling. Farting and fucking are a communal experience here. The constant hum of social noise, of shushed activity, hushed struggles and day-to-day minutiae of twentysomething ambition pressed into a raw factory above an Italian delicacy shop. I worry about the unlikely girls who aren't the right size or shape and whose intelligent minds are unconsidered, who juice veggies and do it all correctly but watch their chances dim as time ticks on. This build-ing is chock-full of novices, four floors of new hopes and delusional dreams.

There is the lucky period in the swank but raw penthouse garret on West Broadway that I land in while taping and painting the walls of an early luxury loft conversion, renovating myself out of a home that I couldn't afford.

There are several other moves that are too quick or dim to recall, but finally there's a break. I score a shareable one-bedroom through a coworker I bond with at FOOD, where I am a pot washer and she is a waitress. **Kinga** is a hot Eastern European redhead who warms to me, and when she procures an apartment through a friend, she offers to share the lease of a floor-through on 95 St. Mark's Place between 1st Avenue and Avenue A (my name remains on the doorbell till 2010). She backs out at the last minute and I score it by default. The rent is $250 a month. While I often have to run home at night for the last half block past aggressive catcalls and snowballs in the winter, I'm happy to have a home on the outer limits. Things change quickly at the beginning as more white artists stream into Alphabet City. The East Village is raging—fashion, art, performance and club/street culture, and I live there on and off for twenty years as the neighborhood gentrifies. Yaffa Cafe eventually locates on the ground floor and there's no turning back. The apartment's rent-controlled price is part of the reason I could build a dance company in Manhattan. The rent makes living on next to nothing viable. 95 St. Mark's Place becomes party central and eventually SPC office/headquarters. Those walls see a lot of dance action in the '80s at an ongoing series of holiday parties for the downtown dance world. All the struggling, restless dancers and future luminaries of the day end up there at some point. Bill T. Jones and his lover Arnie Zane often slept there when I was away on tour. That bedroom is currently writing a memoir of its own.

I love this apartment and its location dearly; it's a home from which to watch the city shift and change around me, the unbelievable gentrification, the Ukrainian stronghold that remains constant during this change, and my life shifting from one in a million artists trying to grab the ring to a working dancer touring the world.

There is a spectacular collection of New York nameless celebrities on St. Mark's Place, omnipresent characters who would seem improbable in a script but are the genuine artifact: the octogenarian music teacher on the ground floor who shuffles the pavement hunched over in all weather, the bite of December or swelter of August, in the black wool overcoat and black fur-trimmed hat with the giant earflaps (the sadness when he finally leaves horizontally with glazed eyes and a weak smile); the homeless street woman with the giant breasts and no teeth, who patrols the street between Third Ave and Tompkins Square Park, offering oral for a fiver when the moon waxes; and the guy with the giant black trash-bin turban and leggings who pushes god-knows-what in his cart 24/7. And the parade of dealers, **Mack** and **Michael** and Mack's brother, the studly **Guy**, as they grow up and revolve in and out of jail with disheartening regularity, give birth to children and soldier on working Avenue A. And **Lissie**, the Ivy League graduate who chose dealing the street over the tennis courts of Connecticut, who blows her cover casually when she mentions she spotted me in *Cosmo*.... I love this place where growing up an artist is the most natural, common even, thing in the world.

Then on to a Chambers Street excursion, where you can't get a roll of toilet paper in those days after 5 o'clock when the office world shuts down. There were no amenities, apart from the Delphi restaurant, a local greasy Greek diner. I build my first loft here from the raw space up, sanding out a dance floor, framing walls and doors, hanging sheetrock and installing the electricals. None of these things are in my skill set (apart from the floor sanding, which I did more times than my sawdust-filled nostrils care to remember), but I needed to prove that I can pull it off and I do this once and put my tools away forever. I weep while dropping a plumb line in the August heat, dripping with frustration and awkwardness, but the door gets framed and is level enough to shut tight and lock and looks relatively like a door should.

I hightail it back to the raging style of St. Mark's Place when I learn that my landlord, a certain Moskowitz, is labeled the Monster of Tribeca and fear that my rent will quadruple in a year when my lease is up.

In 1989 I want to move away from the drug dealers who learn to ring my bell at St. Mark's. I protected my turf there before Michal moved in, but he blows the cover by giving his favorite dealers our bell number and brings publicity to my place. I'm forced to look for an escape from their incessant bell-ringing and offering of their wares. One impossibly hung-over morning I look at a subway map and take a random stab at escape. I get on the LL and fall out at the first stop: Williamsburg. It is so close but so far from the East Village, and I reckon it's a perfect oasis away from Avenue A society. In my effort to outrun the dealers of the East Village, I unwittingly moved Michael and me into the epicenter of crack and heroin across the river. It's impossible to move away from trouble in the city in 1990. Kids throw bottles at us in these Brooklyn days, calling us "Nazi skinheads," stopping only when Michael Jordan shaves his head. Then it's all winks and thumbs-up as we ride on the LL to our new haven on Wythe and North 8th Street.

The split from Michael precipitates the next move, another stop down the LL to the garden cottage on Lorimer St. and Metropolitan Ave, and eventually around the corner into the loft on Union across from Kellogg's diner. The bags of papers and receipts of a life that is still unglued are piled to the ceiling but I am heading toward the big shift to "no to drugs." When I do shift, things refocus. Not too long after I meet Jean-Marc and move back to Avenue A.

Jean-Marc's place on Avenue A is my first elevator building. It's the new construction I used to roll my eyes at on my way down to the bars above Houston. (Gentrification. Tsk-tsk). I'm now riding up the elevator of my resistance to change and getting off at a different life that's looking rather fine from this height. Jean-Marc is neat as a pin and quiet. We are in bed early and up at 5 o'clock to work out before the day begins. Vintage dental artifacts, formaldehyde specimens and taxidermy surround us, long before it hits the trend button in the Style Section of the Times fifteen years later. And of course there is my art, always art all around us, and never enough walls. But the open one-bedroom does have a wall of windows onto an 800-square-foot terrace that Jean-Marc has turned into the most elaborate and beautiful potted world I've ever seen. We begin to ramp up the parties here as well, but it is a new life that is so much brighter at this elevation. Our engagement party is at this apartment, in this garden, with hundreds of friends and Indian food from East 6th Street and a tabla/sitar ensemble setting the vibe. I look around at our life and I am happy and can accept all with openness. My edge doesn't seem to dull in response. Now I'm walking to the gym on Lafayette in a migration of young professional suits with freshly laundered shirts, extra starch. I look around and am struck by how the neighborhood seems to have grown up with me, but all the other lives I've lived here are an odd comfort, a beautiful contradiction that continues down these streets after all that's been said and done.

It's post-9/11. I'm desperate to be off the island. I watch the attacks on TV from London where I am making a dance, *House of Magnet,* for a company called Ricochet Dance. A new height of empty panic hits me as I watch the towers fall and the mayor close down the bridges and tunnels that connect

Manhattan to the rest of the world. The thought of being sealed off and trapped in a home whose isolation is never apparent to me till now, drives me into a claustrophobic jag that I can't shake. I reflexively begin to plot our escape from NY. Upon returning, I cab it home entering Manhattan over The Williamsburg Bridge in a dreamlike state that's permeated with the background smell of barbecue. From the FDR Drive, it's like that dream where you are in some approximated past on the street that you grew up on, but something is slightly off, something is missing or rearranged, and you recognize it but it isn't exactly the same. Something is changed. The world as I know it.

Suddenly I am forty-five and lacking a thing to hold on to, no savings or sense of safety to my life. Before this moment I wasn't aware of a need for these things. Jean-Marc and I are fairly successful people with the same sense of thrift—none. We're a couple who eats every dinner out and enjoys the cultural fruits of New York, but...What? Dinner and drinks at $200-plus a night and a rental apartment in a gentrified Lower East Side luxury apartment that's more like a glorified college dorm. An upscale dormitory for aging professionals—and without warning it seems a fragile and empty world.

I plot our move to Brooklyn is search of a bearable lifestyle as well as a possible escape route for the next juncture of attack that I am shell-shocked into believing is inevitable. I look at over sixty possible places to relocate to but the harder- core choices of neighborhoods on the edge are no longer as viable for us, who are no longer in our twenties and up for anything. Mott Haven is out, as well as the Bushwick migration that is rumbling to life. I stumble onto Windsor Terrace at the south side of Park Slope—it smells like possibility. It is the bedroom community for NYC fireman and policeman; the Brooklyn Battery Tunnel dumps right out from Wall Street into our block on the wrong side of the BQE. It is Italian and Irish and I like that, plus there's a dyke couple down the block and everyone knows that when they show up, a neighborhood can shift.

We take a thirteen-foot-wide, two-story townhouse that allows us to cut our rent in half and start socking away money in hopes of a purchase beyond dinner and drinks. Our landlord, **Mr. Perretti**, drops his asking price over $700 because rentals have ground to a halt after 9/11. He thinks of us as an investment, tells me that he likes "guys like you." When the queers come in, the neighborhood is moving on up; the investment looks more promising. We become chums of a sort and a year after we are there, we begin to see the telltale signs. There are tattoos and piercing creeping into the hood, slowly—apparently I sniffed it out one more time. By the time we are ready to go, queer couples are pushing strollers down the street and by now we know what happens to rents shortly after that.

When the year turns out to be a good one, we're sitting on a down payment, miraculously; the first time in my life that I have *any* savings and am not living week to week. But when I start to look around for a purchase that meets the requirements of two adult males, that includes space and a garden, the market is at its peak. We are priced out of Manhattan. The parts of Brooklyn we will consider? Priced out. Two successful men in the world and we can't live beyond the ken of twenty-year-olds.

I search forever and find a loft in Hoboken. Jean-Marc kills it at the final hour when he stops the purchase cold the afternoon that we're about to go to contract. "It just isn't glam enough for us." I go ballistic and think that nothing is good enough for him so we'll end up with nothing, or that he just doesn't want to commit to a purchase together after all.

He suggests going up the Hudson into Westchester and I laugh out loud, then spit, "I'm an artist and I've lived in New York for thirty years. I will never go up the river." I quietly determine to dump him that night but go along on the ride the next day anyway because the idea of life without him is unthinkable. I'm stewing and quietly planning my exit strategy the whole drive. We get about forty-five minutes into it and the world begins to transform around Mount Vernon into a beautiful pastoral landscape of forest and bodies of water. I can't believe this is so close to Manhattan. It's ever so green and smells uncannily sweet out the window of our black Xterra.

Thus begins the shift north. One year later we are living in a 1700s farmhouse in Putnam County, a castle, estate and dream that costs the same price that a dank one-bedroom would cost on 14th Street. When we leave Manhattan at night and open the car door an hour away, to gulp the sweet air around our new home then walk in to an embracing, tucked-away country haven, it's clear: We escaped. I no longer feel like a disenchanted, disenfranchised loser living under a rug or off the map. By going the farthest out we can imagine without leaving altogether, I become not the loser, but king.

Photo: Claire Flack. With Jean-Marc at our first wedding, San Diego, CA (2010). We married again in in Mahopac, NY in 2012 when Marriage Equality succeeded in the Empire State.

AN ARCHITECTURE OF LOSS

Thirty years of making dances is no small feat. It's hard to fathom I've been at it for such an extended length of time, that I could stay focused on *anything* so long. Yet I remain intent. The regular and daily practice of constructing works of motion remains the overriding and detailed activity of my life, a life that swirls in and out of control through different stages, some that are noteworthy, others that are not. But there is always motion; I count on motion, constant calming and grounding activity to bring my day into sharp focus.

For years I struggled to chisel out a language and style that was indisputably clear and recognizable as an entity of its own, one that functioned as a kinetic form for communicating ideas, literal, abstract, expressive or beyond. Whatever the function, it must be strident and crystal and has often been aggressive in its delivery. Structure is a recognizable anchor for me to launch movement, to reorient its activity and keep it reeling out in a comprehensible or discernible way. It's "Show Business" after all. There can be no mistake. And I got pretty deft at showing my wares. Around the twenty-year mark in the life of Stephen Petronio Company, I felt confident that I had accomplished that goal, and with that came a sense of completion. But this state was inevitably accompanied by every artist's challenge: "Now what?"

Now I have a language and it makes some kind of unmistakable sense. Is that it? Do I just keep using it as a vehicle to say "things," approach an endless litany of themes? With the clarity of accomplishment I crave more—a creative instinct to move beyond or destructive impulse? From my beginnings back at Hampshire College, it was open-ended improvisational investigation that won my undying love. That passion remains molten in my creative need.

I began searching for ways to disappear the steely sureness that's become a hallmark of my work. I had to throw a wrench into my compositional methods, and with that end in mind I plotted works that were less adamant as compositional landscapes, like *Ghostown* and *The Architecture of Loss (TAOL)*. *Ghostown* was conceived as a place that that implies a previous world that no longer exists in the present—a Ghost Town.

I've always been riveted by a Rauschenberg painting called *Erased de Kooning*. As the story goes, Bob idolized **Willem de Kooning** and approached him for a work to use. He felt he needed a work of significance as a starting point for what he intended. De Kooning agreed to give him a work, which Bob then proceeded to paint over with a pure white. Bob erased a potential masterwork. It now only exists as an idea. I loved this concept as a starting point for investigating movement and I had previously erased the opening movements of **George Balanchine**'s masterwork *Serenade* in a dance I made in the late '90s called *Not Garden*. It's a delectable, albeit killer, compositional problem, seemingly impossible to solve with the usual tools I had at hand (movement in time and space).

Ghostown had that beautifully uncomfortable feeling throughout the conception and making that could be so rewarding if I manage not to drop the ball or give up in frustration. Really, how do you show something in real-time dance that's actually no longer there? With the difficulty of the assignment, I begin to get little sleep, not much of a surprise considering my lifelong insomnia. And while up all night doing whatever, reading ghost stories for fun, and roaming the Internet for inspiration/distraction/pleasure, I begin to drift back to my early childhood, reliving memories that seemed incredibly vivid, almost real to me again so many years later. And I drifted with these as entities that are transparent worlds that exist in my mind but not in space. This all seemed apt activity in searching for the tools that might help to inform *Ghostown*.

In pursuing these short memory pictures, or snapshots as I thought of them, I simply attempt to paint them with language. It doesn't really require much effort. I already have a penchant for the reconstruction of images and memories with my imagination in great visual detail. I merely have to "catch" the image much the same way I'm trained to catch movement. The difference is that I am catching with words, words aimed at memories of real actions that linger somewhere in my cells.

The act of remembering and reconstructing these intangible landscapes, jotting them down in small washes of words is tangible and satisfying. I begin to post these nocturnal snapshots on Facebook and almost immediately begin receiving quite a lively level of response in return. People seem to love these mini-descriptives and stories and begin to send back in return ones that my writing tripped off in them. I've been showing dances for a long time but have never felt this kind of reciprocity. Seems the telling of the stories was some kind of a common trigger.

Ghostown eventually takes shape as an airy, gossamer dance, asymmetrical and more fragile than any I have made before. The characteristic drive and aggression in my work was absent, and I believe that I found what I set out in search of. But *Ghostown* is not the end of the line of this direction, of my interest in the temporal nature of my art form.

In the mid-'90s I am at the height of a period of heavy repetitive pattern-making across the space of the stage. I often employ groups of two or three dancers moving in powerful unison, but in counterpoint to their adjacent groups. These counterpoint groups would be woven into tight-braiding, interlacing patterns that filled the stage. I hold the skill of this obsessive pattern-making as an essential component of my idea of an "accomplished" choreographer. It is a phase of reassuring the audience by orienting them in perceivable constructions, repeated over and over in order to allow viewers to have a sense of stability, of "Oh, I can see that pattern, thus am secure in my experience, even if I don't understand where this might be going."

These repetitive forms would kind of lull one into believing in their existence, as performed over time. They hold the moment before disappearing into a past event and finally a memory. They are akin to rooms or buildings. To my mind, this becomes a kind of architecture built of motion. As the nature of motion is temporal, it must slip away and disappear. *An architecture of loss.* This seems to catch the essence of what captivates me as an artist and is at the center of my interest and craft. The Architecture of Loss: The phrase remains in my notebook all these years and it rears its head again in 2011, demanding my attention. (Dance chooses me again.) It's intriguing to take a phrase wrought so long ago and to revisit it, now just a basic premise of my work, and to use it as a central focus for creating a new work.

The Architecture of Loss is a work that eschews the depiction of situations of loss, or the emotive response to the stages of losing those things: "I lost my love, so I'm sad," or "I'm losing my grip, so I'm crazed." Rather, I wanted foremost for the audience to grasp a feeling of temporality that translates as *feeling* actual loss, both visually and kinesthetically. I begin to look for structural devices to produce these results. One simple path is to build a strong recognizable rhythmic field that breaks into a contrasting field. When something changes one feels at the juncture of change a kind of loss of the familiar. It's basic theater. Another tool I use is *erasing* or *blocking*: to build some kind of movement information, "a phrase of movement," then block it partially from the viewers' gaze. Much like the person with the long spine, big cranium or tall hat sitting in front of you at the theater. You know there is something happening on the stage because you're catching glimpses of it, what pokes out around the edges of the blocker, but you lose the actual whole of it, the complete picture. I think that a very real way to provide loss for the viewer. And in this manner and other similar investigations, the piece proceeds.

Then somewhere in the middle of the creative process and without warning, Tom, my eighty-three-year-old lion of a father, begins a series of falls that rapidly diminish his health. One moment he is strong, funny, cranky as all hell, and the next slipping away, losing ground (literally; he couldn't connect down through his legs, unable to use the floor to move).

Somehow, the structural pursuits, the nuts, bolts and girders of the dance under construction, begin to collide with the nuts and bolts of the specifics of my father's health needs, along with the unspoken emotions that are rumbling beneath the surface of the reality that my father is in transition. He is shifting and though he has been a constant in my life for all of my fifty-odd years, he simply might not be permanent.

I'm standing in rehearsal making a delicate transition between sections of movement when my brother calls with a health update or the need for a decision about my father's care or living situation. Or a phone call from **Valgeir Sigurðsson**, my Icelandic composer and collaborator for the dance, with yet another layer of questions about music length or instrumentation; or a call from deliverymen from Ikea about a furniture delivery to my father's new assisted living situation, the one we secured for him and his wife, Kay, followed by a text from **Rannvá Kunoy** or **Guðrun & Guðrun**, who are the visual artist and designers collaborating on *TAOL* from the Faroe Islands. And it continues on like this for a few months, converging alternate paths of reality, intersecting in my rehearsal process for *TAOL*.

What started as an esoteric meditation on the transitory nature of dance, the impermanent art, becomes complicated by concurrent meditations on the transitory and fleeting nature of life. And the joy and pain and lust of being in the singular moment in motion in space begins to resonate with the joy and pain and lust related to my human impermanence.

Watching my father step out into space in his old confident way without the grounding support of his legs is real: a physical state of ungrounded action, unstable and careening. A body without ground. It is not metaphorical by any means, but gives way to much loftier rumination. Or the way he becomes humiliatingly unable to command his Tarzan frame to do his bidding; how he has to sink into his nurses and aides for support. I try to catch that state and build it into the fabric of what I'm making for my dancers' strong young bodies that work daily to *enhance* their own sense of connection to the ground.

Another duet in *TAOL* is built upon two characters, one who blindly supports the other through a slow journey of un-centered postures, always falling through space, never on her own stable center, unable to stand on her own feet. It's part of the journal of this period: the loss of strength, mobility stability, home base, ability, finally temper, then faculty. How could I resist having my father with me in this dance for as long as it is performed?

Tom, Sunny, Sun, Big Daddy. Who could be as big, handsome, funny or generous? Who else moved with a sense of ownership and belonging that seemed genetic? Whose bear-hug could be so warm, whose hands could loom so large and powerful and filled with comfort?

I arrive at the hospital where my brother and his wife **Lucretia** have been standing vigil over my father all week. I'm shocked by how rapidly he has deteriorated. Now in his hospital bed, his breath is labored and gurgling, struggling beyond speech. I approach his side to offer some ice for his beyond-chapped lips and he grips my hand in his, looks into me pleading, through me to some distant beyond. It's not so much a look between father and son, but an odd reversal to a child now searching for his parent, or more simply a human imploring kindness.

These are the hands of my father now, diminished, abdicating rulers, cramped back into stiff, strangled fists, spotted brown with age, pricked and prodded with a litany of ineffectual procedures. Massive calloused hands, but soft, how gentle his touch.

He hit me only once with these hands for some forgettable offense, but can I ever forget the fearsome power in those hands? Hands that reach for me now, reach instinctively for help, child wide eyes searching some far off beyond, eyes that sear into me, his second son, the somewhat troubling one, asking for a help he somehow still understands that I am the only one willing to arrange.

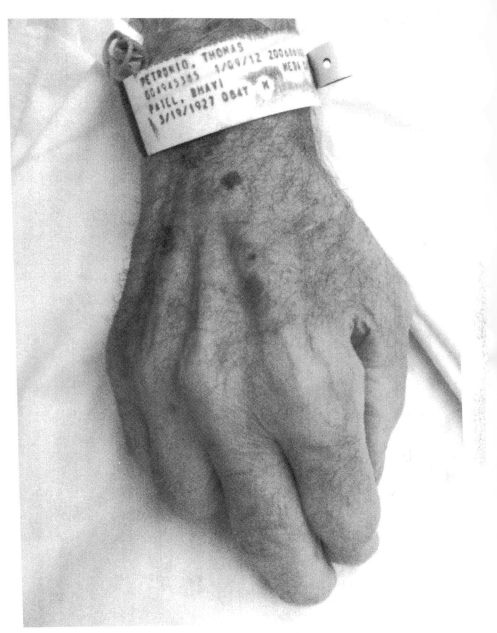

My Father's right hand hours before his death. Jan.12, 2012.

And within a few hours of arriving at his room that afternoon, I demand the Director of the Palliative Care (final stage pain management), the bureaucrat needed in order to ease my father's transition. Frustratingly illusive until now, **Jackie** appears from nowhere, as if by magic. I'm in luck. She's angelic, precisely serene... and transgender. I walk her out into the hall for a private moment and she listens to my frank assessment and adamant request with deep empathy. Within a few minutes she lets me know she has my back and immediately honors my wish to administer the medication that will usher my father through this moment. She informs us that the process, once begun, is irreversible, will keep him relatively comfortable until his passing and will most likely take a few weeks. Dad responds instantly, his agitated struggle easing. He's noticeably calmer and we leave him resting soundly. In the car on the way home I'm certain I made the right choice but it stings badly beneath the knowing, just the same. We barely get home that evening when the call comes. My father is gone.

I can get through my father's death and funeral. I can handle this. He dies a month or two before the premiere of *TAOL* and I can handle it all without missing a rehearsal or a beat. He goes pretty quickly, a matter of a few months, first falling on the rundown farm in Chestertown, Maryland, that he shares with his second wife of twenty-something years. She has severe memory issues and we had tried to move them to an assisted facility for years. His fall is the opportunity. I throw myself into the details of what I know well how to do: organize, plan, shop my father into his new healthier, cleaner life. The thought of failing at these tasks, even at this most busy time in my life is unthinkable. If I can organize this properly, it will all be all right again. And when he does pass shortly before the NY premiere of *TAOL* it's numbing but I cope. I can write and deliver his eulogy (he would find irony, in fact, that the task of delivering his eulogy would fall to his *different* son, the queer, smart-mouthed, troublemaking one—he'd definitely have a good chuckle over that), with my brother Tommy leading the way now, attending to all the details of the wake and party to follow.

These were activities I could mold my sadness into. When it's over, I turn back to the performance looming at hand and without much interruption *The Architecture of Loss* premieres at the Joyce Theater in April 2012.

I'm a consummate professional; capable of whatever I set my mind to. I love a clear goal. I can lean in against a task and fight it, conquer it, complete it; an activity to keep me moving through the pain of my father's death was right up my alley.

But a few months later when things slow down and the summer break rolls around, an unexpected and uninvited anger rumbles up from somewhere to erupt in ugly flashes. Without warning, without reason, there are inconvenient feelings of futility and angst from...I don't know where. And then it becomes obvious: the loss of my father.

After all this: the struggle, the shifting, the battles to define and differentiate, the correction, moving forward to improve and grow beyond, the attempts to reason and win; Death, like gravity, steals the show. We're mortal. I am finite. My father, Tom, is gone and that's final. I have no paternal head to butt up against. And without that tension I'm slightly lost, off-kilter. In my mid-fifties, I find myself, inconveniently, an orphan. Vulnerable. There's emptiness unlike any I've experienced throughout my life. I am, after all these years, a man on my own and it's oddly calming.

Christmas Eve (2007). With Dad and Tom Jr.

Thursday, October 11, 2012

- 5:30 a.m.: Wake up, understand it's me and slide off the bed to stiff-leg it slowly across the room (legs and feet work at only forty percent flexibility in the first ten minutes after waking).
- Bathroom to pee.
- Feed our four sphinx kitties fresh-ground organic chicken prepared and frozen on the weekend.
- Make organic grass-fed milk wheat/probiotic shake with organic low-fat milk and two raw organic eggs (one whole, one just the white). The high-protein/no-carb injection immediately after rising blasts my metabolic furnace on full force.
- Pop daily pills. Allegra D, Astaxanthin, Purple Defense, organic krill and Ubiquinol.
- Feed the fish.
- Triple shot espresso.
- Wake the husband.
- E-mail and news online.
- Tend the cat litter.
- Personal grooming.
- Dress (play with kitties simultaneously).
- Pack my bag for the long day.
- 6 a.m.: Head out to the gym for a thirty-minute swim.

- 7:15 a.m.: Rendezvous with JM in the parking lot to drive to the city (the truck will remain at the gym all day). Commute to Manhattan (Taconic to Saw Mill, Henry Hudson to JM's West Side office at Showroom Seven. En route I read more news constantly, listen to music, write whatever comes (all on iPhone), prepare notes for classes and rehearsal, eavesdrop on morning Bluetooth strategic call between JM and his business partner Karen. Morning car-phone chat with in-laws in Paris.
- 9 a.m.: Arrive in Manhattan: Head for the gym for a short interval and stretching workout.
- Review phrase to be taught in a.m. class at NYU.
- 10:15 a.m.: Walk over to Tisch School of the Arts (2nd Avenue and 5th Street).
- 10:45 a.m.–12-15 p.m.: Teach Morning Technique class for second-year NYU students.
- 12:20 p.m.: Grab organic chicken salad from the Key Food on 2nd Avenue (my chicken is cooked!), eat en route to Joyce SoHo on Mercer and Prince for my company rehearsal, which starts without me at 12:30.
- 12:45 p.m.: Arrive to oversee remounting of company work *UNDERLAND* (music by Nick Cave) and last year's work (*The Architecture of Loss*). Assistant Gino Grenek steers the process with the company, who are fluid about assuming the responsibility for maintaining their roles to a high standard while I oversee the process, interrupting constantly, adjusting and revising as I see fit. Business-related phone calls and e-mails obsessively interspersed throughout.
- 4:15 p.m.: Check in with office to discuss agenda for board meeting looming at 6 p.m.
- 4:30 p.m.: Head up to gym (Crunch) where I've left my clothes in a locker. Shower, shave and dress.
- 5 p.m.: Eat some lentil soup from Bite, a street kiosk 333 Lafayette St..
- 5:50 p.m.: Arrive at Showroom Seven; check the ongoing sample sale.

- 6:00 p.m.–8:20 p.m.: Board meeting with my executive director and marketing director and six of nine board members, including JM, his sister (my sister-in-law Claire), Karen Erickson (chair), **Liz Gerring** (friend, supporter and accomplished choreographer in her own right), **Jill Brienza** (liaison to the visual arts world), Adina Newman (lawyer and former neighbor from Avenue A) and lawyer **Mandie Erickson** (head of Seventh House PR and social wizard who helps elevate all SPC events to a vibrating level) to hash out company budgets, cash flow, new potential board members, upcoming art auction involving fifty amazing visual artists who have donated original works to be auctioned to support the company.
- 8:30 p.m.: Walk over to Bottino on 10th Avenue and 25th Street for a fabulous quiet dinner with JM and Claire.
- 10:15 p.m.: Drive back up to Carmel.
- 11:15 p.m.: Arrive to feed the now voracious kitties.
- Wade through and attend to fifty or so e-mails, usually project- or work-related while catching the end of *Chelsea Lately*, enter notes for draft of memoir.
- 12:30 a.m.: Slip into slumber.

Photo: Sarah Silver. Stephen Petronio Company shoot for *City of Twist* (2003).
Dancers: Jimena Paz and Todd Williams

Photo: Sarah Silver. Stephen Petronio Company *Beauty and the Brut (2008)*.
Dancer: Jonathon Jaffe.

Dance Is A Ravenous Beast

Modern dance is an awkward product. It's invisible. Its tradition is iconoclastic, and often loved by people who are intuitive before rational. Sometimes it's seen as ballet's less valid relative. Its skill is difficult to pin down. How does one qualify in its ever-shifting and multifaceted forms? And who is passing these judgments? What chance has it got of financial gain?

My job as artistic director of a single-vision modern dance company is brutal. It's not that I don't love the fact that I conceive, research, create, direct, rehearse and modify my dance productions. I gather, direct, butt heads with and am transformed by my collaborating artists in music, visual art, fashion and design, graphics and text, and I inspire, mollify and psychoanalyze, empower or overwhelm my invaluable dancers who are like family, children, peers and enablers to me.

It's not that I have to build an organization that supports my vision, find a manager who is skilled, creative, relentlessly hardworking and savvy and social, and whom I just might like enough to have dinner with once in a while, steer her/him in overseeing what little staff we have, someone who is trustworthy and inspired by what we do. The killer is that I have to pay for it!

The sleepless nights in creative, feverish bliss are amazing. The feverish nights in fear of meeting payroll or, worse, fear of financial ruin and ultimate destitution are a drag. Sixty percent of my time is spent trying to

261

raise the money necessary for our endeavors. It's not enough to rise to the top of the extremely competitive and volatile field of choreographers in New York and in the world. I have to be in the smartest and most likeable upper percentile of who can meet the requirements of foundation and corporate sponsorship and have access to private wealth. *Help!*

No one's in this field to make money, though I'm not allergic to it and have done my best to glamorize the perception of this art form in the field at large. And why not? The modern dance world might want to face the zeitgeist being admired for its incredible artistry *and* in being in the right leggings! Does change have to be poorly attired? I think not. (100 per cent how you get there, 100 per cent where you arrive to and 100 per cent what you're wearing when you arrive). But if anyone thinks that not-for-profit dance is rolling in dosh ($), get your dictionary out and look up the meaning of not-for-profit.

Almost everything stems from the original intent of an artist. To make new art, the next discovery, the pushing forward of whatever dialogue she/he happens to be involved in. And this is how art, culture, the world, moves forward: in dialogue, in research, in discovery. So, yes, Dance is a hungry beast and its nature is unpredictable. This beast ALWAYS will need to be fed.

PS: Dancers eat real food!

Photo: Sarah Silver. Stephen Petronio Company Like Lazarus Did (2013).
Dancer: Joshua Tuason.

Top 10 (Questions People Ask Me)

1. What do you think of *So You Think You Can Dance*?
2. Do you mean, like, on Broadway?
3. How did you start?
4. How do you make a living?
5. Where should I look?
6. What does it mean?
7. Is there a story?
8. So how do you do that?
9. Do you eat a special diet?
10. Are dancers as good in bed as rumored?

Photo: Sarah Silver. Stephen Petronio Company *Underland* (2011). Dancers: Tara Lorenzen, Julian Deleon, Amanda Wells, Barrington Hinds and Emily Stone.

Live Man Walking

I'm standing at the edge of the roof of the Whitney Museum, seven towering stories above 75th Street and Madison Avenue in Manhattan. Look up and it's all open sky, look down and it's...

It's September balmy, a blustery day, the wind whipping up against the front of my body and face. Perfect for flight. My mood is pensive, unusually quiet, breath deep and slow. The moment comes and I step out onto a metal scaffold, a portal into nothingness. The front of my body pulses at the free space calling beyond the roof—an empty ache in my stomach and knees, new distance between my skull and scalp.

I'm attached by harness and rope to scaffolding constructed as my support and fixed anchor on the building. I'm also connected to Jason, my fly expert/guide. He's behind and to my left and speaks in a cool authoritative voice, a reassuring whisper in my left ear. Against my headstrong nature I decide to give up control to his prompts, as what I am about to do goes against every survival instinct and thread of logic I have. I clear my mind and do exactly what he says.

"Ready?" he asks.

"Let's go," I respond.

I have a tight grasp the metal frame at either side.

"Step on to the ledge, left foot first," he urges.

Done.

"Now right foot."

Done.

I perch on the four-inch aluminum ledge at the roof perimeter that holds only the heels of my size 10 1/2 feet. My heart syncopates and erupts through my shirt as my toes jut into the void and I grip my heels and calves like never before. Can I grasp with my heels? I wonder, trying to grow instant Achilles talons to do so. The back surfaces of my body open to the space behind me, instinctively in retreat, trying to get closer to the roof behind, to safe ground, my past, "Go back!" comes a voice from the deep.

"Release your left hand," comes Jason's quiet command.

I do, and paste it to my left outer thigh.

"Now release your right hand," he continues.

I obey but a spring trap in my left hand is fired by my lizard mind and I re-grasp the left side of the frame.

"Let go with your left hand," he says more firmly and I slowly comply, freestanding on my heels. The rush and surrender through my body is molten hot.

"Lean forward slightly," he says.

Thump, thump, thump. I know elementally that behind me is all that is safe and solid, before me is ether. I force myself to stop straining back toward the ledge and tip my weight gently forward to lean out a degree or two. The schism between thought and action disappears. Everything unites in the lean. A muffled gasp rises up from the crowd gathered down below to witness the moment that arrives.

"Good to go?" he asks.

"Go."

I stretch out t-a-u-t into the gaping emptiness before me, a slow-motion dive pushing into the wall with my feet and away with the rest of my being. Everything in me, all my instincts scream "WRONG!" but I continue forward and out to shift my standing orientation 90 degrees. I stop. Perpendicular to the building. I am standing in the wrong plane, a perfect right angle.

With the help of a rope and harness we defeat gravity. I reorient myself and proceed to walk calmly down the length of the building to the street below. It's a short walk, perhaps three or four minutes, but it is one of the most significant of my life.

Trisha Brown, renowned postmodern choreographer and my dance mentor, created *Man Walking Down the Side of a Building* in 1971. I performed it once for her as a dancer in her company in the '80s. It was exciting then, three stories up a medieval tower in the south of France. But in 2010, my walk is different. Different beyond the additional height and the urban location, though they both matter. It's not merely a dance reconstructed but a monument to honor the mind that helped to teach me how to challenge rules of perception and physics, the tools of my trade as a dancer and choreographer. In one singular moment I learn to definitively put my body on the line, shift perspectives and venture out into improbable, the unknown.

The next day I feel my body head-to-toe like it's brand-new again, can't stop thinking about the moment of lean. The walk has given me a rush that lasts and transports me to a state of suspended reverie. I am bigger, E X P A N D E D.

I am an artist—a choreographer to be exact. I make movement, dances, visceral things that exist in a moment of real time then disappear—evaporate. Mine is the elusive art of shaping energy into form, of small adjustments, incremental growth and daily disciplined practice.

But stepping out onto the ledge of the Whitney roof and leaning out into Manhattan's slow-motion free fall antigravity space is like taking my molecules to a cosmic high-powered carwash. Renewed again. What more will it take for me to come clean?

The boundaries of *unknown possibility* are thrilling terrain. I've chased these boundaries on the dance floor ever since I started dancing and in my life ever since I can remember. I'm riveted by this focus, the rush and speed of the chase, the high stakes of awareness and the pleasure that can result. *And everybody's addicted to something. Some more than others.* I love these addictions like old friends. For better or worse they belong to me.

With Trisha Brown after Man Walking Down the Side of
the Building @ the Whitney (2010).

Many years of molding, shaping, transforming my body like a costume to suit my needs at every stage of my life. I hate it, love it, wonder at its flexibility and prowess, curse its limitations and weaknesses, but for better or worse, this is my body, fortunate and flexible. This is where I live, where it all plays out, where a career has been built, an endless ocean of dreaming and creation spring forth from these limbs and skin. This is my body and we have struck an amicable deal together. Once in a while a sprain, spasm or break, but I've pretty much been able to work with its shortcomings and run with its strengths. This is my body and for the most part we've been friends.

I'm sitting on the beach in Aquinnah, Massachusetts, down by the clay cliffs of Gay Head, one of the sanctums in America where you can be naked and free with the bluest of oceans. I'm sunning and playing in the wild surf, heart pounding in my chest, contracted with the bracing cold of the water. I run up the beach barefoot and bare-bodied across the sand, having one of those private moments with my body, but in a public space, out into the bright sunshine of a glorious June day. I drop back on my towel to sun-dry and catch my breath. I look down my arm and the camera comes to a screeching halt, then zooms in. Several strands of silver hair glint mockingly in the harsh sun. It's clear: I'm aging. No matter how hard I fight to stay ahead of it all, there is a shift in the tone of my skin and muscle, the outline of my torso and now this.

I'm in my fifties now, growing older by numbers but the gift of my profession is that I have been able to cunningly stave off the signs of wear on the tool I depend on to perform my trade. I am still youthful and strong. I earnestly believe I can beat the mortality thing. Aren't I the one who's heard "How cute your boy is" and later "How handsome" and later still "How strong or lithe and articulate your body is" over and over again like a mantra beating through my life. Can't I freeze the aging while mere mortals expand and sag with each passing decade?

Then one day it pounces with a thud. From a young waitress comes, "Thank you, sir...." Then worse, a compliment is offered somewhere: "How young you look...for your age..."

In the studio, when I'm soaring at top speed, hounding after some illusive physical thought, I'm ageless. My body's open and responsive like a colt in training, riding this superb wave of movement with a pack of twenty-two-year-old dancers from the company beside me, all in full flight. Then I turn to glance in at the mirror and there it is. However I feel, I'm a man grown into maturity, their fathers' age, and there they are, young, fresh and tight. Children. Never mind! Don't stop; keep moving forward, ahead of time and age and into that other place, that timeless cloud.

Then the gap between my age and how I look begins to shrink— fifteen, ten, five years now. Then one day when I let my age slip to a 20 year-old student, there's no discernable surprise response. "Of course" their eyes reveal. "You're that older dude".

Finally, here it is: the undeniable truth of my body on a sun-bleached day on the beach. There's just no turning back. To my surprise, it's a relief.

Mine is a life marked by the deep, lush valleys of a practice in motion, sensual peaks, rushes of excitement, orgies of chaotic action, sexual anarchy.

Concept, thrill, pleasure and extreme; to know I'm still here, to feel my edges, the hunger for more, deeper, faster, pressing beyond each goal reached. This is the life I've come to love, built step by step, moment by moment, wrung from the grips of the yawning void; an awkward boy/obstinate man, the last wrong piece of some detailed, shifting puzzle. I am restless, misfit and squirming into a home in transition, a life in motion.

END

Photo: Sarah Silver: Stephen Petronio Company *I Drink The Air Before Me* (2010).
Dancers: Michael Badger, Shila Tirabasi, Gino Grenek,
Amanda Wells and Barrington Hinds.

A History Of Petronio Repertory

2012   *The Architecture of Loss**
    Original Music: Valgeir Sigurðsson
    Costumes: Guðrun & Guðrun
    Artwork: Rannvá Kunoy

2012   *Intravenous Lecture** by Steve Paxton (1970/2012)
    Costumes: John Bartlett

2012   *Ethersketch I*
    Music: Nick Cave
    Costumes: Erickson Beamon
    Performed by Wendy Whelan (New York City Ballet)

2011   *UNDERLAND**
    Music: Nick Cave
    Costumes: Tara Subkoff
    Video: Mike Daly

2010   *Untitled Man*
    Music: Harold Arlen performed by Jeff Buckley
    Costumes: Michael Angel

2010   *Ghostown*
    Music: Jonny Greenwood
    Costumes: Jillian Lewis

2009   *I Drink the Air Before Me*
       Original Music: Nico Muhly
       Costumes: Adam Kimmel, Cindy Sherman
2008   *This Is the Story of a Girl in a World*
       Music: Antony, Lou Reed, Nico Muhly
       Costumes: Michael Angel, Tony Cohen, Tara Subkoff/Imitation of
       Christ
       Jewelry: Erickson Beamon
2008   *Beauty and the Brut*
       Original Music: Fischerspooner
       Costumes: Benjamin Cho
2007   *Bird Gerhl*
       Music: Antony
       Costumes: Tony Cohen
2007   *Without You II*
       Music: Placebo
       Costumes: H. Petal
2006   *For Today I Am A Boy*
       Music: Antony
       Costumes: Tara Subkoff/Imitation of Christ
2006   *BLOOM*
       Original Music: Rufus Wainwright
       Costumes: Rachel Roy
2006   *Bud Suite*
       Music: Rufus Wainwright
       Costumes: Tara Subkoff/Imitation of Christ, H. Petal
2006   *The Rite Part*
       Music: Igor Stravinsky, Mitchell Lager
       Costumes: Manolo (*Full Half Wrong* 1992)
2005   *bud*
       Music: Rufus Wainwright
       Costumes: Tara Subkoff/Imitation of Christ
2003   *The Island of Misfit Toys*
       Music: Lou Reed
       Set: Cindy Sherman
       Costumes: Tara Subkoff/Imitation of Christ

2002 *City of Twist**
Original Music: Laurie Anderson
Costumes: Tara Subkoff/Imitation of Christ

2002 *Broken Man*
Music: Blixa Bargeld
Costumes: Tara Subkoff/Imitation of Christ

2000 *Strange Attractors (Prelude)*
Music: Placebo with David Bowie
Costumes: Tanya Sarne/Ghost

2000 *Strange Attractors (Part II)*
Original Music: James Lavelle
Costumes: Tanya Sarne/Ghost

1999 *Strange Attractors (Part I)*
Original Music: Michael Nyman
Set: Anish Kapoor
Costumes: Tanya Sarne/Ghost

1998 *Not Garden*
Original Music: David Linton, Sheila Chandra
Music: J.S. Bach/ Charles-Francis Gounod
Set: Stephen Hannock
Costumes: Tanya Sarne/Ghost
Lighting: Axel Morgenthaler

1997 *ReBourne*
Music: The Beastie Boys, Sheila Chandra
Costumes: Paul Compitus

1997 *I Kneel Down Before You*
Music: Hratchik Nigohossian, Djivan Kasparian
Costumes: Gene Meyer

1996 *Drawn That Way*
Original Music: Andy Teirstein
Music: Suede
Costumes: Manolo

1996 *#4*
Music: Diamanda Galas
Set: Arnaldo Ferrara
Costumes: Manolo

1995   *Lareigne*
       Original Music: David Linton
       Music: The Stranglers
       Costumes: Manolo
1995   *X-Obsessed*
       Music: Deborah Harry, The Buzzcocks
1993   *The King Is Dead*
       Music: Elvis Presley, Maurice Ravel
       Set: Cindy Sherman
       Costumes: Manolo
1993   *She Says*
       Music: Yoko Ono
       Costumes: Manolo
1992   *Half Wrong*
       Music: Igor Stravinsky
1992   *Full Half Wrong*
       Music: Igor Stravinsky, Mitchell Lager
       Costumes: Manolo
       Hairpiece: Leigh Bowery
1992   *Half Wrong Plus Laytext*
       Music: Igor Stravinsky, Mitchell Lager
       Costumes: Manolo
1992   *Wet Within Reason*
       Music: Richard Rodgers/Oscar Hammerstein II
       Co-Choreographer: Michael Clark
1991   *Wrong Wrong*
       Music: Igor Stravinsky
       Co-Choreographer: Michael Clark
       Costumes: Leigh Bowery
1990   *Bed Piece*
       Music: silence
       Co-Choreographer: Michael Clark
1990   *MiddleSexGorge*
       Original Music: Wire
       Costumes: H. Petal

1989   *Close Your Eyes and Think of England*
       Original Music: David Linton
       Costumes: H. Petal
       Lighting: Stan Pressner
1988   *AnAmnesia*
       Original Music: Peter Gordon
       Set and Costumes: Justin Terzi
1987   *Simulacrum Reels*
       Original Music: David Linton
       Set: Justin Terzi
       Costumes: Yonson Pak
1986   *#3*
       Original Music: Lenny Pickett
1986   *Walk-In*
       Original Music: David Linton
       Set: Justin Terzi
       Costumes: Yonson Pak
1985   *The Sixth Heaven*
       Original Music: Pat Irwin
       Costumes: Yonson Pak
1984   *Adrift with Clifford Arnell*
       Original Music: Lenny Pickett
1983   *Apollo Object*
       Original Music: Ray Rudd
1982   *Deconstruction*
       Music: Orchestral Manoeuvres in the Dark, live circular saws
1981   *Wistful Vistas*
       Music: Orchestral Manoeuvres in the Dark
1981   *City of Homes*
       Music collage
1980   *Splinter*
       Music collage
1980   *Micronesia*
       Music collage

1978 *Pack Piece*
       in silence
1975 *Wall Piece*
       in silence

*Currently available
All lighting by Ken Tabachnick unless otherwise noted.

Commissions

2011	*The Social Band*	OtherShore, New York, NY
2010	*By Singing Light*	National Dance Company Wales, UK
2009	*Tragic Love*	Ballet de Lorraine, France
2007	*Ride the Beast*	Scottish Ballet, Scotland, UK
2007	*deCapulet*	Washington Ballet, Washington, DC
2006	*He* and *She* (two works)	Norrdans/Harnosand, Sweden
2005	*Photo Booth Project*	Ricochet Dance Company, London, UK
2004	*Quiver*	Second Avenue Dance Company, New York, NY
2004	*Unchained Melodies*	Norrdans/Harnosand, Sweden
2003	*The Human Suite*	CanDoCo, London, UK
2003	*UNDERLAND*	Sydney Dance Company, Sydney, Australia
2002	*La Preza*	A Quo Danza Contemporanea, Morelia, Mexico
2001	*House of Magnet*	Ricochet Dance Company, London, UK
2000	*Secret Ponies*	Axis Dance Company, San Francisco, CA
1998	*Fetch Boy and Fox*	Ricochet Dance Company, London, UK
1995	*A Midsummer Night's Dream*	Maggio Danza, Florence, Italy
1994	*ExtraVenus*	Lyon Opera Ballet, Lyon, France
1992	*Cherry*	Annapolis Ballet, Annapolis, MD

1992	*Laytext*	Deutsche Oper Berlin, Berlin, Germany
1990	*Le Trouvere*	Tulsa Opera, Tulsa, OK
1988	*Surrender*	De Rotterdamse Dansgroep, Rotterdam, The Netherlands
1987	*Simulacrum Court*	Ballet Frankfurt, Frankfurt, Germany

All choreography by Stephen Petronio.

For further information inquiry and welcomed contributions (SPC is a registered Not-For Profit 501c3 Charitable Organization): www.stephenpetronio.com

Made in the USA
Lexington, KY
12 August 2016